# People's Warrior

*Congressman John E. Moss (1915–1997). Photograph courtesy California State University at Sacramento Archives.*

# People's Warrior

## John Moss and the Fight for Freedom of Information and Consumer Rights

Michael R. Lemov

FAIRLEIGH DICKINSON UNIVERSITY PRESS
*Madison • Teaneck*

Published in the United States of America
Published by Fairleigh Dickinson University Press
Co-published with The Rowman & Littlefield Publishing Group, Inc.
4501 Forbes Boulevard, Suite 200, Lanham, Maryland 20706
www.rlpgbooks.com

Estover Road, Plymouth PL6 7PY, United Kingdom

British Library Cataloguing in Publication Information Available

**Library of Congress Cataloging-in-Publication Data**

Lemov, Michael R., 1935-
  The people's warrior : John Moss and the fight for freedom of information and
consumer rights / Michael R. Lemov.
    p. cm.
  Includes bibliographical references and index.
  ISBN 978-1-61147-024-6 (cloth : alk. paper) — ISBN 978-1-61147-471-8 (paper)
— ISBN 978-1-61147-025-3 (ebk.)
  1. Moss, John E. (John Emerson), 1913- 2. Legislators—United States—
Biography. 3. United States Congress. House—Biography. 4. Government
information—United States—History. 5. Freedom of information—United
States—History. 6. Consumer protection—Government policy--United States—
History. I. Title.
  E748.M775L46 2011
  328.73092--dc22
  [B]
                                                                    2011011373

∞™ The paper used in this publication meets the minimum requirements of
American National Standard for Information Sciences—Permanence of Paper
for Printed Library Materials, ANSI/NISO Z39.48-1992.

Printed in the United States of America

For Penny
*Who lived it all with me.*

# Contents

# Foreword

## Ralph Nader

Of all the lawmakers with whom I have worked or interacted over the years, it was Congressman John Moss from California who epitomized best the description of being a "legislator's legislator."

Granted, he conducted his legislative work in consumer protection, securities reform, environmental protections, freedom of information, and watch-dogging executive branch agencies at a time when the public was more engaged in public issues, and the quality of Congress overall was significantly superior to that which prevails today in both his Democratic Party and the Republican Party. Moss had his heyday of success largely between 1966 and 1976 when the Vietnam War, the military draft, the civil rights struggles, and the rise of the women's liberation movement all helped create both an enabling climate and more progressive legislators for what was accomplished in the consumer, environmental, and worker fields of action.

Unlike some of his openly progressive successors today, John Moss invited and worked with citizen groups on one bill after another. His attitude was to do more than diagnose and document a necessity or injustice, drop a bill into the hopper, and be done with it—as is so often the case today. No, Moss did not see his role as being complete, even after laboring to get the bill through all the hurdles in the House and Senate and having it signed by the president. To achieve the desired results, he went on to monitor the agency or department tasked with implementing or enforcing the law. He must have believed in "eternal vigilance" when it came to the executive branch and the ever-hovering corporate lobbyists.

 So, to be in his office, going over details and strategies to pass the historic Freedom of Information Act amendments of 1974 or the effective Magnuson-Moss warranty law, was to be in the presence of a professorial legislator with his feet solidly on the ground and his mind attuned to the myriad of nuances and personalities that had to be negotiated prior to passage. He was a no-nonsense lawmaker. He was informed about the draft of proposed legislation better than just about any lawyer member of Congress of his time. Because he was not a lawyer, he must have felt an extra obligation to read the text of the proposed legislation carefully and suggest refinements. Working with him was a delight, an exercise in what a deliberative democratic process should be in our country.

 Among so many lawmakers whose antennae were always attuned to what the lobbies for commerce want or which campaign contributions could be enhanced, Representative Moss had instincts for what the public interest was—the right to know about our government's doings, the right to health and safety, the right to have our savings secured, the right to be free from toxic substances, and the constitutional duties of the Congress to represent the citizenry.

 At a time when political books become sellers only if they wallow in gossip and shallow personality profiles, it is to the great credit of Michael Lemov that he labored so diligently and knowledgeably to preserve and extend to the future the momentous career of John Moss. With history receding faster and faster from each generation's frame of reference, John Moss could have been lost to our consciousness except for a few academics, friends, and relatives. That risk is lessened with the publication of *People's Warrior*.

 Mike Lemov is uniquely qualified for this biographical initiative. He was the chief counsel to the U.S. House of Representatives' Oversight Committee chaired by Representative Moss from 1975 to 1978, and before that was Special Counsel to Moss's Consumer Protection Subcommittee from 1970 to 1975.

 For young people today, beset with cynicism about Congress or simply "turned off" from politics, this book is an awakening antidote. It reminds that, not so long ago, Congress did significant things for the people of this country. Our *First Branch* enacted major civil rights legislation and Medicare/Medicaid in a two-year period. It enacted the comprehensive auto and highway safety laws just nine months after the publication of my book *Unsafe at Any Speed*. These great lifesaving laws were signed by President Lyndon Johnson in 1966. Mr. Moss had an important role in their enactment.

 Within three years—from 1970 through 1972—groundbreaking product safety and air and water pollution laws were enacted and given to newly formed agencies to implement.

It is important for young people today, who see procrastination, cowardliness, evasions, corporate-indentured stagnation, and arrogance running through members of Congress like an epidemic, to read about a different time when many more legislators knew why they were sent to Washington by the voters back home.

The younger generation should always bear in mind that their predecessors marched and rallied—they showed up—to demand and support these redirections by Congress and the White House. The first Earth Day of 1970, stimulated by Senator Gaylord Nelson and others, led to fifteen hundred events that April day on college campuses, and included many millions of people at rallies and marches. These young Americans put the environmental issue on the front pages and the television news with their public citizenry.

As you read this book and feel the passions and performances of those years, you might ask yourself what advantages our forebears possessed over us today. The answer, I submit, is that they had emotional intelligence—what community organizers call "fire in their bellies." All other advantages—plus being able to stand on their shoulders in an efficient and inexpensive communication age—are present today.

I hope that *People's Warrior* will shear away any excuses you might have about the futility of trying to change our society for the better. For the legacy of John Moss affects you beneficially every day and can motivate you to assure that his kind of intense and courageous labors continue to have legs, arms, and brains for the relentless struggle for justice.

Ralph Nader
Washington, DC

# Acknowledgments

No book can be written alone. This book, about an extraordinary life and unique era, is no exception.

From the day I promised John Moss—by then, elderly and ill—that I would write about his work and his life, I have been aided and encouraged by the Moss family: primarily John Moss's wife, Jean, and his daughters, Allison and Jennifer. They have given me their unfailing assistance with information and insights about the life and times of their husband and father.

So, too, have members of Congress, public officials, former congressional staff members, journalists, and public citizens who knew or worked with John Moss given freely of their time and energy to furnish interviews, read chapters, and make important contributions and suggestions.

My great appreciation and thanks go to many others outside the circle of Moss's family and friends: to Zoe Davis and the dedicated staff of the United States Senate Library; to Julie Thomas and Sheila O'Neill of the Department of Special Collections and University Archives of the California State University, Sacramento, where John Moss's papers are well preserved and carefully indexed for future historians; to Sharon Davis, Chief Legislative Clerk of the House Energy and Commerce Committee; Bill Mahannah of the Library of Congress Law Library; to Kassy Benson, John Moss's able administrative assistant and to all the Board Members of the John E. Moss Foundation; to Carol Anderson and Elizabeth Alesbury who double checked my facts; and to Tami White and Katrina Stirn who produced the manuscript. My thanks also to Harry Keyishian at Fairleigh Dickenson University Press for his confidence in this book and in me; to the editors at Rowman & Littlefield who assisted me, particularly Elaine McGarraugh who carefully read the final manuscript.

To my author-children, Rebecca Lemov and Doug Lemov, who took time out from their own busy lives and their own books, to help and encourage me along the way, a loving thank you.

To my wife, editor, and adviser, Penelope Lemov, who aided and encouraged me throughout the writing of this history, my love and lasting appreciation.

And most of all my gratitude to John Emerson Moss for living so bravely a turbulent and productive life, for his successes and near misses, and for his leaving us with lasting proof that, in the words of Franklin Roosevelt, public servants are tribunes of the people.

April 2011

# People's Warrior

# Prologue

## *The Consumer Decade*

A shocking article appeared in the *New Yorker* magazine in May 2004. It described the torture of Iraqi prisoners by American soldiers at Abu Ghraib prison near Bagdad. Based on a leaked report, the article stated that Major General Antonio Taguba, who had investigated the torture allegations on behalf of the U.S. Army, concluded that American soldiers had engaged in "sadistic and criminal abuses." Taguba's report was never intended to be made public.

In the firestorm of outrage that followed the revelations of torture, President George W. Bush, Defense Secretary Donald Rumsfeld, and others in the Bush administration denounced the conduct at Abu Ghraib and said the fault lay with a few low-level bad apples. None said anything about how and why Abu Ghraib happened in the first place.

What Americans learned several years later—because of a law called the Freedom of Information Act—was that the torture was authorized at the highest levels of the American government. It was approved by officials at the Departments of Justice and Defense and the White House and opposed by some military officers who were overruled by their political superiors.

That Americans learned the truth about their government's actions was due mostly to a crusade and the tactical brilliance of a virtually forgotten California congressman. In 1954, John E. Moss wrote an open government bill, then spent twelve years pushing his fellow congressmen to pass it and three presidents to sign it.

Moss, who was also the driving force behind other major consumer protection laws, served during an all-too-brief time when our political system seemed to work for the benefit of ordinary Americans. During Moss's time in Congress and due in great measure to his efforts, American citizens gained a new right to challenge secrecy by their government and unprecedented new power in the marketplace. This book is the story of that man and that time.

* * *

John Moss started out as a little-known congressman from California's Central Valley. He had no father or mother to help him as a young boy. He made his way through the hardship of the Great Depression on his own. From abandonment and poverty, he rose to become the chairman of three congressional subcommittees that, under his leadership, were among the most effective in U.S. history. Although never chairman of a full committee, Moss was indispensable in pushing through Congress some of the most notable and far-reaching legislation of the twentieth century, including the Freedom of Information Act, the Consumer Product Safety Act, and major reforms of the capital markets.

To win these reforms for the American people, Moss had to fight, at different times, five U.S. presidents, congressional leaders of his own party, and entrenched industry and government interests.

He had important allies in his battles—Senators Warren Magnuson and Phil Hart, Congressmen Bob Eckhardt and John Dingell, among others. But it was Moss, single-minded, stubborn, and incorruptible, who made the changes finally possible.

Although the 1970s were golden years for the consumer movement, the beginnings of the consumer revolution surfaced in the 1960s, starting with the release of a Consumer Bill of Rights by President John F. Kennedy. Kennedy and Esther Peterson, the first White House consumer adviser, announced four basic rights of American consumers: the right to be informed, the right to choose, the right to safety, and the right to be heard.

Ironically, the right to be informed brought Kennedy and his successor Lyndon Johnson into direct conflict with Moss, a member of their own party. Moss, then in the seventh year of a twenty-six-year congressional career, was in the midst of an unprecedented battle with the federal bureaucracy over repeated agency refusals to provide public information to the press, the public, and even to Moss as a member of Congress. The battle between Moss and the Executive Branch continued through the Eisenhower, Kennedy, and Johnson administrations. Ultimately, it established what Americans now assume is a basic right—the right to access government information. But the fight, over who owns government information and when government information rightly should be kept secret, continues to this day.

In 1954, when Moss first took up the cause of open government, existing policy was dubbed by some congressional staff members as "silly secrecy." At the height of the Cold War, this involved stamping "secret" on everything from the Department of the Navy telephone directory to a study of modern adaptations of the bow and arrow.

Moss's determined—some would say bull-headed—investigation of government information restrictions ultimately led Congress to pass the Freedom of Information Act in 1966. The new law, commonly known as FOIA, implemented a big part of the first of Kennedy's consumer rights: the right of citizens to be informed about the actions of their government. But a major problem for Eisenhower, Kennedy, Johnson, and for succeeding presidents of both political parties was that the target of FOIA was disclosure about government itself, warts and all. It was information that could embarrass a lot of people, especially those in power.

In moving FOIA from an investigative idea to legislative reality, Moss faced roadblocks, end runs, and veto threats. But en route, the young congressman also received a stunning legislative gift from an octogenarian committee chairman from Brooklyn. Finally, despite charges that he had sold out with a last-minute compromise, the stubborn Californian delivered his Freedom of Information Act to a reluctant White House, or rather to LBJ at his Texas ranch on the Pedernales River. There, in July 1966, the president had every intention of letting it turn to dust in the hot Texas sun. Why it did not die involves a surprising twist of history and a lesson in American politics.

Even more surprising is what Moss did next. Rather than rest on his FOIA laurels—more than enough to cap most congressional careers—Moss teamed up with Senator Warren Magnuson, the powerful chair of the Senate Commerce Committee, and a handful of other legislators and advocates. Together, they targeted problems consumers were having in the marketplace. Moss, "Maggie," and a few others, with help from a young consumer advocate named Ralph Nader, initiated a wave of consumer protection legislation unrivaled in the twentieth century. Their efforts were supported by public interest groups, labor unions, and the laserlike attention of the American press.

Moss's legislative logic was common-sense simple: there should be a way to prevent deceptive advertising, to require enforceable product warranties, to require recall and payment for dangerous automobiles, and to ensure that consumer products are tested first in the laboratory and not on the bodies of unsuspecting buyers; there ought to be a law requiring stocks to be sold to investors at competitive commission rates, not at rates fixed by the New York Stock Exchange.

Ultimately, Democratic Congresses enacted and Republican presidents signed the Consumer Product Safety Act, the Magnuson-Moss Act that includes enhanced Federal Trade Commission powers and warranty protections for consumers, as well as legislation to promote truth-in-lending, fair packaging and labeling, toxic substances control, damage-resistant automobile bumpers, new motor vehicle safety regulation, investor protection, and securities market reform.

These laws implemented much of Kennedy's Consumer Bill of Rights, and they did it over the determined opposition of most, but not all, of American business. For a time, the consumer was king.

While Moss and his allies were seemingly overmatched, they managed to prevail. How and why they did it is at the heart of this story. New laws were passed; some commemorative pens were given out. But turning those consumer and public information victories into ongoing reality was another matter.

Ultimately, public attention turned elsewhere. Opposition grew, based on free-market ideas and deregulatory fervor. The consumer revolution was at first slowed, then starved——then mostly forgotten. Michael Pertschuk, one of Magnuson's most savvy tacticians and powerful aides, captured it best in the title of his book: *Revolt Against Regulation: The Rise and Pause of the Consumer Movement.*

Also forgotten during that extended pause were most of its leaders, including Moss. The California progressive—so key to the success of consumer protection and the driving force behind the Freedom of Information Act—was the son of a Utah coal miner. Three years after the family moved to California, he watched his mother die of an infection. A year later, when he was twelve, his father abandoned him and his brother.

Moss was mostly self-educated, forced to drop out of college during the Great Depression for lack of money. He became an appliance dealer and a real estate salesman. He knew hard times and lean years. An ally of California's Republican Governor Earl Warren, a liberal Democrat in the midst of the Red-baiting McCarthy era, Moss overcame erratic health and called on a reservoir of bravery to fight for individual consumers and against entrenched, powerful interests.

Toward the end of his congressional career, Moss led a series of oversight investigations that proved prescient. He warned of Enron-Madoff-type securities frauds decades before they cost investors billions of dollars. He fought a lonely battle to create a stock market that would be free from uncontrolled speculation. His hearings in 1978 on defective Firestone 500 tires and the lack of effective motor vehicle safety regulation foreshadowed the deaths twenty years later of more than 240 Americans from another Firestone tire model and the failure of Toyota to report repeated cases of unintended acceleration in 2009.

Moss retired with a legacy of progressive legislative achievements, as did Magnuson and other leaders of the consumer revolution of the 1960s and 1970s. Some of them even lived to see the rising influence of anti-government views, unlimited political money, and public apathy erode what they had built.

In telling the story of the consumer decade and of John Moss, one of its towering leaders, this book attempts to shed light on that long-ago era. Is the consumer-information revolution that Moss, Magnuson, and their allies fought for dead or only forgotten?

The story of John Moss and the consumer wars of only yesterday is a David and Goliath tale. This story of amazing success, coupled with failure, may offer a reflection on where we as a nation are today.

# 1

# Troubled Roots

## *A Little Town in the Valley*

High above California's Central Valley, the American River rises in the peaks of the Sierra Nevada Mountains. The three forks of the American converge violently and plunge down the rocky slopes, gathering power as they sweep toward the valley below. At the foot of the Sierras—at the junction of the American and Sacramento rivers—lies the city of Sacramento and the fertile farmlands of the four-hundred-mile-long Central Valley, the heartland of California agriculture.

From the time Sacramento was settled in 1839, until the middle of the twentieth century, the American River made the city a dangerous place to live. Each spring, despite levees, dams, and dikes, as much as two million acre-feet of water—enough to cover the state of Rhode Island to a depth of three feet—roared down the American River, pointed like a dagger at the heart of Sacramento. The result was deadly flooding.

In 1935, during President Franklin Roosevelt's New Deal, years of state efforts culminated in federal approval and funding for the massive Central Valley Project. It was designed to provide flood control, water for irrigating the valley's crops, and cheap hydroelectric power for the homes and businesses of Sacramento and the valley. The Folsom Dam, an integral part of the project, was intended to do much of the heavy lifting, primarily by holding back the waters of the American River when they reached flood stage—if Folsom could ever get built.

Although the dam was approved by Congress in 1944, it stood incomplete nearly a decade later. Anger over the failure to finish Folsom ran high in Sacramento and the Central Valley. The potential for life-threatening floods fed local fears. Frustration over the dam spurred the area's newly elected congressman, John E. Moss, a thirty-seven-year-old appliance dealer, sometime real estate broker, college dropout, and Navy veteran. Elected to Congress in 1952, he headed off to Washington in January of 1953 with Folsom on his mind.

It was clear to Moss that failure to complete the dam as part of the Central Valley Project was the result of some kind of breakdown in the nation's capital. Congressmen, senators, and federal agencies did not appear to appreciate the urgency of putting up the money to finish it.

The first thing Moss did when he arrived in Washington—right after settling his wife, Jean, and two young daughters, Jennifer and Allison, in a small apartment off Connecticut avenue in the northwest part of town—was to dial the White House. He was an unknown congressman-elect from what was then a small city in northern California. He had not yet taken the oath of office. That did not deter Moss. He had, after all, met President Harry Truman briefly when Truman and his vice-presidential running mate, Alben Barkley, whistle-stopped through Northern California on the road to their upset victory over Governor Thomas Dewey of New York in the 1948 presidential race.

Four years later, however, Truman was about to leave office, having served a total of seven years as chief executive. During the 1952 presidential race, it had become clear that the New Deal, the Fair Deal, and the Democrats were running out of steam. Dwight Eisenhower had won a resounding victory over Adlai Stevenson in the November presidential contest and would be sworn in on January 21, 1953.

Moss did not let the constraints of time or changing politics slow him down. He asked Truman's secretary for a meeting with the president and was granted a fifteen-minute "courtesy" appointment. It lasted much longer. Like Moss, Truman made up for a minimum of formal education with political savvy and an innate ability to judge the cut of a man's jib. Truman must have thought the new congressman-elect sitting across the desk from him had a determined look, or maybe some decent ideas. Or he might have been impressed by Moss's victory in a tough district. Moss had wrested control of the city of Sacramento and five surrounding counties from a decade of Republican Party control. Whatever his motivation, at the end of the conversation, Truman asked,

"Congressman, is there anything I can help you with?"

"Yes, Mr. President, as a matter of fact there is one big thing," Moss said. In recalling that conversation, Moss said he told Truman, "We have been trying to get the Folsom Dam completed for many years. The money is being held up by the Department of the Interior, in Mr. Chapman's office. Once you leave the presidency I believe the chances of our completing the Folsom Dam any time soon will be lost."[1]

Truman reached over and took a little piece of paper from his desk. He wrote something on it, stood up, shook Moss's hand and told him he would do the best he could.[2]

Before Truman left office six days later, the Department of the Interior had furnished final approval for the funding and completion of the dam and its connection to the Central Valley Project. The approval landed on House Speaker Sam Rayburn's desk. Shortly, Congress put the Folsom money into a big appropriations bill. Construction resumed out in the Central Valley.

Two years later, the Folsom Dam across the American River was almost finished. It still had not been tested for flood containment by the Army Corps of Engineers. The waters in the American River above Sacramento would not wait. Record-breaking winter and spring floods struck Northern California. Unprecedented amounts of water roared down the rivers of the Sierra Nevada. The American, Sacramento, and Feather rivers carried cascades of water into the Central Valley. The "Marysville flood," as it came to be known, was the worst natural disaster in California since the San Francisco earthquake of 1906. In parts of the Central Valley raging waters swept away railroads and highways, inundated farmlands and orchards, drowned animals, and destroyed thousands of homes. In Marysville and Yuba City, which are just north of Sacramento on the Feather River, the disaster killed eighty people, injured forty-three hundred, and forced fifty thousand residents to flee their homes.[3] President Eisenhower declared a national disaster in the region.

But on the American River high above Sacramento, the newly completed, as yet untested Folsom Dam held fast. Thanks to Moss and his talk with Harry Truman, the city and the surrounding parts of the Central Valley escaped disaster. "It saved our city," said one elderly resident, decades later. "It saved the valley."[4]

* * *

Folsom Dam had been a major issue in Moss's first campaign for the California State Assembly four years before he ran for Congress. The former appliance dealer appeared willing to support costly new public works projects if he thought they offered a long-run benefit to his constituents. Campaigning for office for the first time, Moss told the voters that the Folsom Dam must be finished without further bickering. He pointed out that the project would not only be a means of flood control and irrigation, but also a source of public—not private—electric power.[5] Even before Moss was elected to anything, he had staked out a dangerous position. He stood in opposition to one of Sacramento's biggest economic power centers: the privately owned Pacific Gas and Electric Company. As a young candidate, Moss did not always temper his positions. In that first campaign, he said Sacramento was feeling the effects of a "blindly selfish policy carried out over a period of years by the private utility interests."[6]

From the very beginning, Moss demonstrated—as he did throughout his career—a willingness to tackle big economic interests. Sometimes wisely, occasionally impetuously, he fought to keep big interests—government as well as the private sector—accountable to the voters of his district and the country.

\* \* \*

John Emerson Moss was born on April 13, 1915, in Carbon County, Utah, in the small town of Hiawatha. True to its name, Carbon County was coal country. Moss, one of five children, was the son of a coal miner. His father, Henry, had trouble supporting his wife, Orta, and their children. That may be why he took to hard drinking.

Moss's mother's parents came West in the 1850s and landed in Sanpete County, Utah. Their roots were in Pennsylvania and western Maryland, where, as English and Scottish emigrants, they had settled before the American Revolution. Moss's mother's family, the Mauers and the Coxes, became Utah farmers and led a hard, simple life. They were practicing Mormons and members of the Church of Jesus Christ of Latter-day Saints.

John's father's family, the Mosses, had come from England by way of Australia. They arrived in Carbon County in the 1870s. There is some question about why they wound up in Australia. Escaping English justice is one possibility. The search for something better than they could find in class-dominated England is another. Years later in Utah, in the 1920s, Moss's grandfather became a cabinetmaker for Utah Fuel, a mining company. It was not a bad job—compared to digging coal. He could even afford a car now and then. When he did buy one, it was always a Studebaker.

John Moss's Uncle Curly was the sheriff of Carbon County. As family legend has it, Curly needed to get around the county but was too stubborn to learn to drive. So law enforcement in Carbon County was dependent on someone chauffeuring the sheriff around in Moss's grandfather's Studebaker.[7]

Moss's father, Henry, sometimes made a living in the mines. But nobody in the family had any real money. Few in Carbon County did, except the mine owners.

In the 1920s, when Moss was a boy, Carbon County was a violent place. The miners, working for low wages in dangerous conditions, tried to organize unions. Among the unions active in the state were the sometimes violent Industrial Workers of the World, known as the Wobblies. The radicalism of the Wobblies was crushed by the mine owners. The United Mine Workers were more successful, but the mine owners fought the miners and their unions with strikebreakers and police. The Utah state government did not intervene.

The words of a contemporary song probably capture the tenor of the times generally in coal country: "They say in Harlan County, there are no neutrals there; you either are a union man or a scab for D. H. Blair."

Down the road in Salt Lake City, the union organizer Joe Hill was tried on what some believe was a trumped-up murder charge. He was executed by firing squad on November 19, 1915. It is said he went to his death with a message for his fellow workers: "Don't waste time mourning, organize."[8]

As a boy, Moss lived through tough times. He saw national guard troops with machine guns camped on the porches of the homes around his family's small wooden house. He was not too young to feel the fear in Carbon County. But Moss liked the woods and open spaces of Utah. As a man, he remembered their tranquility.[9] Perhaps he remembered them because they were in sharp contrast to the tumultuous, challenging life he came to lead as a young man in Depression-ridden California, and later in the nation's capital.

The tough times in Carbon County were a burden for Moss's parents, Henry and Orta, who had five children to take care of. And they were very concerned about John's asthma, which troubled him all his life and was greatly aggravated by the coal dust-laced air in Carbon County. So Henry and Orta decided to pack up their family and leave Utah for Sacramento, where Moss's mother had two sisters.

The Sacramento where John Moss's family moved in 1923 was still a small river town—despite its "status" as the capital of California. The city was marked by rough streets, brackish water, a nonexistent cultural life, and the miles of farms that surrounded it. It would have been called a cow town if it had been located somewhere else. Although it had been the permanent capital since 1854, the state legislators disliked staying there long. They complained that the city was hot, smelly, and disease ridden.

The legislators particularly resented the critical comments of one of the town's two major newspapers, the *Sacramento Bee*. Adding to the discontent over legislative sessions in the dull little place was the continuous needling of the politicians by the *Bee*'s founder and editor, James McClatchy. The *Bee* once sarcastically celebrated the end of a legislative session with a two-word headline: "Thank God." The legislators became so incensed over the slight that they threatened to retaliate by moving the capital somewhere else. Fortunately for the city, the effort to move to San Francisco or elsewhere faltered, as did later attempts by a vengeful Southern Pacific Railroad to force the capital to relocate. But the very possibility that the state government might pull out of town galvanized city leaders and reformers to attempt to clean up Sacramento.[10]

not stay small for long. It experienced dramatic expansion.
s mostly based on government jobs—federal and state—
before and after World War II. But, from the days of the
_____ century gold rush and the legendary forty-niners mining for
gold up in the Sierra's, the region was divided by basic economic and
political differences.

Since settlement by the Spanish, vast tracts of land in Northern California had been controlled by large land-owning families. Settlers arriving
in California in the 1850s—after the first years of the gold rush—badly
wanted land. They confronted a confusing legal situation.[11] Much of the
land in the Central Valley was divided into vast private claims as big as
fourteen million acres each, a heritage from the Spanish American period.
The newcomers refused to recognize the Spanish land grants and squat-
ted on the land. They claimed it as theirs based on the old frontier tradition of the right of possession. Tensions between landowners and settlers
rose to a white heat by 1850.

James McClatchy arrived in Sacramento from New York in the same
year. McClatchy had been a correspondent for the *New York Herald Tribune*, edited by the abolitionist and populist Horace Greeley. McClatchy
started a newspaper in Sacramento called the *Settlers and Miners Tribune*.
He was a "Free Soil" advocate, as was his new newspaper. In August
1850, McClatchy was arrested by court order and thrown in the Sacramento jail for inciting a riot. His allies—squatters and settlers—marched
on the jail in an attempt to free him. Other citizens recruited by the mayor
and city leaders barred the way. A fierce gun battle erupted. The mayor,
the city assessor, the sheriff, and several settlers were shot dead. In all,
eight people died, six were wounded. One of the leaders of the Free
Soil group, James Robinson, was arraigned for the murder of the sheriff.
Robinson was never brought to trial. Instead, he was elected to the state
legislature, while still in jail.

There are some in Sacramento who believe that Horace Greeley urged
McClatchy to go west specifically to start a populist newspaper. A few
years later McClatchy founded the *Sacramento Bee*, which became an advocate of voiding the large land claims and placing land in the public domain.
The *Bee* became an influential opponent of concentrated power of all kinds.

The "squatters' riot" and landowner–settler violence left their mark
on Sacramento. Even after the settlers and the courts forced the breakup
of the large land tracts, a rebellious, populist streak remained. Farm and
railroad workers followed the forty-niners into town in the early twentieth century. They helped make Sacramento prosperous. Many of the
new immigrants were Italian, Eastern European, Portuguese, and Asian.
They were mostly poor. Their interests were not those of the investors,
businessmen, and middle-class homeowners who had preceded them to
the growing metropolis.

Despite Sacramento's growing prosperity, the *Bee* continued to reflect the populist views of its founder, McClatchy. That tradition was one of the reasons that the *Bee* and Walter Jones, its editor in 1948, looked with some favor on the candidacy of young John Moss for the state assembly and later for Congress.[12]

* * *

When Moss and his family arrived in Sacramento in 1923, the city was in the midst of transition. The progressive movement, spearheaded by politicians such as Hiram Johnson, was a powerful force in the city and in California. Johnson was elected California's governor, founded the Progressive Party, and was Theodore Roosevelt's vice-presidential running mate in 1912. The Progressive ticket, advocating more direct power for the voters, carried the state. The movement was given voice by McClatchy's son, C. K., and the *Sacramento Bee*. The movement and the *Bee* sparked reforms in the city, helping to change it from a small farm town isolated from the rest of the state to a growing urban center.

After World War I, the city experienced a building boom. True to their roots, city voters in 1923 authorized a public power authority, the Sacramento Municipal Utility District—or SMUD—to compete with the privately owned Pacific Gas and Electric. It did not gain full control of the city electric system until 1946, after years of litigation.

By the late 1920s, the city's population was nearing one hundred thousand. By all accounts, from new municipal water hook-ups to rising school enrollment, the future seemed bright for California's small capital.[13] But when the Depression hit, all parts of the city's economy were hurt. Agriculture, the economic driving force in the region, was crippled by plummeting prices. The canning industry suffered massive layoffs in 1932.[14] The Western Pacific Railroad fired two-thirds of its workforce. Two Sacramento banks—California National Bank and California Trust and Savings Bank—failed in January 1933, causing a run by depositors.

In 1930, 10 percent of Sacramento's residents were out of work. In February 1932, there was a job riot. Two hundred men fought for twenty temporary jobs unloading granite from Southern Pacific flatcars onto river barges.[15] As the unemployment numbers increased, so did the number of transient camps. People from other parts of the country, even harder hit than California, flocked to the Central Valley in search of seasonal work.[16] Rough shacks of tar paper and scrap metal sprung up along rail lines and highways, under bridges and overpasses, and in city parks and empty lots. The private sector, responsible for Sacramento's earlier prosperity, was overwhelmed. The government could not deal with the large number of unemployed. In July 1933, hundreds of homeless stormed the office of the Registrar of Charities, which had declared that only permanent Sacramento residents could receive relief.[17]

Progressive ideas were still strong in both the Democratic and the Republican parties. Communists, Socialists, and utopian groups thrived. The Communist Party, which in 1931 had begun organizing agricultural workers, had a small but committed following in Sacramento. Its size was unequal to the fear its presence generated. Eventually, run-ins with the local police culminated in a raid of party headquarters. Fourteen men were arrested. They were brought to trial on charges of "vagrancy" and the now forgotten crime: "criminal syndicalism." Amidst widespread public hysteria over the red menace, eight Communists were convicted. They were sentenced to jail for up to fourteen years.

Radical agendas were not the monopoly of the Communist Party. Author Upton Sinclair ran for governor in 1934. He lost narrowly on a socialist platform, a platform that would have turned most private industry over to state control.

The politics of the Depression years were tumultuous in Sacramento. The economic downturn helped fuel a resurgence of progressive ideals in the region. Some programs, such as the progressive state income tax and unemployment compensation, were ultimately approved by the voters and remain law today.[18]

* * *

The unstable political environment, combined with the failure of government and industry to solve the problems created by the Depression, made it painfully obvious to many that something larger and more comprehensive than state efforts was needed. Roosevelt's New Deal was broadly endorsed by citizens of Sacramento and Northern California. The New Deal initiated programs that helped with the city's most pressing problems and also laid the foundation and infrastructure for the area's future growth. Through programs implemented by the New Deal, Sacramento's water delivery and storage system was upgraded, and its flood-controlling levees were expanded and made significantly larger. And the Central Valley Project was started. It included plans for the Folsom Dam and more. John Moss, as a high school and college student in the 1930s, was impressed by the New Deal programs.

With the onset of World War II, Sacramento's unemployment faded overnight. The city became a major center for military bases to support the Pacific war. Two Air Force bases, McClellan and Mather, employed a large civilian workforce and brought streams of trainees and career military personnel to the area. Mather was soon bringing as much as $4 million a year to the local economy. Moss later played a major role in the growth of federal facilities in Sacramento and in federal support for building a deep-water port on the Sacramento River.

* * *

As the region grew, voting patterns changed. The conservative, rural vote was balanced by workers and middle-class government employees. They tended to be more liberal. After Roosevelt, the voters within the city were predominantly Democrats.[19] There was a Sacramento Democratic Central Committee that had some political clout in the 1930s and 1940s. But it was definitely not the basis of Moss's political career.

As a young man, Moss was deeply affected by the Depression and the advent of the New Deal. Moss said he admired Roosevelt because of his determination to get the country out of the Depression. He saw Roosevelt as a man who was willing to try different things until something worked. Most of all, Moss admired Roosevelt because he believed that FDR—called by some a "traitor to his class"—thought first about the lives of ordinary citizens.[20]

\* \* \*

Life in Sacramento did not at first go well for Moss. The family arrived in 1923 when he was eight. Four years later, Moss's mother, Orta, died suddenly at the age of thirty-two of acute peritonitis, an infection Moss said was caused by a cut from a minor fall on the back steps of the family's house. He said that sulfa or penicillin—not yet discovered—would probably have saved her. A year later, polio or spinal meningitis killed his youngest sister, Afton. She had been the closest to him of his four brothers and sisters. Sorrow over the deaths stayed within him. Many years later, when he talked about his mother and sister, his eyes would grow sad and distant.

After the death of his mother and sister, some of Moss's Mormon relatives said that John's lack of interest in the Mormon Church—the faith of his mother's family—may have been the cause of a divine intervention visited on his mother and Afton. That suggestion did not sit well with Moss. Neither did the politics of the Mormon Church, nor an attempt a few years later by its leaders to suggest how he should vote. As an adult, Moss mostly ignored the Mormon Church.

Moss's father Henry, alone in a strange city, was a miner in an agricultural town. He was often drunk. Eventually he abandoned his children. John's sisters went to live with an aunt. That left Moss and his brother, Henry, living alone in a little loft they rented in Sacramento. Moss was twelve; Henry was fourteen.

Moss claimed he was not really angry with his father for deserting them—just very disappointed. He saw his father rarely. He had no use for him, Moss said, particularly when he showed up in town drunk and had to be escorted to the railroad station by the sheriff. Moss said his father was just not up to his responsibilities as a father or a man.[21] Living up to responsibilities became a driving force in Moss's life.

The two brothers looked for ways to support themselves. John worked as a stock clerk, and, as he grew a little older, a tire salesman, repossession agent, department store clerk, and at odd jobs. At one point, he drove a hearse to make extra money. Moss had so little money that, when he attended Sacramento Junior College for a while, he walked several miles across town to save the ten-cent bus fare. He used the dime to pay for gas to light an oven in the loft to heat canned spaghetti for dinner with Henry. Sometimes the brothers ate the spaghetti cold for lack of a dime.

Moss went to Sacramento Junior College, now Sacramento City College, for almost two years. Some biographies incorrectly state that Moss received a college degree there. But Moss dropped out in 1933 a few months short of his degree. He said he just ran out of money. There were no programs, state or federal, to help him get through even a few more months of school. Education was important. So was eating. But he continued to read a lot: Blackstone and Holmes on the law, and every newspaper he could get his hands on. He got an education, but not the usual way. Moss learned about people who had little or no money and no one to turn to for help. He was one of them. He seems never to have forgotten that there was no safety net in those years.[22] The lack of a college degree did not seem to handicap him in dealing with PhDs, lawyers, and other highly educated people later in his life.

\* \* \*

Moss's political career started in the Depression years. After dropping out of Sacramento Junior College, he took a job as credit manager for a couple of tire dealers in Sacramento. One of the dealers was Schwab Tire, a distributor for B. F. Goodrich. His work was collecting payments from people who had purchased tires on the installment plan and could not make the payments. There was plenty to do.

The hours at Schwab were long. Jobs were not easy to come by in the 1930s; the pay was not much. And Moss did not like pursuing people for the tire money they owed to Schwab. So, when Schwab's branch manager told Moss and everyone else who worked there that they would have to work on Christmas Day in 1934, Moss balked. He told the branch manager he felt he had earned a day off and so had all the other employees at Schwab. He said he had "worked as hard as hell" and wanted Christmas off. The manager said he was sorry, but "you can't have it." As Moss told the story years later, he told his boss, "Oh, yes I can." When asked what he meant by that, Moss answered, "I mean I quit. That is the choice I have and I will exercise it."

So Moss hit the bricks in the middle of the Depression. He was out of work for a year.[23]

Moss combined careers in business and politics. By 1938, he was in the retail business, owning and managing the Moss Appliance Company in Sacramento. In the same year, he became a member of the Democratic State Committee and secretary of its education division. He was elected a national committeeman of the California Young Democrats. He worked hard to elect a Democratic governor and lieutenant governor in 1938. He was a young man who wanted to move up. He wrote to Ellis Patterson, the newly elected lieutenant governor, that he would be interested in moving to a staff job with the California State Senate.[24] Patterson thanked Moss for his hard work in the campaign. But, as far as a political job was concerned, Patterson suggested that Moss file an application with the local Democratic Central Committee, no friends of Moss's.

In a few years, Moss would find his own job, one that would eclipse the lieutenant governor in power, as well as accomplishment.

* * *

Moss married Jean Kueny in 1935. They were introduced by Jean's sister, Merle, at a dance at the Hotel Senator in Sacramento. There was instant attraction. They were married one month later in Carson City, Nevada. When they told Jean's Aunt Effie—a power in the Kueny clan—that they had gotten married, her evaluation of Moss was lukewarm: "A nice young man, but sort of an innocuous fellow."[25]

She may have been misled by his appearance. Moss, at five feet, seven inches in height, was not physically intimidating. He was a serious man with strong features and a square jaw. He had dark brown hair and brown eyes and wore steel-rimmed glasses most of his life, which added to his serious appearance. He could be funny at times, but usually he gave the appearance of being stern.

Jean was a fourth-generation Sacramentan. She came from a well-established local family. Financially, the Keunys had experienced good times and bad. Moss's daughter Allison recalled being told that during the Depression, Jean's dad, who was then in his late fifties, farmed all night and then went out and worked for ten cents a day to make ends meet. His second job was operating a jack hammer for the state highway department.[26]

Jean's family may not have had money, but they had an important gift they brought to Moss's political prospects: they were known as people of integrity. Jean's father, it seemed, never turned anybody away, even in the depths of the Depression. If someone needed food, they could work on his farm. If they needed a place to sleep, there was always the barn. He was known to keep his word. A handshake sealed it. That was the family's reputation. One of his brothers, Jean's uncle, was elected to the

Sacramento County Board of Supervisors. The family had been in the Sacramento area since the gold rush.[27]

It was a good marriage for John and Jean. She was his closest advisor for fifty-three years. She was also the boss at home. You didn't cross her for love or money, the daughters said—although John's steel backbone resulted in family showdowns once in awhile.

John and Jean did not believe in fighting in front of Allison and Jennifer, so they would go upstairs in their little house on Marty Way in Sacramento and battle it out. As Allison and Jennifer recalled, you could hear the screaming downstairs and probably next door as well. This would be followed by a long silence. John Moss would then stomp out of the house and go for a walk or a drive. Once, he drove around the block twenty-five or thirty times in the middle of a storm to cool down, but came back more upset than ever. He had managed to run the car out of gas and had to leave it several blocks away.[28] According to Allison, "Father had a long fuse. But when it went off, you were wise to stay clear."[29]

Moss's personality was unusual for a politician. He was serious and not overly friendly with colleagues. He did not party or pal around with legislators or lobbyists after the legislative sessions ended. He went home to Jean. He could be fierce and tenacious in public, but was mostly gentle with his family and his staff. There are pictures of Moss hammering the gavel when a witness at a hearing went on too long or did not answer a question directly. He is sometimes shown wearing a surgical collar—for a neck injury aggravated in an automobile accident—making him look even more bullish and fearsome. He once ordered a lawyer escorted out of a congressional hearing by the U.S. Capitol police because he was whispering to his client, something lawyers are prone to do. Moss wanted the witness—in this instance the chairman of the Federal Power Commission—to answer his questions without any coaching.

Some people in Washington thought Moss was antibusiness because of his stubbornness in adhering to positions that favored disclosure of government information or tough consumer protection laws. Almost instinctively, Moss took the position of the underdog, perhaps because he remembered being one himself. It did not make him popular with lobbyists or even some fellow members of Congress. But he was respected, perhaps even feared.

Moss's staff more than liked him. "Revered" is a description that many former staffers use. He invariably backed them up when they ran into trouble and were challenged by government agencies or private interests as they pursued his sweeping agenda. With his staff he was not the stern, hard-driving leader he seemed to be in public.

Once when a young staffer was threatened with personal retaliation by a big manufacturer for planning a hearing on the injuries possible to athletes from synthetic turf, Moss said kindly, "Don't worry about that. They can't hurt you. Put them right at the top of the witness list." And when another staff member visited his home late one night to review the facts of the next day's particularly contentious hearing about Firestone 500 tire blowouts, he spent half an hour showing the awed young man his prized glass collection before getting down to business. Once when he noticed a member of his staff eyeing an attractive female employee, he joked, "Why Lowell, I didn't know you could be distracted by things like that."

\* \* \*

Moss's dogged performance as an owner of the Moss Appliance Company, and later with Henry in Moss & Moss Real Estate, was eclipsed by his natural ability in politics and his driving ambition. He became friendly with faculty members at Sacramento Junior College. One of them was Professor Carson Sheets, who ran unsuccessfully for Congress in 1948, the year Moss launched his first campaign for state assembly. Another was Professor Albert Rodda, an early Moss mentor, who later served several terms in the California State Senate.

The college group was progressive. They were influenced primarily by two things: the Depression that lay upon Sacramento with a heavy hand; and the sorry state of the local Democratic Party. At the time, it was dominated by a group of business people who were closely affiliated with the "Third House." This was a sarcastic title elevating Sacramento's lobbying community to legislative status.

Moss and a number of the college faculty wanted to get involved in the activities of the local Democratic Party. In view of their low estimation of the local Party, Moss and the faculty group started Democratic clubs to give local activists and reformers a chance to make the party more responsive to their ideas. In a flashback to the squatters' riots of the previous century and the progressive reform movement of Hiram Johnson in the early twentieth century, Moss and his fellow activists of the 1940s fought for and gained control of the Democratic Central Committee. The college community, the clubs, and Sacramento's progressive tradition were the foundation upon which John Moss gambled his political future.[30]

Moss volunteered during World War II and served without particular distinction in the Navy for two years. He did not care for military life. He had a tendency to question the way things were done. It did not make him a good recruit. He made it through and was discharged for physical disability in 1944. This was not surprising. As his daughter Allison recalled, he had suffered from asthma and lung ailments since he was a child in Utah. Those diseases would continue to plague him throughout his life.

When he announced his candidacy for the state assembly in 1948, it probably came as a surprise to most Sacramentans. He was not well known. He did not have any money to speak of. He was not a favorite of the Democratic Central Committee. He ran an independent campaign in the Democratic and Republican primary elections for the nomination for the Ninth Assembly District seat, which covered most of the city.

Moss faced a four-term incumbent, Republican Dwight Stephenson. The race in both the primary and the general elections looked like it would be a real cliff-hanger. Under the cross-filing procedures then in effect in California, candidates could file for the nominations of all political parties. Moss and Stephenson both cross-filed in the Democratic and Republican primary elections.

A couple of months after Moss announced his candidacy for the state assembly, he received a boost with the endorsement of McClatchy's *Sacramento Bee*. Sacramento's other major paper, the *Sacramento Union*, endorsed Stephenson.

The *Bee* called Moss a "businessman"—which was a bit of a stretch— "whose social conscience and concepts of governmental duty are broad." The *Bee* also commented on Stephenson, calling his record "ultra conservative, negative, and ineffectual." The comparison did not hurt Moss.

The *Bee* noted that Moss favored many of the social programs of Republican Governor Earl Warren. For instance, Moss supported universal public health insurance for California, for which Warren had done battle with the medical lobby in the state. And the *Bee* noted that Moss was supporting Warren's highway construction program over the protests of the powerful oil industry lobby. The *Bee,* reflecting its progressive traditions, said Moss's support for public power was another reason to elect him. That and the fact that Moss, according to the newspaper, appeared willing to state his public positions without "pussyfooting."[31] It was a characteristic that Moss would not lose.

The *Sacramento Union,* the city's more conservative newspaper, saw things otherwise. In its editorials, it linked Moss to both the then-unpopular President Truman and to third-party presidential candidate Henry A. Wallace: "Election of the Trumanite would hamstring the administration's program. Election of the Wallaceite would be good news for Joe Stalin."[32]

Moss won some Republican votes, but lost the Republican primary to Stephenson. He did, however, narrowly win the Democratic primary by about a thousand votes. That set up a rematch between Moss and Stephenson in the general election of November 1948. Moss was again endorsed by the *Bee* and by some labor unions, the carpenters, trainmen, and teachers. He raised the grand sum of $1,250 for his campaign war chest.

In November 1948, with a small majority of the votes on the Democratic line and a good showing among Republican voters, Moss won a narrow victory in the general election by about fifteen hundred votes out of thirty thousand cast.[33] It was definitely not a landslide beginning.

A few weeks later, Moss walked across town from his little house on Marty Way in the modest Land Park neighborhood to the state capitol. He was sworn in as a very junior assemblyman. He immediately demonstrated characteristics that would remain with him throughout his political career. First, through his votes, his legislative proposals, and his public statements, Moss challenged major Sacramento political interests: Pacific Gas and Electric Company and the Southern Pacific Railroad. And then he went on to demonstrate that he was one fiery, combative legislator.

In the election of 1950, when Moss ran for a second term in the state assembly, he won both the Democratic and the Republican primaries and swept to victory unopposed in the general election. Upon returning to the state assembly in January 1950, he was elected deputy Democratic leader. He was now a second-term veteran. More importantly, he was a marked man in the California capital.

Many people with a lot of money wanted to see an early end to John Moss's political career.[34]

# 2

# Dangerous Ground

## *The California Legislature*

John Moss's four years in the California Assembly were filled with conflict, controversy, and—surprisingly—increasing political stature.

Moss's exceedingly narrow win in his first race for public office, for the California Assembly in 1948, did not stop him from taking on major issues. He seemed fearless—perhaps foolhardy—in his first term as a state legislator. He appeared willing to tackle almost any issue, any economic power, regardless of the possible political cost, if the issue was consistent with his progressive values. His friend, Congressman John Dingell, later called him a populist, who "had a sense of outrage about any issue that hurt ordinary people."[1] But, it is not clear, even now, what impelled Moss to take so many chances so early in his political career.

Moss had telegraphed some of his progressive positions clearly in the 1948 campaign. In announcing his candidacy for the Ninth Assembly District in Sacramento, he had opposed the "rule or ruin policy" of private utility groups and their "blatant lobbying tactics," and urged rapid completion of the Central Valley hydroelectric flood control project and the Folsom Dam. He favored public power, "security in old age," and adequate medical care for all citizens.[2]

And, in a preview of his long struggle against government secrecy, he urged more openness in California legislative proceedings. In particular, he wanted all bills introduced to be published and for the public to have an opportunity to comment on those bills. His goal was to prevent special interest lobbyists from succeeding in what he termed their "underhanded purposes" in the rush and confusion at the end of each legislative session.[3]

As a first-term assemblyman, Moss did what he said he would do. He championed public power and new flood control projects over the determined opposition of the area's private utility, Pacific Gas and Electric. Although the California Medical Association opposed it vigorously, he supported Governor Earl Warren's proposed universal health care plan. He sponsored a "full crew" law for railroad brakemen, which put him in direct conflict with the dominant Southern Pacific railroad, one of the largest employers in his district. He proposed slum-clearance legislation for the crumbling, crime-ridden west end of Sacramento, even though nobody then in power was ready to spend state money to do it. He backed subpoena power for the Warren Crime Commission, designed to root out corruption in California government, thus alienating a lot of ranking politicians and state officials.

First-term state legislators do not usually do such things. Taking on such a collection of controversial issues in a member's first term—or at any time—can be dangerous. Issues such as Moss involved himself in are usually avoided like an electrified third rail by elected politicians, particularly if they are opposed by large commercial interests. New legislators who take on such issues can expect short political careers. Moss took them on—and survived.

Part of the reason was diligence. He was known even to his opponents as a hard worker who was well prepared. It didn't hurt that he was smart and doggedly determined. Those factors appeared to count for something with the leadership of the California Assembly.

There was a revealing incident involving Moss, lobbyists, and eventually Republican Assembly Speaker Sam Collins during that first term in the legislature. It was clear to the freshman that powerful lobbyists for California's business interests, such as Pacific Telephone, the insurance companies, and the railroads, had a large role in the content of the legislation that made it through the legislature and to Governor Warren's desk. California's lobbyists then were no different from lobbyists now. They learned fast that money is the mother's milk of politics and that buying access to legislators is the basic first step to success for their paying clients.

In California, the money flowed freely. Lobbyists wined and dined the lawmakers. When the legislature was in session, they hosted a regular free buffet every night at a high-class restaurant at the Senator Hotel just down the street from the capitol. Most of the legislators were happy to drop by for the free food, the drinks, and, of course, the political talk. The California lobbyists did not discriminate between Democrats and Republicans. Everybody was on a first-name basis, and everybody was invited. Moss invariably declined their invitations. It seemed clear, he thought, that the lobbies had way too much influence over the California legislature.[4]

The issue, which Moss had addressed in his campaign, reached a boiling point after he took his seat in August 1949. It was then that a front-page article appeared in *Collier's* magazine with the headline, "The Secret Boss of California." *Collier's*, which had a big national circulation back then, wrote an exposé about the power of a Sacramento lobbyist named Artie Samish who successfully worked the halls of the state assembly and senate. *Collier's* said that Samish was armed with a commanding block of votes, a friendly Speaker, and control of key committees. The magazine reprinted some admiring comments about Samish:

A distinguished corporation lawyer said, "Artie is a one-man Tammany Hall."

A California political strategist said, "More than any man in California, he can deliver the legislature."

A successful corporation lawyer and author said, "Artie's the real governor of California."[5]

The *Collier's* article must have angered Governor Earl Warren. It seemed to anger Moss even more. In a speech a day or two later, Moss said the article should become the "memoirs of the last of the ruthless super lobbyists who make a mockery of representative government."[6] He wrote to Governor Warren calling for a special session of the legislature to pass new legislation curbing the big money lobbies. He promised to back Warren in restricting lobbying power. And in 1949, he combined with Warren and other legislators to push through new legislation requiring disclosure of campaign financing and lobbying expenses.

Moss wanted to go even further. He introduced his own bill to criminalize some lobbying activities. It went nowhere. Years later he conceded that, as he gained experience, he became "a little more reasonable" about regulating the use and misuse of lobbying.[7]

The lobbying registration bill was a major step forward for political reform in California. But, as Moss observed in his first term as an assemblyman, mere disclosure requirements would not really solve the problem of the overwhelming influence of money and lobbying on the legislative process.[8] In particular, he did not see how anything would change if the press did not care enough to make an issue of it, and the voters did not care who was paying money to whom—and what the money was buying them.

Moss's battle with lobbyists went to the core of what he found troubling—the way special interests threw around their influence and their attitude when they did so. He thought he could deal with the complex issues facing the state and the legislature, and he was ready to try. It was the dismissive, even degrading manner these fellows displayed toward the people's elected representatives that bothered young Moss.

The California Assembly met for only a few months each year in those days, starting in January and generally finishing its business in the spring or early summer. Because of the short session and the great amount of legislative business in the growing state, the legislature often stayed in session late at night. Almost everybody—legislators and lobbyists—were from somewhere else, like Los Angeles or San Francisco. So there was almost always a party thrown for the away-from-home members after the gavel came down on assembly sessions.

Moss noticed the parties even started while the assembly was still in session. The hip flasks up in the gallery came out early. The people in the gallery were not voters—they were well-paid lobbyists. They liked to enjoy themselves while they were working. In fact, they made so much noise that Moss could not concentrate at his desk on the assembly floor below. He had no staff; the California government did not furnish legislators with professional staff at the time. Most legislators relied on lobbyists for information and advice. Moss did not. In later years, he mellowed a bit and acknowledged that lobbyists could sometimes provide useful information.[9]

Moss got fed up with the distractions from the gallery. As a first-termer, he had little standing to speak up. But he complained privately to Sam Collins, the Speaker of the House. Nothing came of it. Finally, he rose publicly on the floor and raised a "point of order."

Making a point of order is the right of any member of a legislative body. It asserts that the rules are not being followed. It is a privileged motion and must be considered at any time under the rules. It requires immediate recognition by the presiding officer and a ruling on whether or not the rules are being violated.

Collins refused to look at Moss or recognize him to state his point of order. Moss repeated that he had a point of order. As he recalled, he stated it loudly. It was then that the Speaker turned off Moss's microphone. Perhaps the gentleman in the chair knew something touchy might be coming from the tone of the young assemblyman's voice or the expression on his face. Perhaps he just wanted to get on with the regular business. Whatever the reason, Collins elected to ignore Moss.

Risking the wrath of the leadership and perhaps all future invitations to after-hour buffets, Moss strode down to the well of the chamber. He stood directly in front of Speaker Collins.

Here is his description of that evening session and what happened:

> There were some occasions where I made a lot of noise. I remember one night towards the end of a session; all of the lobbyists up in the galleries had been out to receptions over at the Senator Hotel, and some excessive drinking had gone on. They were up there acting like a bunch of clowns and making noise and disrupting the orderly business of the legislature. I rose to make a point of order, and Sam Collins kept ignoring me, and he turned off my mike.
>
> And I remember saying, "Mr. Speaker, that won't do you one damn bit of good, because I can be heard over the mike."

And I kept on until he had to recognize me. And I said, "I demand that the sergeant-at-arms be instructed to take that bunch of monkeys out of the . . . gallery."[10]

Collins ruled that Moss's point of order was well taken. The gallery was cleared. And John Moss became even more of a marked man in the California Assembly from that day on—at least when the big lobbyists were in town.[11]

Despite his sometimes undiplomatic approach, Moss was appointed deputy Democratic floor leader after only two years in the legislature.[12] One reason may have been his reelection to a second term, with *both* the Democratic and the Republican nominations. The voters of Sacramento seemed to like their feisty young assemblyman. Although the Republican Party controlled both the assembly and the senate, Moss could claim a role in getting some important legislation passed—sometimes with support from both parties.

His record, particularly for a new member, bordered on impressive. Often, he did not tackle small issues. He had campaigned for the assembly focusing on electric rates charged to consumers by the giant Pacific Gas and Electric Company and on the weak public utility commission that was supposed to regulate the company. He continued to press for expansion of public power and flood control in the Central Valley.

Inadequate highways in Sacramento and the Valley were another Moss issue. Because of the postwar population surge, everyone thought the road system needed to be modernized and expanded. Governor Earl Warren wanted to pay for new roads with increased gasoline taxes. Moss backed Warren. That brought him into direct conflict with another powerful industry, major oil companies that sold gasoline to California drivers. The oil companies did not have any problem with building new roads. But they opposed the gasoline tax that Warren wanted to fund the roads. It was the first time, but would not be the last, that Moss was to tangle with Big Oil.

Moss also aligned himself with the governor over the establishment of a state crime commission. Warren and his staff wanted to pursue charges of corruption in the state government. They wanted a crime commission with subpoena power in order to do it. Many incumbent office holders— Republicans and Democrats alike—did not want the commission to have that power. A crime commission without the ability to subpoena books and records would, Moss thought, be a toothless tiger. But access to public and private records just might prove embarrassing to some people in government. Moss and Republican Assemblyman Gordon Fleury, who represented part of Sacramento, successfully led a fight to get subpoena power for Warren's crime commission.

Moss worked hard to obtain slum-clearance money to build publicly subsidized housing that would permit rebuilding some of the poorest areas of West Sacramento. Many of these neighborhoods were in his district, which included most of the city proper and some agricultural areas to the south in Sacramento County. He failed in his effort to start an urban renewal program in Sacramento. It was not until 1950 that the federal government did just that nationally, with the enactment of the Federal Housing Act and federal funding.

A major issue for Moss in his first term was a proposal for a universal, prepaid state health insurance program, known as the Salsman Plan, after its author. It was supported by Moss and Governor Warren and vigorously opposed by the California Medical Association—despite the potential for many new patients.

As with Pacific Gas and Electric and the oil industry, this was another preview of a fight thirty years later—between Moss and the American Medical Association—over rising health care costs and an issue Moss grew very interested in, so-called "unnecessary surgery." But in 1949, Moss and Warren failed to obtain approval for a state health insurance plan. Something like it—the Medicare-Medicaid program—was enacted nationally in 1964 during Lyndon Johnson's administration.[13]

Moss's stands on health care, electric rates, slum clearance, gasoline taxes, and the crime commission did not endear him to a lot of powerful interests in Sacramento. He was warned by other members of the assembly that he had been put on a "blacklist" maintained by some of Sacramento's big lobbys.[14] Its purpose was to recognize certain assembly members—like Moss—who should be guaranteed a short political career.

California lobbys would not soon forget another of Moss's actions immediately after he was elected in 1948: he called publicly for a special session to secure enactment of the "strongest possible" lobbying control law.[15] Despite significant opposition, a lobbying registration law sponsored by Assemblyman John "Bud" Collier, of Los Angeles, and strongly backed by Moss, was enacted during a special session of the legislature in 1949 that Moss had asked Warren to convene.

Moss's early legislative successes were not wholly accidental. There was a general perception at the time that many members of the legislature did not work very hard. Moss was different. Moss, neither a college graduate nor a lawyer, said that his willingness to put in long hours and get into the details of legislation was one of the reasons for his rise in the state assembly.[16]

Historian Donald B. Seney, of the Center for California Studies at California State University, interviewed Moss in 1989 about his career. Seney said he was "flabbergasted" at the amount and depth of Moss's research on legislative issues both as a candidate and as an assembly member. Seney located a chart that Moss compiled during his first campaign for the assembly. It listed every vote cast or missed by his opponent Republican Dwight Stephenson over the entire course of Stephenson's long career in the assembly.

During that campaign, he had issued a statement, carried in the *Bee*, noting that Stephenson had been absent for a vote on the crime control bill "on June 16, 1947, when SB 641 was passed by the Assembly . . . Page 4682 of the Assembly Journal shows that at 11:15 a.m. the sergeant-at-arms was ordered to go out and bring in Stephenson."[17]

Moss definitely liked getting into details then and later—such as the profit and rate of return of the Pacific Telephone Company. He said it made him more effective and—he might have added—more dangerous.

Hard work paid off from the beginning. Despite his aggressive stands on controversial issues, Moss made remarkable gains in power and committee assignments between his first and second terms in the assembly. In his first term, he was assigned—perhaps because of his obvious interest in electric and telephone rates—to the Public Utilities Committee. Despite the committee's imposing name, Moss was disappointed. It was in the hands of the utilities. Moss called the chairman "an errand boy for the utilities." Nothing the utilities opposed—including bills authored by the freshman legislator—ever got out of the Public Utilities Committee.[18] Moss was also put on the Civil Service Committee. That was normally a minor assignment, but it was an important one for Moss because of its potential impact on state employees. A lot of them lived in Sacramento. The Civil Service Committee was a political plus for him.

Surprisingly, in Moss's second term in the assembly, which started in 1951, he was promoted by the Democratic leadership to membership on the powerful Budget Committee, which controlled government spending in the state. He was also put on the Ways and Means Committee, which set state tax policy.[19] Overall, it was not a bad start for a poor kid with no money and no statewide contacts to speak of.

At the beginning of his second term, Moss did something that reflected both a personal characteristic and, over time, something of a problem. For most young politicians, the road to political power lies in building a good relationship with the party leadership and waiting patiently for a promotion. Not for Moss. He joined and then led what became known as the "Rules Committee Revolt." It directly targeted the Republican leadership of the assembly.

In 1950, the Rules Committee in the assembly controlled every bill that any member wanted to get to the floor for a vote. Nothing passed without the approval of Rules. Even the governor's priority legislation had to clear the Rules Committee. Its members were appointed by the Speaker, Sam Collins. Collins was a senior Republican and a powerful, elder statesman, who Moss claimed he got along with quite well.

The revolt came about because Moss and other junior members—of both parties—thought Rules Committee members should be elected by the assembly, not appointed by the Speaker. Moss and a group of young rebels secretly plotted to surprise the leadership at the beginning of the 1951 session and change the process. They won the organizing vote—making Rules Committee membership elective and reducing the Speaker's power. And Moss, at least initially, seemed to have avoided the usual political retaliation. The Rules Committee became an elective position. Moss was elected as one of its new members. The *Sacramento Bee* referred to the "Rules Revolt" in an article noting that Moss was considering a run for Congress.[20]

Moss's political prestige had advanced substantially during the 1951 legislative session. But for all his ability and apparent success, Moss admitted he could be disruptive and annoying.[21] He stepped on some large toes in the California legislature. The traditional, smiling, back-slapping approach was not a part of Moss's personality. He was a serious legislator. He had a temper. He had an inner impatience. It showed—even more in the years to come.

A lobbyist for Pacific Telephone once criticized Moss over a bill he had introduced to limit the company's management fees, which were, of course, reflected in consumer telephone bills. Moss had discovered that the fees were set at a fixed percentage of total company revenues. As nearly as he could calculate, the services the company rendered did not vary much and had little to do with total revenues. It was, Moss believed, a kind of hidden subsidy for the telephone monopoly and a tax on users. Moss thought the public utility commission should be required to set a management fee based on Pacific Telephone's actual management costs, plus a fair rate of return as determined by the Utility Commission—not a fee based on revenues.

At one point, the telephone company's lobbyist, a former army colonel named Howes, came into Moss's small office and told him: "You know young man, I've lived a long time. And I've learned you've got to have respect for free enterprise."

Moss said that what followed went something like this: "Look Colonel, I do. I have the utmost respect for free enterprise. But your monopoly is no free enterprise. You operate under a charter that gives you an exclusive right to serve and nobody can compete with you. And you're guaranteed a profit. I don't know anybody else that has that deal. . . . So, if you people want to become a free, competitive enterprise, then I'll certainly play the game under those rules."[22]

Moss's telephone rate bill got absolutely nowhere. And it began to look like Moss would go nowhere himself. His persistent support for bills opposed by big business interests helped to keep Moss on the "blacklist" and made further advancement of his political career appear very unlikely.

* * *

Moss angered powerful California economic interests. Often his fights were over consumer rates or service. Sometimes it was worker wages or safety. One of his pet projects involved the "full crew law," something the railroad unions badly wanted and the railroads opposed. The full crew law would have required the railroads to maintain a brakeman on freight trains as well as the engineer and other crew members. It was really a jobs bill, a union priority, and, according to the railroads, totally unnecessary "featherbedding."

When he was interviewed by historian Seney forty years later, Moss was still vigorously defending his full crew bill, arguing that the long-gone brakeman, riding the caboose, would have prevented some deadly railroad accidents.

But at the top of the list of Moss's transgressions was the lobbying registration and disclosure law passed in 1949 by Moss, Warren, and their reform-minded allies. That success was, in turn, based on the "Boss of California" scandal triggered by *Collier's* revelations about the power of lobbyist Artie Samish.

Samish worked the halls of the legislature effectively for interests as diversified as liquor, outdoor advertising, and horse racing—the basis for *Collier's* naming him the "real governor" of California.[23] Moss considered the situation a disgrace to his state and said so in the *Bee* and on the floor of the legislature.

To say that his initial positions did not endear him to many California power centers would be an understatement. There was a social element as well. Moss kept himself apart. He failed to talk much with the established economic and political powers at the chamber of commerce and the Sutter Club. The Sutter Club was the finest upper-crust establishment in town at the time. It was the gathering place of the city's power elite. Moss was not a member. In fact, he did not mix particularly well with anyone, except a few friends, family, and perhaps the voters. He was known as an "anti-lobbyist," but he denied any motive except a desire to limit lobbyists to their "appropriate" role.[24] In a later era of even bigger political money—or in a place bigger than Sacramento—his approach might have done him in. One might have thought the young assemblyman had a political death wish.

Moss's political friendship with Earl Warren, forged in the battles over California's roads, health care, the crime commission, and lobbying regulation, continued for years. Later, when the governor was appointed

Chief Justice of the United States Supreme Court and Moss was a congressman, the Warrens and the Mosses lived near each other in Washington. The families remained friendly. Allison, Moss's younger daughter, was a babysitter for Warren's children. She sometimes returned home late at night in his long, black limousine.

Although he was close to Warren on many issues, their friendship in Sacramento did not extend to social activities. His colleague from Sacramento, Republican Assemblyman Gordon Fleury, lunched with the governor several times a month, mostly at the Sutter Club. Moss was not invited. His position as a progressive and an "outsider" was why, according to Moss, the crowd at the Sutter Club "tried to plot my downfall."[25] The Sutter Club was an influential organization. It played a major role in ensuring that one of its best-known members mounted a well-financed and ominous challenge to Moss's 1952 attempt to win election to Congress.

Moss's promotion to deputy Democratic floor leader in his second term showed about how far he could go without completely alienating both the Democratic and the Republican leadership of the state legislature. He could have stayed on as a power in state politics for many years. But he had other ideas.

# 3

# I Went to Bed a Loser

## *Rough Road to Congress*

Nobody drafted John Moss to run for Congress in 1952. He drafted himself after talks with his main political adviser, Jean.

One day, when word got around that Moss was considering a run for Congress, he was approached by Earl Kelly, an officer of the Bank of America in Sacramento and a leading local Republican. Kelly invited Moss to his office for a serious talk. Moss had, after all, been the Republican candidate, as well as the Democratic candidate, in the 1950 election for the California Assembly.

As Moss recounted the conversation, Kelly started it off with a suggestion: "John, you know I have always been a supporter of yours. And you have made a remarkable record for yourself here. You stay in the assembly. You can stay there just about as long as you want. But you shouldn't go out and get in this race for Congress. Look for someone who is more seasoned."[1]

The advice was given in a friendly, fatherly way, Moss said, but he was having none of it. "Now Earl," he said, "you know that you have not always supported me. You live over in the Eighth Assembly District, and I represent the Ninth, so you couldn't possibly have voted for me. And I know you never gave my campaign five cents."

Moss said he would let the voters decide whether he had enough experience to run for Congress.[2]

The young legislator's motives for giving up a relatively safe seat in the state assembly and running in the newly created Third Congressional District were decidedly mixed. On one hand, he was a born activist. That much was apparent from his ambitious, progressive agenda in four years in the assembly. On the other hand, he needed the larger salary that went with being in Congress. He could not pay his bills while continuing as a state legislator.

"We didn't have adequate income," he recalled years later. "We couldn't afford all the time away from the appliance business for the regular and special sessions. You just couldn't attend to business. My wife and I decided we had to either get in or get out."[3] He was paid, as were all other assemblymen, the munificent sum of $100 a month. He could not live on that. In fact, Moss was so hard up for money that when the legislature voted an additional $10 a day for living expenses and many of the members refused to take the raise for fear that the voters would retaliate against them, Moss broke with them. "I'm going to take it," he said. "I need it. God knows it is not excessive."[4]

If he hadn't left the legislature to roll the dice on Congress, Moss probably would have gone back to the appliance business, or the real estate business with his brother Henry. But he seemed to want to make an impact. Something drove Moss. Perhaps he was angry about the difficulties of life in America as he lived it during the years of the Great Depression and afterward. He was forced to drop out of college. He was poor as a boy, then struggled to get by with a series of dull jobs. He saw poverty, slums, and joblessness all around him. He did not have an easy path as a small businessman. He wanted to change things.

Moss saw an opening in a new congressional district created by the 1950 census. It was a rare opportunity. California was awarded seven new congressional seats in 1952 because of its enormous postwar growth in population. One of the new seats was centered in Sacramento and surrounding counties. The city was a likely Democratic stronghold, but the district also included five rural, conservative counties. Created by the Republican legislature, it was intended to lean Republican. And based on voting patterns in past elections, Moss knew it was a close district, definitely not designed for an assemblyman that one local newspaper called a "fearless liberal."[5]

Many state legislators wait decades for an open seat in the U.S. House of Representatives. The newly created seat presented an opening for him after only four years of legislative experience. It was almost too soon to run. But he decided he wanted to be in Congress. He ignored the approaching torpedoes and forged ahead.

This first run for federal office was not going to be any cake walk—politically or financially. John and Jean did not have any real money. They sold the building that had housed the Moss Appliance Company for $10,000 and put that into their campaign fund. They raised a little bit of money from their families, mostly Henry, John's brother, and Jean's dad. Moss's campaign statement for the primary election of 1950, just before he declared his candidacy for Congress, is revealing. He raised a total of $2,338.65. The Carpenter's Union gave him the largest contribution: $500. The state and county Democratic committees kicked in a combined $300. The Cannery Workers Political Action and Education Committee donated $150. The balance came in small sums from assorted individual backers and Moss-Kueny relatives. No contribution from any business association, corporation, or lobbyist is listed in Moss's campaign finance statement.[6] Moss financed his first congressional campaign on about $20,000.

He announced his candidacy for Congress on December 3, 1951.[7] His statement said he would seek the nominations of both the Democratic and the Republican parties under the cross-filing procedures California then had. He emphasized the immediate need of the sprawling new district for the development of the Folsom Dam flood control project, an improved irrigation system for farmers, and more hydroelectric power for its growing population. It was not the usual platform for an urban liberal.

Moss faced a well-funded, well-established, and popular opponent in Les Wood, later elected mayor of Sacramento, which was the heart of the new Third Congressional District. Wood was not only well known and well financed, he was a grand master of the Sacramento Masonic Lodge. And that meant, according to Moss's campaign manager, Jerry Wymore, that Wood had a tremendous network of contacts up and down the Central Valley. Wood was also a member of the establishment Sutter Club and had been the president of the Sacramento Chamber of Commerce. He was a very prominent Republican. And he had once been a close, personal friend.

In 1949, when he was a rising Republican politician, Wood had told Moss that he would serve as the chairman of a "Republicans for Moss" congressional committee. So Moss was somewhat stunned when Wood reversed himself and decided to get into the congressional race, not *for* him, but against him. It seemed clear that the Chamber of Commerce, the Sutter Club, and other interests in Sacramento had decided that Moss's positions on key issues and his unwillingness to accept much guidance from business leaders was a bit too radical for them. They were motivated enough to ensure that he had a well-known and well-funded Republican opponent. Moss had received an early lesson about political friendships.

And then Arthur Coats, a Democratic assemblyman from Sutter County—an important part of the new congressional district—made things even more difficult by announcing he would also jump into the race against Moss. Coats was a lawyer from a prominent family. His father was a superior court judge. Moss now had opposition within his own party, which would obviously split the Democratic vote, and also for the large GOP vote. It was a classic squeeze play—and it usually worked.

Even more ominous forces were opposing Moss. In 1952, Dwight Eisenhower, the hero-general of World War II, was at the top of the Republican ticket as its candidate for president. Californian Richard M. Nixon was the vice-presidential candidate. It looked like any Democrat would have a hard time in California that year. The previous election in 1950 had been an almost complete Republican sweep of the state. Republicans controlled all but one of the six statewide elective offices, starting with the governor. Both of California's United States senators were Republicans. So were thirteen of the state's twenty-three representatives in Congress. Republicans had strong majorities in both houses of the state legislature.[8]

Maybe the Third could be a competitive district for a moderate Democrat, in a normal year. But not in 1952. Not for John Moss.

Meanwhile, the Democrats in Washington were running out of steam. They had controlled the federal government since FDR's election in 1932. Harry Truman had been president for seven years, and the country had grown tired of him and his administration. The economy was not doing well. The New Deal and Fair Deal programs that had helped pull America out of the Depression and win World War II did not look as good in 1952 to the American public.

Then there was the problem of the Democratic Central Committee in Sacramento. It had become clear that Moss did not take direction very well from senior party leaders. The chairman of the Democratic Central Committee, Bob Zarick, did not like Moss at all. He did not intend to support him for Congress. That may have been why Democrat Arthur Coats jumped into both primaries.

Looming problems and long odds did not appear to deter Moss. He and Jean, with support from their family and a few friends at Sacramento City College, decided he would leave the security of deputy minority leader of the assembly and run for Congress.

* * *

Jerry Wymore lived in Sacramento all his life. He worked as a real estate broker at Moss & Moss Real Estate, Henry's company, where John had hung out a shingle after his military service in World War II. While John Moss had a desk at Moss & Moss, as well as an appliance business, his real work was politics. Wymore and Moss got along well. There was something about Moss that moved Wymore, who was a registered Republican with no political experience, to take a chance on him. He became his almost full-time campaign manager—without pay.[9]

At Moss's memorial service nearly fifty years later, Wymore recalled that his life and that of John Moss had been intertwined for half a century. And the passion of his recollections about the man made it clear that it had been a strong relationship. Wymore was particularly sad that Moss's image had become one of a stern, combative political leader.

Wymore said Moss had really been a fun guy. He talked about traveling the Third District with John to get out and meet the voters. They raised campaign money by having ham-and-bean dinners for fifty cents a person—a sum that, at that time, almost anyone could afford. They would get a couple of hundred people together and make a hundred dollars for the campaign fund. There were no check bundlers and six-figure "Pioneers" in those days.

Despite his limited personal skills as an inside politician, Moss loved to get out and talk to voters. It did not matter whether they agreed with him or not. He was frank. Sometimes he was blunt. When he did not agree with someone, he tended to say so. It is not a trait that is particularly helpful to young politicians. But Moss was willing to listen to anyone. In later years, that habit held true even for some lobbyists, who were generally opposed to his consumer and investor protection legislation.

Wymore said Moss quit smoking during the race, and, in order to show solidarity, Wymore quit too. Instead of smoking, they ate candy constantly as they traveled around the new Third Congressional District. Wymore said they both gained ten or fifteen pounds. But they had fun. One of Wymore's favorite memories of that first campaign took place at Moss's house when Wymore and his wife, Mary Fran, got a man from the Arthur Murray dance studio to come over and teach John, Jean, and a bunch of Moss supporters how to do this new dance—an early version of the Twist.

People could not believe it. The serious candidate and his pretty young wife doing the Twist? Along with a bunch of youthful volunteers?

"Well, they kind of did it," Wymore said. "There was a big loveseat in the living room. So John and Jean went behind the loveseat, where people couldn't really see them shake very much, and they danced over in the corner." But they did do the dance, along with the rest of the Moss-for-Congress committee.

The issue of communism was a factor in the campaign. Senator Joseph McCarthy was at the peak of his political power in Washington and the nation. His purported list of communists in government and his charges of widespread disloyalty had a powerful impact on American public opinion in 1952. It was a year when the menace of Russian power, the danger of another world war, and deep fears over possible disloyalty in the American government were growing. In 1950, Richard Nixon skillfully used the issue in California to win election to the United States Senate over Democrat Helen Gahagan Douglas. He denounced Douglas as a Communist dupe and a pinko.

Tucked away in Moss's files is a handwritten note he sent to the defeated Douglas after Nixon's Senate victory: "I have not written sooner to express my admiration for your battle for decency during the recent campaign because I felt so deeply the shame of California for the representatives we now have in the Senate. . . . Wisconsin has only one McCarthy, we have two. I hope to God that 1952 will be a year of redemption for the Democratic Party and the people of California."[10]

In 1952, the same tactics were tried against Moss in Sacramento. Word was spread that his progressive voting record in the California state legislature suggested that he was at the very least a Communist sympathizer. Moss would not stand for it. He was a businessman and a veteran. He had fought his way up from nothing. He had sold appliances and real estate. He might have ideas about improving things, but he was no Communist sympathizer.

Moss walked into the Sacramento bank, whose president had been referring to him as a "Red." He stood in front of the banker's desk and looked directly at him without saying anything. "Good morning, John," said the banker, "I'm glad to see you." "No, you're not glad to see me," Moss told him. "And if you ever suggest anywhere that I am a Communist, the next time you see me will be in court." The banker's jaw dropped. Moss did not say another word. He turned on his heel and walked out.[11]

Then, at a public meeting in Elk Grove, a tiny place some fifteen miles south of Sacramento where the Southern Pacific still rumbles through the middle of town, an elderly voter stood up during the question period. He said he thought that Moss might have Communist sympathies. Moss's response was blunt. "Well maybe I am one," he said, "and let me tell you the kind of Communist I am. I love to own property. I want to get ahead. I want to make money. I want to be free of any political influence that isn't absolutely necessary. I want my children to have a great many opportunities. . . . Now if that's a Communist, I guess I'm guilty."[12]

Despite his liberal voting record in the legislature and the red-baiting tenor of the times, nobody could ever hang the label of Communist sympathizer, pinko, or dupe on Moss in that first campaign, or at any time afterward.

Moss did have at least one big thing going for him in the campaign. It was the *Sacramento Bee*, the larger of the two daily newspapers in town. Moss said he never sought the *Bee*'s endorsement, but they did ask to interview him when he announced his candidacy for Congress. He spent a lot of time talking to their editorial board, after which he was invited to meet with Herb Phillips, the political editor of the *Bee*. When he got there, Phillips's first question was, "Who writes your stuff?" Moss said, "I do." Given Moss's lack of formal education, Phillips may have had doubts. He proceeded to question Moss closely to see if the claim could possibly be true. The discussion went on for a long time.

According to Moss, nothing was asked of him, and the *Bee* editor gave him no commitment. He said he did not leave the meeting with any strong conviction as to what the *Bee's* interest in him might be. A couple of days later, on the Saturday before the primary election, which was held on the first Tuesday in June, the *Bee* endorsed him for Congress. It gave him a lot of positive press coverage.

The *Sacramento Union*, the more conservative Sacramento newspaper, did not give him anything. It attacked him repeatedly and endorsed his opponent Les Wood.

Nonetheless, Moss developed strength in the conservative agricultural area south of the city, known as the Delta. There were large and small vegetable farms down there and lots of farm workers. Jean's dad, who was a farmer in the area, had been helpful to a lot of people in trouble in the Depression. As Moss recalled years later, you get "a lot of brownie points" for doing things like that.[13]

Moss got an unexpected break from a comment by Walter Jones, the editor of the *Bee*. Some years before the 1952 election, there had been a proposition on the California ballot to allow the state to tax parochial schools for the general public school fund. Moss's opponent Les Wood, as it turned out, had signed a petition in support of the proposition. It had been all but forgotten, but Moss's novice campaign manager Wymore and Albert Rhoda, from Sacramento City College, dug up a copy. Wymore took it over to the *Sacramento Bee* and asked Walter Jones if it was newsworthy. Jones, who at first did not really want to take a partisan position in the campaign, looked it over anyway. Then he read it again. Wymore told him they were going to print about one thousand copies of the petition with Wood's name on it supporting the tax on Catholic schools and distribute them around the district. Jones said, "Hell no. Don't do that. Print 10,000 copies."

So Wymore had ten thousand copies of the petition printed. The Sunday before the election, Bill Merrick, another Moss supporter, went to all the Catholic parishes in the city and handed out Wood's endorsement of a tax on the parochial schools. "It was a crazy thing for Wood to do," said Wymore. "But, you know, the Masons never did have any time for the Catholics."[14]

The three-way primary campaign in June was fiercely contested and very close. Wood had a well-funded campaign. Moss ran on a shoestring, his assembly record, and the endorsement of the *Bee*.

All of the ghosts of Sacramento past—miners, squatters, speculators, progressives, unions, business—sharply divided the vote in the Third Congressional District that year.

All three candidates—Moss, Wood, and Coats—were running in both the Democratic and the Republican primaries. Moss *lost* the total vote count. He finished more than ten thousand votes behind Wood, out of one hundred and twenty thousand votes cast overall. But in the Democratic primary, he narrowly won the nomination by a few thousand votes. If Wood had gotten a few more votes in the Democratic primary—a switch of fewer than twenty-five hundred votes—he would have been nominated in both the party primary elections, and no general election would have been necessary under the California electoral rules then in effect. But since Moss had eked out a narrow win in the Democratic primary, that forced a second confrontation between Moss and Wood in the general election.

The votes in the 1952 primary looked like this:[15]

| Candidate | Democrat | Republican | Totals |
|-----------|----------|------------|--------|
| Moss | 30,381 | 14,244 | 44,625 |
| Wood | 25,679 | 29,129 | 54,808 |
| Coats | 13,943 | 4,980 | 18,923 |

With such a narrow win in the Democratic primary, Moss's political future looked very doubtful. The big question: which way would the Coats votes go? November—election day—was fast approaching. So Jean and her sister, Margaret Anderson, and several friends went out and campaigned among the farm workers and small farmers in the rural counties around Sacramento and in the Delta. So did the candidate. They worked Sutter, Glenn, Yolo, Colusa, and Yuba—counties that rarely saw a campaign worker, let alone the candidate or his wife. They walked through the hick towns and muddy fields. Sometimes, Jean and her friends had to slog through the fields dressed in high heels and stockings. Jean said they must have been a sight.[16]

When they were in the fields and small towns, they talked to farm workers and local people. They did not discuss issues or anything like that, Jean said. She just told them about what a really nice guy John was and that he was her husband. Her pitch went like this: "He was a very ordinary guy with a nice wife, and, by God, he needed a break."[17]

They also spent time walking through the poor sections of West Sacramento. They worked the red-light district—there were plenty of voters there, Jean said. And they were voters who nobody talked to much. Sometimes, Jean went out with a Portuguese friend of hers named Roberta. Jean's dad had some Portuguese friends in the large immigrant community in Sacramento, and that gave them a little bit of a toehold.[18]

One day, Jean and Roberta were in a rundown area in West Sacramento early in the morning. They wanted to put a "Moss for Congress" sign in the window of a somewhat seedy bar and grill. It had just opened—at 8:00

a.m. Jean was feeling pretty down about leaving her two young daughters crying at home. Neither Jean nor Roberta drank much. They realized that they probably ought to order something if they were going to ask the owner for a favor. So, they joined a few early morning drinkers and asked for a couple of whiskies. The owner seemed stunned. "Ladies," he said, "Don't you think that a cup of coffee would be better?" So Jean and Roberta told the owner that what they really wanted was to put up their sign in the bar's window. "No problem," said the owner. He proved to be a strong supporter of Moss for Congress.[19]

"We needed everything we could get," Jean said.[20] That is why the Moss entourage talked to small-town newspaper editors in towns like Woodland and Colusa. Once they stayed overnight as the guests of the editor of a small newspaper and ended up drinking more than they should have. It turned out to be a weird drinking bout. A lot of local people dropped in. The "evening" lasted almost all night. "The most fun I ever had in my life," Jean said later. "John and I really got a charge out of it."

So did the campaign. Jean said that, "after that evening, you could hardly have an editorial down that way that wasn't favorable."[21]

Moss was not above using some negative campaigning. He linked his Republican opponent for Congress with California's Senator Richard Nixon, who was not particularly popular in Sacramento. By then, Nixon was the Republican vice-presidential nominee on the Eisenhower ticket. Moss issued a statement shortly before the election referring to a "slush fund," which had been raised by wealthy Republican donors for Nixon. He called it the "outright purchase of a United States Senator by the Millionaires Club of Southern California." He did not stop there. "Here in Sacramento," he added, "at a series of meetings in the Sutter Club last spring, attended by men of the same type as those who previously selected Nixon . . . Les Wood was selected, drafted, or grafted as a candidate of the Republican Party for Congress. And after the most costly primary campaign ever conducted in this Third District, he was nominated by the Republican Party. . . . I ask Mr. Wood: how much money has been promised, if you are elected, as supplemental income?"[22]

Moss was also willing to associate himself with Adlai Stevenson, who was trailing Eisenhower in the presidential race. Moss said he believed Stevenson had brought to the campaign "a frankness most refreshing and unusual in these times."[23]

So the November election came down to the Democratic base in Sacramento County—including labor support—against the rural Republican base, the Chamber of Commerce, and most of the business community.

Election day, November 4, 1952, rolled around. John and Jean, with Jerry and Mary Fran Wymore, worked the polls all day, then decided to go out to dinner and, after that, to the Eaglet Theatre in downtown

Sacramento to relax a bit while the votes were being counted. The returns were not due in until about 10:30 p.m., so the Eaglet was a way of passing the time. After all those weeks and months of ceaseless effort, they had to take their minds off the voting and Moss's imminent fate. At intermission, they got the returns from the East Coast in the presidential race. Eisenhower was, according to Wymore, swamping Stevenson. That was not a good sign.[24]

They got out of the play about eleven p.m. The more affluent neighborhoods in the city reported their returns early. They were always first, Wymore said, because those people voted early. They had a lot of disciplined voters and they were mostly Republicans. Plus, they had experienced people running the polls, and they counted the vote quickly. The returns were devastating for Moss. He was way behind Wood.

They went back to Moss's house on Moss Drive, so named because brother Henry had built some tract houses in the neighborhood. A campaign worker named Sue Newman, who was usually at headquarters answering the telephone, was at the door when people arrived for the election night party. As the campaign workers piled in, Sue would shake her head sadly, and they would all just stand around or drop into a chair exhausted. It was like a wake, not a party. Things were going terribly.[25]

At about midnight, Moss concluded he was beaten. He wrote telegrams to the *Bee* and to Les Wood conceding defeat. Wymore urged him to wait. "We owe it to all of the people who helped us," he said. "Let's go down to headquarters and talk to the people there. Maybe we'll learn something new."[26]

So they went to Moss's downtown headquarters at about 1 a.m. on November 5. They felt they had strength in the old Ninth Assembly District, which Moss had represented for four years, and which was part of the new congressional district. They thought people there knew him and liked him.

The returns were slow coming in from the rural districts south and west of Sacramento and from far out Yolo County. It was a long way from the center of the city, and they were not counting votes very fast. It was an ominous sign in unknown territory. When Moss and Wymore got to campaign headquarters, they were still way behind. But the gap was narrowing a little.

At 1:30 in the morning, Moss, still trailing badly in the returns, said good-night to his volunteer campaign manager, went home, and went to sleep. "I went to bed a loser," he said years later. He thought he would have to go back to the appliance business.[27]

Dwight Eisenhower was elected president in 1952, carrying the state of California by more than six hundred thousand votes. William Knowland, a Republican, was elected United States senator on both the Republican and the Democratic tickets, with 3.9 million votes. Republicans won control of the California House delegation, by two to one. Of the seven new congressional districts, five were won by Republicans; only two by Democrats. Republicans added to their majorities in the state senate and assembly.[28]

But in Sacramento's new Third Congressional District, John Moss had come from behind in the small hours of the morning. Based on the votes from rural farm workers in the Delta and from the poorer, late-reporting parts of Sacramento County, Moss nosed out Sacramento's future mayor by a few thousand votes—0.4 percent of the total cast.

John Moss was on his way to Washington. His combative, progressive record in the California Assembly was already well known. So was his drive and ambition, if anyone in Washington had cared to check.

*Moss at Folsom Dam circa 1953. Moss's first act in Washington, D.C., was to obtain funding to complete the dam—just before devastating floods in California. Credit: courtesy, California State University at Sacramento Archives.*

Folsom Dam at flood stage, protecting Sacramento and the Central Valley. Credit: courtesy, National Oceanic and Atmospheric Administration.

1948 campaign flyer, complete with typographical error, from Moss's first run for California Assembly. Credit: courtesy, California State University at Sacramento Archives.

*President Harry Truman greets Moss on a campaign swing through California circa 1948. They would soon meet again. Credit: courtesy, California State University at Sacramento Archives.*

*Moss (far left) and Earl Warren (seated), who was the Republican governor of California at the time, cooperated on key California legislation and remained friends when both were in Washington. Credit: courtesy, California State University at Sacramento Archives*

*Moss, right, with presidential candidate Adlai Stevenson during the 1952 presidential campaign. Moss stood by Stevenson despite Dwight Eisenhower's commanding lead in the polls. Credit: courtesy, Moss family.*

# 4

# The People's Right to Know

## *A Distant Shore*

When John Moss arrived in Washington, D.C., in January 1953, it was still a sleepy southern-oriented town, mocked for being a city of southern efficiency and northern charm. In his book *Loyalties*, Carl Bernstein, who grew up in Washington, wrote of the "slow, drawled, hazy, small-town atmosphere of mid-century Washington."[1] It was also a racially divided city. The schools, playgrounds, and swimming pools of the capital, he recalled, were all segregated, as were the hotels. Only the Gayety Burlesque Theater, on Ninth Street, allowed blacks and whites to mix freely.[2]

Beyond segregation, there was a poisonous political atmosphere in the city. It was not yet a time when K Street lobbyists had the immense power they have today to influence Congress, but Senator Joseph McCarthy had frightening power. He was riding anti-Communist fears that he had helped arouse and that propelled him to great power in the Senate and in the nation. The House Un-American Activities Committee was making headlines too, with its endless investigations of security risks, supposed Russian spies, and disloyalty in dozens of government agencies and American industries.[3]

Congress was a different place then—smaller, slower moving, and somehow more personal. One former administrative assistant for Senator Mark Gillette, a long-forgotten Democrat from Iowa, said the senator's staff consisted of one caseworker and a couple of secretaries—all tucked into a grand old office with a big fireplace that overlooked the Washington Monument and the Mall. When the Senate went out of session, the measured pace slowed to a complete stop. "For months you didn't have anything to do," Gillette's staffer recalled. "There just wasn't the volume of business there is now."[4]

President Harry Truman, in an effort to blunt or perhaps ride the wave of anti-Communist hysteria of the times, issued an Executive Order establishing the administration's Loyalty Program. It directed Truman's attorney general to compile a list of Communist organizations and "front" organizations, and to investigate the loyalty of federal government employees. The targets could, based on the results of these investigations, be fired from their government jobs, prosecuted, and made virtually unemployable. They faced public condemnation and personal humiliation in the process. People investigated under the Loyalty Program were not allowed to confront their accusers or see the charges against them—many based on hearsay evidence—in secret files compiled by the Federal Bureau of Investigation.

United States Court of Appeals Judge Henry Edgerton wrote an opinion concerning the firing of one such government employee: "Without trial by jury, without evidence, and without even being allowed to confront her accusers or to know their identity, a citizen of the United States has been found disloyal to the government of the United States."[5]

Edgerton found the proceedings to be unconstitutional. "Whatever her actual thoughts may have been," he wrote, "to oust her as disloyal without trial is to pay too much for protection against any harm that could possibly be done."

Edgerton's views did not prevail. He was the lone dissenter on the District of Columbia Court of Appeals. The court affirmed the employee's firing from government service. The United States Supreme Court divided evenly in the case, four to four, thus upholding the legality of the Truman Loyalty Program. The result was fear, even hysteria permeating Washington.

* * *

McCarthy began his rise to prominence toward the end of the Truman Administration. In 1950, he made his infamous announcement that he possessed—in fact, held in his hand—a list of 205 card-carrying Communists working at the State Department. The shocking charge was made in a speech in Wheeling, West Virginia, and it swept across the nation.

Moss knew all about the McCarthy approach. He had been a target of similar charges—of being a Communist or a Communist sympathizer—in his California campaigns, for both the state assembly and Congress. He had survived the attacks. But he did not forget them. In fact, they played a key role in his long campaign to secure freedom of information in government—a campaign that was, in part, grounded in his anger at being attacked with such potentially devastating charges, and by the attempt to use unsubstantiated smears against him. Moss's information battle was also based, coincidentally, on his assignment to a very obscure congressional committee. It had legislative responsibility for federal civil service employees.

When he took his seat in Congress in January 1953, representing California's new Third Congressional District, there was no evidence in Moss's political history that limiting government secrecy and protecting freedom of the press would be causes he would champion for twelve long years—and for the rest of his life. In fact, as he settled in as a first-term congressman, he thought he would not last long in Washington. "By all that was holy," he said, "I was destined to be a one-termer."[6]

The reason for this pessimism was his almost inexplicable stand on the Tidelands Oil bill, a major issue in his first term in Congress. The Tidelands controversy involved a dispute between the federal government and several states, including California, over the ownership of the tidelands—the underwater land immediately off the coasts of the Pacific Ocean, Atlantic Ocean, and the Gulf of Mexico.[7] Truman issued a proclamation supporting federal ownership, a position that would have resulted in denying hundreds of millions of dollars annually in oil royalties to the coastal states—including California.

California claimed ownership of all land within three miles of its coast. It and other coastal states sued the federal government to confirm their title to the tidelands and, most of all, to their mineral resources. The states lost when the Supreme Court held in 1947 that the federal government had established ownership of the tidelands up to the high water mark on the beaches. Congress did not agree. It promptly voted in favor of the Tidelands Oil bill, giving the states clear title to offshore land, oil, and minerals under the seabed for three miles offshore—and overruling both the Supreme Court and the president.[8]

It was an easy vote for any representative from a coastal state. They had a decent argument that the states historically claimed ownership of the seabed off shore—and besides, the bill meant major money for state coffers. It should have been even easier for an untested, vulnerable freshman representative: just follow the lead of the state delegation and the majority in Congress.

Every member of the California delegation, regardless of party, voted in favor of the Tidelands Oil bill—and in favor of state revenues. Not Moss. He voted against the bill, which later became federal law over Truman's veto. Moss had read the constitution and historical documents and decided the oil belonged to the people of the United States, not just to those who happened to live in California, Florida, or Texas. That is how he voted. It looked like political suicide at the time. His opponents hammered him over his vote for years.

There had, however, been an almost instant bonding between Moss and the voters of Sacramento. He seemed to fit the district perfectly, according to Wymore, his chief California strategist. They must have liked hard-nosed politicians with strong opinions. He won a second term in Congress, despite his apparently suicidal Tidelands Oil vote.

The Sacramento-Moss connection had started with his election to the California Assembly. Moss had a clear record there. He favored lower utility rates for consumers, public power to compete with the giant Pacific Gas and Electric Company, increased wages for government workers, and better working conditions for railroad employees.[9] His stands on the issues seemed a natural fit for Sacramento's voters over the course of many years.

Moss's state legislative record, his combative personality and hard-luck early life suggested he might stand up to big interests when he got to Washington. The young congressman knew about everyday problems from his own experience—especially the sudden death of his mother and subsequent abandonment by his father when he was twelve years old. He had to struggle to go to school and never finished college. He said later it was "almost a crime to deprive people who have the will to seek education of the opportunity to do it." He acknowledged, "[I] gained all of my bits and pieces of knowledge and understanding the more difficult way . . . but at the same time, it made me appreciate them more, and I probably dug deeper to get some of the facts."[10]

\* \* \*

In the nation's capital, in 1953, Moss was a nobody. He tried for appointment to the powerful House Commerce Committee or to the Government Operations Committee, but he was assigned instead to the Post Office and Civil Service and the House Administration Committees. These were not exactly major appointments for a member from a large state. But freshmen are typically placed on such minor committees. Moss knew that. So he waited and did his best to make something of his position. He served out his sentence stoically, and, as it turned out, productively. On the Administration Committee, his big proposal was to furnish electric typewriters to all of the members of the House. At the time, the members' offices still typed bills and correspondence on ordinary typewriters. Moss succeeded—and thus, it could be said, he was an author at least in part, of the communications revolution in Congress. The members were very appreciative of their new electric typewriters.[11]

Over in the House Post Office and Civil Service Committee, things were not much more exciting. Moss appears to have ignored the tradition that freshmen remain silent. The chairman of the Post Office Committee was a Republican—the GOP was then in control of Congress. He was described by Moss as "bored and mousy." He may have thought of Moss as an overly aggressive cat down at the junior end of the long row of members that circled half the ornate hearing room.

Arthur Summerfield, Ike's postmaster general, had proposed postal re-classification legislation that would establish higher rates of pay for post-office workers and also give them arbitration and grievance rights. Moss wanted to help the post-office workers, if he could. He later said he had to wait three or four days to get a chance to talk, since everything in the com-mittee was done in the order of seniority—and Moss did not have any.

When he got his chance, he said he had a couple of "small amend-ments" that would give the post-office workers arbitration rights and higher pay. The committee was not interested. He lost big time.

In the next Congress, with the Democrats now in the majority, his amendment was again rejected by the committee. Moss was persistent. He approached Howard Smith, of Virginia, chairman of the House Rules Committee. Smith was a conservative, segregationist Democrat. He was in no sense politically aligned with, or close to Moss. He must have been sur-prised at Moss's audacity in approaching him about his post-office worker amendments. The results of the meeting were, however, surprising.

The post-office bill was on the way to the floor. As with all bills, it needed a rule from Smith's committee before it could be reported to the full House. None of the more senior members of the Post Office Commit-tee seemed to be able to explain the content of the bill to the satisfaction of Smith, who was chairing the hearing. So Smith called on second-termer Moss to explain it. He appeared satisfied with Moss's statement. Smith then asked the Californian whether there would be any amendments offered on the floor. This is normally a decision of the chairman of the committee that writes a bill, subject to approval of the Rules Committee.[12]

Moss, without consulting the chairman of his own committee, pressed his case. He said, as a matter of fact, he had one or two amendments he would like to offer: his defeated employee arbitration and pay provisions. Smith, who had bigger fish to fry than post-office workers, said, "Okay, we'll write the rule so the gentleman's amendments will be in order." The final rule provided that the gentleman from California would be recog-nized for two amendments. He was. They passed on the House floor. This was heady stuff for a second-term congressman.[13]

At the end of Moss's second term he received a promotion, becoming a member of the more powerful Government Operations Committee, which had jurisdiction over government information practices. He was to serve on Government Operations for twenty-two years. But the promo-tion and his growing interest in the impact of government secrecy did not seem to satisfy Moss. Some inner compulsion drove him to try to put himself in an even more influential position.

Moss repeated to the California delegation his interest in membership on the Interstate and Foreign Commerce Committee. He wanted Commerce because it had jurisdiction over major parts of business and industry in the United States, and trade with foreign nations. Moss, who had been in the appliance and real estate businesses, thought he knew something about commerce. So the committee's jurisdiction over transportation, communications, securities markets, consumer protection, weather, time, energy, environment, and health care was appealing to him.

When the selections of the Democratic caucus were announced, Moss was again disappointed. "Sam Rayburn always liked to pick Texans for key committees," he said. "He didn't particularly look to California."[14] So Moss, fresh from his productive discussion with Chairman Howard Smith of the Rules Committee, and still feeling pleased with his role in getting federal money for completion of the Folsom Dam—tried again.

He walked from the House office building across the street to the Capitol to talk to the Speaker of the House, Texas's Rayburn. From the way Moss described it later, he did not exactly argue with Rayburn, but it does appear he may have been a bit aggressive for a young member. He reminded Rayburn that there was no Californian on the Interstate and Foreign Commerce Committee; that he was from the growing northern part of the state; and that he probably would have the nomination of both parties in the next election—something he did not actually get until 1958. Moss told Rayburn he knew about business issues, that he could handle the job, and that he *really* wanted it. And, oh yes, putting a Californian on Commerce might be good for the Democratic Party. Rayburn, who was nobody's pushover, appeared friendly, but noncommittal.

A day or two later, Moss got a telephone call from the chairman of the California delegation: "You're on the Commerce Committee, John. What the hell did you say to Sam Rayburn?"[15]

The meeting began a strong relationship between Moss and Rayburn. It turned out that it had not hurt Moss to go to the top to make his case. Moss worked with Rayburn and won his support. It was Rayburn who placed Moss on the leadership track as deputy House whip and perhaps as a future Speaker.[16] It was Rayburn who oversaw the appointment of Moss as chairman of the Special Subcommittee on Government Information, which was soon to be established as a part of the Government Operations Committee. And it was Rayburn who, directly or indirectly, triggered Moss's long freedom-of-information battle.

Despite his progressive stands on many issues, Moss demonstrated an ability to work with members of Congress of vastly different persuasions.

He said he respected Howard Smith, for many years the very conservative chairman of the House Rules Committee. Smith was the *bête noir* of liberals across the country because of his opposition to civil rights and other liberal legislation. Yet Moss found him a member he could go to and talk over the legislative tactics of a particular proposal:

"You could go to him and ask his advice. He might be way over at the opposite end, but you could bank on it; if he told you something, you could believe it. He was a thoroughly honorable person and respected because of it."

Ultimately, despite Moss's respect for Smith, it was Speaker Sam Rayburn who he would look to for early political guidance. Moss said when politicians told Rayburn they couldn't vote with him because "my people would never stand for it." Rayburn would say:

"Your people will continue to send you back here as long as they know you know more about the problems that you face than they do. They want you to lead, not follow them."

* * *

What caused Moss, now in his second term in Congress, to become involved, not in commerce but in government secrecy and freedom of the press? What started him down a different road and, many years later, to an appointment with legislative destiny?

World War II witnessed an immense growth of the federal government and the wartime need for a high degree of secrecy—at least as to military security information. Winning the war took precedence over everything. In the years immediately following World War II, military necessity declined, but secrecy and censorship limiting the flow of government information to the public continued. During the Cold War and the anti-Communist hysteria that followed, both the Truman and the Eisenhower administrations responded with many restrictions— including the Truman Loyalty Program. Some became a permanent apparatus for state secrecy.

Government and public reaction to the uncertainties of the Cold War caused thousands of documents to be classified as secret. The prevailing attitude toward government records was, "when in doubt, classify."[17] Secrecy labels were placed everywhere. The amount of peanut butter consumed by the armed forces was classified as secret because the government feared this information might enable an enemy to determine the nation's military preparedness. A twenty-year-old report describing shark attacks on shipwrecked sailors was classified as secret, as was a description of modern adaptations of the bow and arrow.[18]

In the midst of this wave of Cold War hysteria, Moss confronted executive branch intransigence for the first time. It was while he was serving his first term on the House Post Office and Civil Service Committee. He was then thirty-nine years old.

Moss had defended the rights of civil service employees when he was a member of the California legislature four years before.[19] So it was no surprise that, on the Civil Service Committee, he would became involved with the discharge of some twenty-eight hundred federal employees for alleged "security reasons." Moss felt that the dismissals ought to be explained more thoroughly by the Civil Service Commission because the firings reflected badly on the employees and on the Civil Service in general.

Moss later explained that he knew the majority of the people dismissed had probably not been let go because they were disloyal, but because they had been involved in minor incidents over things like drinking problems or parking tickets, or maybe because they disagreed with their supervisor. An instinctive civil libertarian, who had himself been charged with being a Communist sympathizer, Moss was sensitive to possible smears and questionable charges of disloyalty. So the young congressman, a member of the committee with jurisdiction over such an issue—the Post Office and Civil Service Committee—formally requested that the Civil Service Commission produce the records relating to the discharge of all twenty-eight hundred employees for claimed security reasons. Moss's request was flatly denied by the Civil Service Commission. That, it seemed, was the end of it. With the Republicans now in control of both the Executive Branch and Congress, he was stymied.[20]

Moss was not a person who liked to be stymied, particularly in an area where he believed he was acting within his rights. He did not forget the issue or the affront.

Meanwhile, the Cold War, the Red scare, and concerns over national security continued to broaden government control over information. Kent Cooper, the executive director of the Associated Press at the time, probably popularized the phrase "right to know" in his 1956 book by the same name. He wrote, "American newspapers do have the constitutional right to print . . . but they cannot properly serve the people if governments suppress the news."[21] Cooper alluded to a 1945 *New York Times* editorial that referred to the "right to know" as a "good new phrase for an old freedom."[22]

The American Society of Newspaper Editors (ASNE) had organized a freedom-of-information committee in the late 1940s. The committee pressed to obtain access to government information, but the levels of secrecy and the complexity of attempting to get information from the now-bloated federal government caused one of its chairmen to say that the situation "frightened [him] very, very much," because it posed a threat to basic rights in the nation. The editors became so concerned about the denial of information to the press and the public that they commissioned

Harold Cross, a leading newspaper lawyer and counsel to the *New York Herald Tribune*, to prepare a report on federal, state, and local government information rights. Cross's report was published in 1953 under the title, "The People's Right to Know." It was funded by ASNE.[23]

The Cross report confirmed press fears that there was systematic denial of government information, and asserted that the press and the public have an enforceable legal right to inspect government records for a lawful or proper purpose. In ringing terms, Cross spelled out a new constitutional and legal principle: "Public business is the public's business. The people have the right to know. Freedom of information is their just heritage. Without that, the citizens of a democracy have but changed their kings."[24]

The Cross report looked mainly at the state of the law as reflected in court decisions either granting or denying the right to access. It also focused primarily on state and local law because, under existing federal law, "absent a general or specific act of Congress," there was absolutely no enforceable right to public or press access to government documents.[25]

The federal government was, in fact, subject to a series of statutes and regulations essentially making federal records and information the private property of each federal agency and ultimately of the White House. Thus, Cross's book, which became the Bible of the press and ultimately a roadmap for the Congress regarding freedom of information, opened the way toward a more open government—but only in general terms. Cross said the First Amendment points the way; the function of the press is to carry the torch.[26] Where to carry the torch and how to secure such a public right to government information remained unclear.

Just after the publication of the Cross book, the Eisenhower administration precipitated an incident that gave the issue of public information national publicity and a new political leader. In 1954, the voters returned a Democratic Congress to Washington. At about the same time, President Eisenhower chose to create the Office of Strategic Information (OSI). It was officially established in the Department of Commerce at the request of the National Security Council. It quickly became controversial.

The idea was to ask industry and the press to "voluntarily" refrain from disclosing any strategic information that might assist enemies of the United States. At that time, the primary enemy was, of course, the Soviet Union. The chill of the Cold War dominated the American consciousness. OSI's new director was R. Karl Honaman, who later moved to the Department of Defense under Secretary of Defense Charles Wilson. Honaman had previously been director of publications for Bell Telephone Laboratories.

On March 29, 1955, government secrecy policies were raised to an even higher level when Defense Secretary Wilson issued a directive to government officials and defense contractors stating that, for an item to be

cleared for publication or released to the public, it not only had to meet security requirements, but also had to make a "constructive contribution" to
the Defense Department's efforts.[27] Under this standard, the government
would have had almost total control over what information was released.
At the time, there was no possibility of court review of such decisions.
This new level of government secrecy infuriated editors, reporters, and
the press generally. Editorials were published opposing the Eisenhower
administration's information policy. *Time* magazine commented that,
"such a policy is just the thing for government officials who want to cover
up their own mistakes by withholding non-constructive news."[28]

J. R. Wiggins, of the *Washington Post*, and chairman of the ASNE committee, said, "newspapers will not join in the conspiracy with this or any
other administration to withhold from the American people non-classi-
fied information."[29]

The public battle between the Eisenhower administration and the press
could not help but come to the attention of the newly elected Democratic
Congress—and to members like Moss who had recently been denied
information. The Wilson-Honaman information policy was front-page
news. One historian later noted that the battle may have precipitated the
*most* important event on the path to the Freedom of Information Act. That
event was the creation of a Special Subcommittee on Government Information, thereafter known as the "Moss Subcommittee."[30]

Some evidence suggests that Moss became interested in the denial of
information to the press and public in 1955 when he met with newspaper attorney and author Cross. It was perhaps his own experience with
the Civil Service Commission roadblock to his information requests and
Cross's eloquence that merged the strands of the issue for Moss. The
controversy also came up at a moment in time when the political climate
was ripe for at least an inquiry into the problem of access to government
information.

From his new position as a junior member of the Government Operations Committee, Moss saw a chance to deal with an issue that affected
a lot of people—and one he cared about. A short time after his appointment, he talked with William Dawson, the chairman of the Government
Operations Committee, and suggested that the committee authorize a
"study" to determine the extent of information withholding by the Executive Branch.[31]

Moss's sense of the rights of the public, as well as the prerogatives of
the Congress, undoubtedly fueled his interest in freedom of information.
His meetings with editors, reporters, and Harold Cross increased his interest. And he read the newspapers, as did Rayburn and the House leadership. They thought that secrecy in government could be a potentially

powerful political issue. Under Moss's direction, Wallace Parks, a committee counsel, was asked to undertake a preliminary inquiry. Parks, who later became counsel to Moss's subcommittee, wrote a memorandum—undoubtedly with Moss's supervision—to the committee chair, Dawson, indicating that there was indeed a trend toward suppression and denial of access to government information; that it was growing; and that it affected areas of government untouched by security considerations.[32] What happened next can only have been authorized by Speaker Rayburn, who, a few years later, appointed Moss House deputy whip.

Moss and Parks, armed with Parks's memorandum, approached the House leadership through Majority Leader John McCormack, of Massachusetts, in an effort to solicit support for creation of a new subcommittee on government information withholding. According to a committee staff member at the time, McCormick and others in the leadership were "pushed out of shape because the administration was withholding information from Congress. They wanted the press to get aroused over the issue so that the administration would be pressured on behalf of Congress."[33] Moss, with his populist attitude and the willingness to tackle big interests, was clearly thinking more broadly than access only by the Congress.[34]

With the support of McCormick and Rayburn, a new Special Subcommittee on Government Information was established on June 9, 1955, by a memorandum from Chairman Dawson. Dawson wrote, "An informed public makes the difference between mob rule and democratic government. . . . I am asking your subcommittee to make such an investigation as will verify or refute these charges."[35]

The chairman of the new and potentially powerful Special Subcommittee on Government Information might have been one of several senior members of the House. It was, instead, the very junior representative from California, John Moss.

Why would the Democratic leadership of the new Congress place responsibility for the chairmanship of such a potentially powerful subcommittee in the hands of a second-term congressman? Only Rayburn, McCormick, and Moss know the answer to that question, and they are long gone. But Moss's early willingness to tackle big problems, demonstrated both in the California legislature and on the Post Office and Civil Service Committee, may have played a role. His intense interest in the subject might have been noted. Or else, perhaps, Rayburn just liked the young congressman.

Moss's sudden rise to a key House position may also have been a case of the right leader appearing at the right time. One thing is certain: Moss thought there was a job to be done and he wanted the job "desperately."[36]

Whatever the reason, Moss could not have known then the true extent of the immense struggle that he had embarked upon. How long, and how difficult that battle would be, even Moss could not possibly have foreseen in 1955, when he assumed the chairmanship of the new Special Subcommittee on Government Information.

# 5

# The Freedom
# of Information Act

## *Perilous Journey*

On a spring day in early April 1965, the House Democratic leadership arrived at the White House for the regular weekly meeting with President Lyndon Johnson. The president asked Speaker John McCormack, Majority Leader Carl Albert, and Majority whip Hale Boggs to explain the status of Congressman John Moss's government information bill. When Johnson was told that it was moving forward and was in the hearing stages in the House, the president said it was "terrible" legislation. "What is Moss trying to do to me?" he said. "I thought Moss was one of our boys, but the Justice Department tells me this goddamn bill will screw the Johnson Administration." Johnson suggested that Moss ought to be "brought into line."[1]

Within an hour, Moss was summoned from a hearing of his subcommittee by McCormack. The president, Moss was told, was mad as hell about the information bill. It was shocking. Congressmen are not usually hauled out of a subcommittee hearing by the House leadership. Presidents do not often intervene in the details of emerging legislation—and certainly not at the subcommittee level.

McCormack may not have specifically directed Moss to kill the proposed legislation but that was the clear implication. It was obvious to Moss that the Executive Branch had "no enthusiasm for the bill."[2] Despite the warning, Moss was not deterred. Even if he had been approached directly by the president, Moss said years later, he would not have given up on the Freedom of Information Act.[3] The hearings went on.

Ten years after being named chairman of a newly created Special Subcommittee on Government Information, eleven years after confronting the federal government's wall of secrecy, Moss was still struggling to move a freedom-of-information bill out of the House of Representatives. He had spent most of his years in Congress immersed in a seemingly endless investigation of government refusals to give up information, and in an effort to write a bill that could become law. He had targeted what his staff called "silly secrecy," the refusal to disclose such vital data, as modern uses of the bow and arrow and the amount of peanut butter consumed by U.S. soldiers. Most of the subcommittee investigations, hearings, and reports had resulted in confrontations with federal agencies that did not want to give his subcommittee information from agency files. Every federal agency that testified before the subcommittee opposed what was then known as the "federal records law."

Moss understood that what he was fighting was a denial of a basic American right.[4] But that right is not spelled out in the Constitution—the right to obtain information can only be inferred from the right to speak freely. Moss wondered—perhaps doubted—if Congress would ever guarantee what most people incorrectly thought was already a part of the right to free speech under the First Amendment to the Constitution.

In 1965, as he opened yet another year of hearings on his information bill, Moss seemed somewhat weary. Ten years of study by his subcommittee had proved "the unfortunate fact that governmental secrecy tends to grow as government itself grows,"[5] he said. In a brief statement that opened the final, dramatic struggle over the public information law, he noted that there now was a "legal void" into which executive agencies had moved because of the failure of Congress to guarantee a fundamental right.[6]

Moss also signaled that he understood that the issue touched a very sensitive executive branch nerve, especially with the president. Johnson's dominant, controlling personality was not favorably inclined toward increased access to government information. The respected *New York Times* columnist Arthur Krock described Johnson's attitude as "tight official lip."[7] Johnson not only distrusted the press but, Krock added, "was convinced that the press hated him and wanted to bring him down."[8]

Moss, responding to such concerns, said no one would want to throw open government files that exposed national defense secrets to enemy eyes. But he contrasted that situation with the fact that government should not want to impose the iron hand of censorship on routine information. Between these extremes, Moss suggested, there might be an opening for compromise, one that had thus far eluded Congress and Moss's subcommittee. Moss knew, if the bill ever made it to the White House, he did not have the votes to override a presidential veto.

The final round of hearings was courteously conducted. Beneath the calm lurked a major confrontation between the president and Congress—

led primarily by John Moss. A key witness for the executive point of view came from the Department of Justice. Assistant Attorney General Norbert A. Schlei stated that the proposed law was unconstitutional because it impinged on the power of the president to keep information secret when release was "not in accord with his judgment of what was in the public interest."

Because of the "scope and complexity of modern government," Schlei said, "there are literally an infinite number of situations where information in the hands of government must be afforded varying degrees of protection against public disclosure. The possibilities of injury to private and public interests through ill-considered publication are limitless."[9]

Highly sensitive FBI reports containing the names of undercover agents and informers, for example, were protected only by the president's claimed right of "executive privilege" and ancient legal precedent. The subject was just too complicated, too changing, to be covered by any system of legal rules, said the assistant attorney general.[10]

Schlei predicted that the delicate balance that existed between the Congress and the executive branch would be destroyed by Moss's bill. He said the legislation would eliminate "any application of judgment to questions of disclosure or nondisclosure." It would substitute a single legal rule that would automatically determine the availability, to any person, of all records in the possession of federal agencies—except Congress and the courts, which were excluded from Moss's bill. That approach, said Schlei, was impossible and could only be fatal. There was no way of eliminating judgment from the process used to resolve the problem. "The problem is too vast, too protean to yield to any such solution."[11]

Schlei concluded with an apparent veto threat. Moss's bill, he said, impinged on the authority of the president to withhold documents where he determined that secrecy is in the public interest. Since the bill would contravene the Separation of Powers Doctrine, it would be unconstitutional.[12] Neither the Department of Justice, nor its spokesman discussed the scope of the claimed executive privilege—which is not explicitly referred to in the Constitution. Nor did Justice indicate how the term "in the public interest" would be defined.

Moss listened. Then he challenged Schlei and, through him, the president. He said the problem they were dealing with would not go away anytime soon. He recalled that the House and the Senate had been working on a freedom-of-information law for many years. The Senate had recently passed a bill similar to Moss's House proposal—it had been written largely by Moss's staff.

"Ten years is not impetuous . . . but a rather long time. This step will be taken now and it will succeed," he said.[13] One of Moss's strongest congressional backers was a second-term Republican congressman from

Illinois named Donald Rumsfeld. Rumsfeld, years later a secretary of defense with a different perspective on information disclosure, not only supported Moss at the hearings, he also maintained his support with speeches on the House floor. According to Bruce Ladd, a member of his staff, it was Rumsfeld who convinced Minority Leader Gerald Ford and the House Republican Policy Committee to back the bill. They attacked the Johnson administration for not supporting it, although the Republican Policy Committee had been strangely silent on the issue during the Eisenhower administration. The political stakes over the proposed Freedom of Information Act were growing.[14]

* * *

Ten years earlier, the Special Subcommittee on Government Information had been created by a memorandum from the Government Operations Committee Chairman William Dawson to a younger Moss. The action had attracted little public notice. The issue of freedom of information versus government secrecy had not yet gained public traction.

The press, however, had long been frustrated by its inability to get government documents. As far back as the 1940s, the American Society of Newspaper Editors (ASNE) established a Freedom of Information Committee. Initially chaired by James Pope, editor of the *Louisville Journal*, it commissioned a landmark study by Columbia University journalism professor Harold Cross, which was published in 1953. Pope said in a forward to the Cross book, "We had only the foggiest idea of whence sprang the blossoming Washington legend that agency and department heads enjoyed a sort of personal ownership of news about their units. We knew it was all wrong, but we didn't know how to start the battle for reformation."[15]

Cross opened his report with ringing statements of conviction: "Citizens of a self-governing society must have the legal right to examine and investigate the conduct of its affairs, subject only to those limitations imposed by the most urgent necessity. To that end, they must have the right to simple, speedy enforcement."[16]

Cross cited Patrick Henry's statement at the dawn of the Republic: "To cover with the veil of secrecy the common routine of business is an abomination in the eyes of every intelligent man."[17]

All that was missing was a workable plan of action.

Even when Moss and his special subcommittee got started in November 1955, the press did not focus much on Moss's early hearings. *Congressional Quarterly* reported that representatives of the press were asked to testify first before the subcommittee. This was consistent with a strategy Moss used repeatedly in later battles: demonstrating a pervasive problem and then calling on the government—or on various industries—to explain why the problem should not be fixed by Congress. Russell Wiggins of the *Washington Post* told the subcommittee that newspaper editors were disturbed by the withholding of information in many areas of government. "We think it is due to the size of government . . . and to declining faith in the wisdom of the people."[18] James Reston, chief of the *New York Times* Washington bureau, asserted that withholding of information was part of a growing tendency by government officials to "manage" news that might harm their image. It was a barely concealed jab at Johnson.[19]

Philip Young, chairman of the Civil Service Commission, countered that the commission, not just the president, had inherent power under the Constitution to withhold information from Congress, the press, and the public. Officials of several government agencies testified that, if transactions or even conferences with private businesses were made public, it would be difficult to obtain frank disclosures and recommendations.[20]

Less than a year after its creation, the Moss subcommittee forwarded its first "interim" report to the House. The idea was to energize members of Congress by telling them what the executive branch was doing. The staff report noted that the heads of departments often failed to furnish information even to Congress, based on a "naked claim of privilege." The staff, at the time, was headed by two newspapermen, Sam Archibald and Jack Matteson. Their report argued, with Moss's endorsement, that "judicial precedent recognizes the power of Congress to grant control over official government information. . . . If Congress can grant control . . . it follows that it can also regulate the release of such information."[21]

The Department of Justice submitted a 102-page rebuttal. It is hard to conceive of a federal agency asserting any similar definition of unbridled executive power today: "Congress cannot under the Constitution compel heads of departments to make public what the president desires to keep a secret in the public interest. The president alone is the judge of that interest and is accountable only to his country . . . and to his conscience."[22]

As the dispute grew more intense, Moss's temper showed. He said that if the Department of Justice was right, "Congress might as well fold up its tent and go home."[23]

Defense Department officials were prominent witnesses before the Moss subcommittee. With the Vietnam War expanding and the Cold War still raging, national security fears were a major part of the information debate. The Department of Defense sought to limit access to any negative information about the war. Assistant Secretary Robert Ross did offer a minor concession. He said that in the department's recently issued directive, information must make a "constructive contribution to the defense effort or it could not be released." That said, he added that it did *not* apply to press inquiries. He did not mention inquires by Congress or members of the public.

Another witness, Trevor Gardner, former assistant secretary of the Air Force, had resigned a few months before in protest against Defense Department information policies. He stunned the subcommittee, testifying that at least half of all currently classified Defense Department documents were *not* properly secret. Gardner gave an example of excessive secrecy by noting that a leading nuclear physicist—Robert Oppenheimer—had been denied security clearance by the Atomic Energy Commission in 1954. Inconveniently, Oppenheimer kept coming up with valuable, top-secret nuclear ideas. Gardner thought keeping Oppenheimer uninformed was absurd.[24]

In July 1956, the Moss subcommittee issued its first formal report, which summed up its initial year of work. Despite the opposition of every federal agency that testified, the report concluded, "It is incumbent upon Congress to bring order out of chaos. Congress should establish uniform rules on information practices. These rules should require full disclosure of information except for specific exceptions defined by statute. The withholding of information should be subject to traditional review by the courts. The burden of proof should be on the Executive Branch official who withholds the information."[25]

Republican Congressman Clare Hoffman filed vigorous dissenting views to the report, asserting that the information powers of the president—then Eisenhower—could not be lawfully limited.[26]

But the brief conclusion of the report by Moss and a nearly unanimous subcommittee neatly summarized the heart of what was to become the Freedom of Information Act, an act that could not pass Congress for another ten long years. Moss's vision never varied. But the obstacles faced by Moss and his few allies were immense. Even small victories seemed to go nowhere.

In 1958, for instance, when the Moss subcommittee was three years old, Moss introduced legislation in the House, which was simultaneously offered in the Senate by Thomas Hennings of Missouri. They hoped it would solve the information deadlock. It had to do with a statute that harked back to the early days of the Republic. Federal law included a statute that allowed federal department heads to regulate the storage and use of government records. The "Housekeeping Law"—as it was known—did not specifically say anything about what the agencies might do upon request for these records. But the law was often used by federal agency authorities as a basis for preventing the public from obtaining government records.

So, Moss and Hennings decided to change the Housekeeping Law. The amendment of 1958 passed both the House and the Senate easily. It was signed by President Eisenhower—with a sweeping qualifying statement asserting the "inherent" power of the "heads of executive departments to keep appropriate papers confidential."[27] Still, Moss and his allies were optimistic. The new law said that nothing in the old Housekeeping Law authorized any "withholding of information by federal agencies." The optimism was premature.

The Moss-Hennings amendment did not change other federal laws that could be used to deny information. This meant that the Administrative Procedure Act, which placed additional conditions on the release of data, still applied. Moss, Hennings, and their allies also failed to bargain on the tenacity of the federal bureaucracy—which had, of course, noted the reluctance voiced in Eisenhower's signing statement. The Housekeeping Law amendment was ignored. Federal agencies continued to cite other provisions of law as authorizing them to withhold information, either because it was not in the "public interest," or the person claiming the information did not have a legitimate right to get it, or the information might impair national security. Rarely did President Eisenhower have to make a formal claim of executive privilege. That authority was delegated down the line to relatively low-level bureaucrats, who routinely slammed the door on the public, the press, and Congress.

Another report, issued in 1966 by the full Committee on Government Operations in support of Moss's proposed Freedom of Information Act, said that improper denials of information requests had occurred again and again for more than ten years through the administrations of both political parties. Case after case of improper withholding of information was documented. There was no adequate remedy.[28]

The 1966 report, approved by the full Government Operations Committee, noted many instances of questionable agency roadblocks:

- the National Science Foundation decided it would not be in the "public interest" to disclose competing cost estimates submitted by bidders for the award of a multi-million-dollar deep sea study;
- the Department of the Navy ruled that telephone directories fell within the category of information relating to "internal management" of the Navy and could not be released;
- the Postmaster General ruled that the public was not "directly concerned" in knowing the names and salaries of postal employees;
- many federal agencies refused to disclose the opinions of dissenting members, even where a vote on an issue had been taken;
- the Board of Engineers for Rivers and Harbors, which ruled on billions of dollars of federal construction projects, said that "good cause" had not been shown to disclose the minutes of its meetings and the votes of its members on awarding contracts.

The committee seemed stunned to report that requirements for publication were so hedged with restrictions that twenty-four separate terms were used by federal agencies to deny information. These included "top secret," "secret," "confidential," "official use only," "non-public," "individual company data," and a seemingly endless list of other words and phrases.

Along the road to that April 1965 confrontation with the leadership of his own party, Moss had other hurdles to overcome. There were efforts to deny his subcommittee funds or completely abolish it.[29] Here, the newspaper editors intervened, urging that Moss's subcommittee not be abolished. James Pope wrote to Chairman Dawson that the "importance of the committee's work cannot be exaggerated . . . we have seen the danger and the need and are greatly heartened, and we would like to see the committee's funds, its powers, and it influence vastly expanded.[30]

The effort to de-fund the Moss committee did not succeed, but Moss faced other attempts to take away his committee powers. In 1965, near the end of his long investigation, Moss and his staff wrote and introduced a public information bill—identical to a Senate bill sponsored by Senator Edward Long of Missouri (after Senator Hennings's death in 1960)—which would enact a freedom-of-information law similar to the one outlined in the subcommittee's first report in 1955. But Moss's progress was halted when, suddenly, he was unable to muster a quorum of subcommittee members necessary to vote on the bill.

The meeting had been scheduled in May 1965. It was attended only by Moss and one other member, Republican Donald Rumsfeld. Rumsfeld was beginning his second term in Congress. He had specifically requested assignment to the Moss subcommittee. It was not the last time a member seeking to make an impact—or to gain public attention—on major, controversial issues asked to be placed on a Moss-chaired subcommittee. A decade later, freshman Congressman Al Gore did the same thing when Moss was generating headlines about consumer protection legislation.

Rumsfeld co-sponsored Moss's information bill and remained a strong supporter. Looking back, Rumsfeld remembered Moss at the time as "a straight shooter. He would look you in the eye and if he told you something, you could count on it. He did not take me into his confidence about his relationship with the Democratic leadership, or the committee, and that was fine with me. Moss was not a hail-fellow-well-met man. He was more formal, vastly more senior than me, but smart and businesslike."[31]

But Moss and Rumsfeld could not act without a majority of the members being present (a quorum). In July, Moss prevailed upon Dawson to replace two absent members of the reluctant subcommittee with Democrats David King, of Utah, and Henry Helstoski, of New Jersey, who Moss thought would vote in favor of the information bill.

When interviewed by the *Albuquerque Journal* about what was happening to the Moss bill, his ally Rumsfeld suggested that President Johnson's opposition was the problem. According to the *Journal* reporter, when asked why the subcommittee could not get members to meet and vote on the bill, Rumsfeld answered, "We always managed to meet before."[32]

On July 31, newspaper columnists Robert Alan and Paul Scott, writing in the *Tulsa World,* reported that the Johnson administration was pushing to rewrite the bill to give the heads of all departments and agencies authority to bar publication of official information.[33] An Associated Press story said that the president had passed the word to jettison the bill.[34] Moss's actions in continuing to force a quorum and in replacing the two absent subcommittee members showed he was determined to push the bill through, despite the apparent opposition of a president of his own party and, perhaps, of the seemingly conflicted House leadership as well.

By now, newspaper editors, reporters, and publishers were among the biggest supporters of the freedom-of-information law. The *Washington Post* editorialized in 1965 that "Congress should promptly approve the federal public records law now introduced by Senator Edward V. Long, of Missouri, and Representative John Moss, of California. The principles it involves have been extensively debated for the last decade. . . . Its great contribution to the law is its express acknowledgement that citizens may resort to the courts to compel disclosure where withholding violates the law."[35]

The widely read columnist Drew Pearson used his syndicated column, "Washington Merry-Go-Round," to attack government secrecy. Pearson wrote that it took a lengthy barrage of correspondence from Representative John Moss, "crusader for freedom of information," to get the Defense Department to reveal the facts about the use of plush private airplanes by defense department officials, even to the Congress.

Benny Kass, Moss's subcommittee counsel at the time, recalled that Moss had a good relationship with President Kennedy, whom he had supported in the 1960 election. Kennedy was sympathetic to the Moss bill. According to Kass, they would see each other from time to time. The president would come by Moss's office when he was in the Capitol. [36] Kennedy's personal attitude favoring the freedom-of-information principle did not always reach officials in his administration, who mostly disliked the idea. "No government agency, no president likes to be told what to release and what not to release," Kass said. [37]

Thus, despite Moss's positive relations with Kennedy, the basic problem of federal agency opposition did not change. Kass illustrated how close the Moss subcommittee was to the Kennedy administration by recounting a telephone call he received from White House Press Secretary Pierre Salinger. Salinger said the president was about to order an embargo against Communist Cuba. Russian ships, with missiles on board, were on the way to a country ninety miles from Florida. The Cuban missile crisis was about to grip the nation. Salinger wanted to make sure the press was supportive of the embargo, which would help ensure congressional support. Could a member of Moss's staff come over to help? As Kass remembers it, Salinger said words to the effect that, "We'll give you credentials. You can be our contact between the White House, the press, and the Hill." So it happened that Kass, a Moss staff member, went to press conferences with reporters and officials of the Department of State and Department of Defense at the White House's direction, to assist with press and congressional relations.[38]

The relationship between Kennedy and Moss led to charges that Moss was being "soft" on an administration of his own party when it came to freedom of information. In his defense, Bruce Ladd, who worked for Rumsfeld at the time, says that Kennedy was a supporter of the principle of freedom of information, and that Moss was actually trying to work within the administration to change the attitude of federal agencies. Sigma Delta Chi, the national journalism society, nonetheless charged that it was a "gentle" Moss who chided the Democratic bureaucrats over secrecy, instead of the old fire-eating Moss of 1955 to 1960 who put scores of Republican bureaucrats on the witness stand and hammered them relentlessly and publicly.[39]

Ladd wrote that the Moss critics had overlooked the subcommittee's exhaustive hearings over five years, which had defined the secrecy problem. He thought Moss had moved to a less colorful phase of his investigation and toward a final legislative remedy. Ladd said that Moss was able to establish a working relationship with the new Democratic administration, thus permitting "quiet persuasion" to sometimes take the place of public outcries.[40]

Moss's response to the criticism was to repeat that he knew he was exposing himself to the charge of being partisan when he pressed the Eisenhower administration for information, but, allegedly, went easy on Kennedy. He had tried, he said, to carefully avoid giving any support to that charge: "I think it is frequently true that it is much easier to have a fight with your own family than with neighbors," he said.[41] A family fight was, however, fast approaching.

Kennedy did initiate one important change in government information policy. He gave Moss a letter—at Moss's request—agreeing to assert executive privilege only personally and not to delegate the power to lower-level officials of his administration. President Richard Nixon, Moss's old California adversary, later furnished a similar pledge.

Nonetheless, battles with Kennedy administration officials went on. Moss had repeated disagreements with Salinger and with Defense Secretary Robert McNamara over information requests by the subcommittee. Salinger even attempted to have Sam Archibald, the subcommittee staff director, fired.[42]

Republican support for a freedom-of-information bill, fueled by Rumsfeld and then Minority Leader Gerald Ford, was new. It was something that had been decidedly absent during the Eisenhower administration. Growing press coverage made the issue better known to the public. The tide gradually began to turn. Moss waited, looking for a way to overcome the hesitation—or opposition—of the House leadership. He decided to let the Senate move first.

Moss's decision to cede the leadership of an issue he had pursued for ten years was important. With the backing of Democrat Edward Long, Republican Everett Dirksen, and—surprisingly—the Communist-hunting Joseph McCarthy, the Senate passed a bill designed to be identical to the Moss bill in October 1965. The House, however, still refused to act on its own bill. So the Senate bill was sent over to the House.

In a stunning defeat for information advocates, it was not referred to Moss's information subcommittee. It was, instead, sent by the Speaker to the House Judiciary Committee. And there it languished.

When the Senate passed the Long bill and sent it to the House, *Editor and Publisher*, the newspaper industry journal, observed that House members were too involved in "mending fences" to offer the public hope that anything could be accomplished to get the information bill out of the House Judiciary Committee. *Editor and Publisher* added, "It might be worth a try if enough newspapers were to build a bonfire under that august body."[43]

It was Moss, not the newspapers, who built the bonfire. He arranged a meeting with the chairman of the House Judiciary Committee, the dignified, white-haired Emanuel Celler, of Brooklyn. Celler was seventy-six years old when Moss met with him in 1965. He had been elected to Congress from Brooklyn's Tenth Congressional District in 1922, when he was in his mid-thirties.

* * *

A graduate of Columbia College and its eminent law school, Celler had all the formal education that Moss lacked. Ultimately, Celler served fifty years in Congress, many as chairman of the House Judiciary Committee. He was stern, straight-backed, and liberal. He looked more like a federal judge than a politician.[44]

Despite differences in their backgrounds, Celler had some things in common with Moss. His father, Henry, had owned a whiskey business during Emanuel's childhood. When the whisky business failed, Celler's father was forced to take a lower-paying job selling wine door-to-door to the citizens of Brooklyn.[45]

The come-down was painful. Henry Celler did not do well financially. Emanuel graduated from Boys High School and somehow started college. Shortly after Celler started at Columbia, Henry died. His mother, Josephine, passed away five months later.[46] In his autobiography, *You Never Leave Brooklyn*, he wrote, "I became the head of the household. . . . I took up my father's wine route. I went to school in the morning and sold wine all afternoon until 7 o'clock in the evening."[47]

The wine route took him through some poor, tough neighborhoods in Brooklyn. "While we ourselves were not poor," Celler wrote, "I had only to walk a few streets away to find the sounds and smells of poverty. We were respectable and middle-class. But we were not very far from the Brooklyn dockyards."[48]

His background was German-Jewish with a Catholic grandmother thrown in. His family were immigrants. Nondiscrimination in the immigration laws was a cause he fought for throughout his fifty years in Congress. When Moss met with him in 1965, Celler was still struggling to reverse the immigration quota system of the Johnson Act of 1924. The system sharply limited entry of Eastern Europeans, many of whom were Jewish. At the same time, Celler was custodian—through his chairmanship of the House Judiciary Committee—of some of LBJ's great and lasting domestic priorities: the Civil Rights Act and the Voting Rights Act. They both became law in 1964 and 1965, respectively. Celler was at the pinnacle of his power.

Years before, when he finished working his way through college and law school, Celler had a decision to make. Celler had an uncle named Sam Grabfelder, known to the family as "Uncle Sam," who had made a small fortune distilling and selling Kentucky Bourbon. He helped young Celler financially in college and in law school. But now Celler had to make a decision about his future. Should he continue with the wine business, maybe getting rich—possibly expanding into bourbon? Or should he become a practicing lawyer? Uncle Sam was the key. Without his financial help, Celler would have a difficult time becoming a successful lawyer. So in 1912 he went to Sam with his fiancée and asked two questions: Should I get married? Should I go into the wine business, or start my own law practice?

Uncle Sam did not hesitate. On question one, "Get married now," he said. As to the second question, he asked the youngster, "What do you want to be?" Emanuel answered that in his heart he really wanted to be a lawyer.

"Then be one," said Sam. "I will help you. But, I am not giving the money to you. It will be a loan and this is how you will pay me back. Someday, when someone stands before you in need of help, you will help him as I will help you. In this way only, will I consider the loan repaid."[49]

Benny Kass remembers that his daughter was born on the day of the Celler-Moss meeting. He gave cigars to the two congressmen. Kass also gave Moss a "talking paper" he had prepared on all the reasons why Celler and his Judiciary Committee should surrender jurisdiction of the Freedom of Information Act and hand it over to Moss's subcommittee. He was not confident that the appeal would succeed. [50]

One would like to think that when John Moss came to see the powerful committee chairman, that Celler remembered his long-dead Uncle Sam. Moss was a junior congressman. He was not a full committee chairman. Celler far outranked him. The position of the Democratic leadership—and President Johnson—on the Freedom of Information Act was unclear. But Moss was asking for help.

Celler gave it to him. He turned jurisdiction of the Freedom of Information Act over to Moss's subcommittee.

Celler's gift to Moss is almost unheard of in Congress. Chairmen of major committees do not turn over significant legislation to a junior member, especially one who is only the chair of a subcommittee. But somehow, Moss persuaded Celler to give him the bill. Perhaps Celler felt that Moss's ten-year effort to get a freedom-of-information law through the Congress should not go unrecognized. Perhaps the liberal from Brooklyn found something in common with the progressive from California. Perhaps Celler wanted to get rid of a hot potato that might threaten his relations with the White House. And perhaps he remembered what his uncle had said years before about paying back. Whatever the reason, Celler's gift proved to be a momentous one. The result, ultimately, was a law as far-reaching as Celler's other great legislative achievements.

So the bonfire that newspapers wanted to build was constructed by John Moss with help from Celler, Rumsfeld, and the House Republicans. In politics, things sometimes come together at just the right time. With jurisdiction, and at least a grudging green light from the House leadership, the Government Operations Committee favorably reported out the Moss information bill in May 1966.

The fact that Moss had been willing to wait for the Senate to act and to take up the Senate bill—not a potentially different House bill—was a key decision. It meant that there would not have to be a possibly divisive conference committee meeting between the two bodies. The bills were the same. Moss's bill unanimously passed the House on June 20, 1966. Having passed both the House and the Senate, it was promptly sent to the White House for the president's signature.

\* \* \*

The stage was now set for either the final chapter or yet another defeat for the unborn Freedom of Information Act. The bill was delivered on

June 26, 1966, to President Lyndon Johnson at his Texas ranch near Johnson City on the Pedernales River. And there it sat as the hot summer days
dragged by.

Neither Moss nor Senator Edward Long knew whether Johnson would
sign the Freedom of Information Act. The testimony of the Department of
Justice in 1965 had said the bill was unconstitutional. What better reason
for a veto than that?

The message delivered by Majority Leader McCormack that the president was displeased with the information bill had let Moss know that
the executive branch did not like it. He had moved forward against the
wishes of the president.

The press reported in early July 1966 that things were looking bleak for
the Freedom of Information Act. In an effort to reach an agreement with
the White House that would get the bill signed by Johnson, Moss and his
counsel, Kass, met with Attorney General Nicholas Katzenbach.

Kass remembered the meeting well forty-one years later. "This was a
very important meeting," he said. On behalf of the administration, Katzenbach reported, "We cannot support the bill. The president will not
sign it. There are just too many problems."[51] Moss and Long felt they
could not modify the bill further, particularly the right to court review of
agency denials of public requests for information and the bill's presumption favoring public disclosure.

At the meeting, Moss suggested that the Justice Department give the
House some language that they would like to see in the House committee report, which explains the history and intent of a bill. Such language,
he added, might suggest a more acceptable interpretation of the parts of
the legislation that the White House opposed. While offering to accept
changes in the House report, Moss stood his ground on the terms of the
bill itself: "I want this bill to be passed. If counsel and the Justice Department can work out reasonable report language and my committee goes
along with it, I'll support it—with the bill as written."[52]

So the House report was written jointly by Moss's staff and Justice
Department lawyers. It was approved by the committee and released. It
was somewhat different than the text of the legislation. It suggested that
executive branch officials had more leeway in deciding whether they were
authorized to apply some of the bill's exemptions, to deny requests for information. Moss went along with what some people called a "sellout." Kass
later said, "We believed the clear language of the law would override any
negative comments in the House report. If the statute is clear, you don't look
to the legislative history."[53] More important, it was the price of getting a bill.
Moss knew they did not have the votes to override a Johnson veto.

Moss and his allies now waited. The bill was on Johnson's desk in
Texas. Moss was not sure whether his agreement with the Department

of Justice, which resulted in the House report language, would lead to a presidential signature. He had personally explained the bill to President Johnson during at least two meetings at the White House. Whether his explanations had been satisfactory to the president remained unclear.

Congress adjourned that year, rather than recessing, for the July 4 holiday. The adjournment was significant. Under the Constitution, if Congress is in adjournment, rather than only in recess, and the president fails to sign legislation delivered to him within ten days, the bill is "pocket vetoed." No congressional vote to override is possible. Thus, if Johnson did not sign the bill by midnight July 4, 1966, the Freedom of Information Act would be dead. The entire process would have to be repeated again, perhaps in some future Congress. Perhaps never.

Bill Moyers was Lyndon Johnson's press secretary at the time. He had initially been skeptical of the need for a Freedom of Information Act and had sided with all federal agencies in opposition to the bill. But over time, noting broad press support and growing congressional support for the legislation, Moyers changed his position. By July 1966, he had become a supporter. Moyers was in touch with Moss's staff regarding the chance of Johnson signing it.

Moss told his staff to talk to the press; not only to write editorials, but to contact Johnson directly to pressure him to sign. Moss's people spoke to Russell Wiggins of the *Washington Post*, to columnist Jack Anderson, and to whomever they could get in touch with urging them to telegraph or telephone Johnson and ask for a presidential signature, not a veto. Moss personally called newspaper editors all over the country regarding the fate of the Act.

On July 4, the last possible day, it appeared that Johnson would not sign the bill because of his objections to its impact on the powers of the presidency. Pressure from the press and Congress was intense. The issue had become political. The Republican Policy Committee had announced support for the legislation. The midterm congressional elections were approaching in the fall. The president was focused on problems of foreign policy, mostly the growing Vietnam conflict. Domestic issues were no longer Johnson's priority. At the last minute, Moyers went to Johnson's office and recommended that he sign the bill. Years later, Moyers described what happened next:

> In language that was almost lyrical, he said he was signing with a deep sense of pride that the United States is an open society in which the people's right to know is cherished and guarded. But as press secretary at the time, I knew something that few others did not.
>
> LBJ had to be dragged, kicking and screaming, to the signing ceremony. He hated the very idea of open government, hated the thought of journalists rummaging in government closets, hated them challenging the official view

of reality. He dug in his heels and even threatened to pocket veto the bill after it reached the White House.

Only the tenacity of a congressman named John Moss got the bill passed at all, and that was after a 12-year battle against his elders in Congress who blinked every time the sun shined in the dark corners of power. They managed to cripple the bill Moss had drafted and even then only some last minute calls to LBJ from a handful of newspaper editors overcame the President's reluctance. He signed "the f—ing thing" as he called it and then set out to claim credit for it.[54]

So the Freedom of Information Act (FOIA) became law. Johnson issued a signing statement that, on one hand praised the bill, and on the other vigorously asserted the prerogatives of the president to keep most things secret.[55]

In an interview some forty-five years later, Rumsfeld said that passage of FOIA "was the right thing to do. Obviously one can see instances where mischief is made, fishing expeditions can occur. There are costs involved in reviewing requests, and there are some hard decisions the Executive Branch must make on what should be kept confidential. But, overall it is a good law."[56]

The concerns of Moyers that the bill had been crippled, and of others that Moss had sold out to the Justice Department, did not prove to be correct. Over the years, the courts have generally adhered to the broad principles of disclosure enunciated in the bill and have been critical of agencies attempting to withhold information. The exception has been in cases involving national security. It is primarily in that area or where there is a presidential claim of executive privilege—which is not recognized as an exemption from FOIA—that the law has failed to broadly open government information to public scrutiny. Executive branch delays in furnishing documents, and the cost of a citizen or newspaper going to court to get them, remain major problems and a deterrent to greater use of the Act.

\* \* \*

The legislative struggle that was commenced by Moss in 1954 ended successfully in 1966. There was no signing ceremony. There were no commemorative pens handed out by the president. But the press rejoiced. "Twas a sparkling Fourth of July for information crusaders," said J. Edward Murray, chairman of the American Society of Newspaper Editors' Freedom of Information Act Committee. The long campaign in the never-ending war for freedom of information was crowned by a signal triumph, he said. The "dead hero" of the battle was the distinguished newspaper lawyer Harold Cross, who wrote the basic treatise in 1953. The "living hero," said Murray, "was the distinguished California Representative John E. Moss, Congress's most inveterate FOIA champion."[57]

The Freedom of Information Act has been amended several times since 1966. It has mostly been strengthened by Congress—particularly in 1974—to make withholding of information by the federal government *more* difficult and to permit attorneys' fees to be awarded to those whose requests for government data are improperly denied. As Moss understood, despite the list of exemptions, the principle of openness had been firmly established. The law is used each year by hundreds of thousands of private citizens, newspaper reporters, and businesses to obtain government information.

Moss knew the Act was not perfect. "Sometimes you have to compromise," he said.[58] A decade after FOIA's enactment, he added, "If you compare it with today, we've made vast progress. If you ask me if we've made enough, the answer is no." [59]

Before he died in 1997, Moss recalled that he knew from the beginning that the Freedom of Information Act would require continuing change. It would be, he predicted, a never-ending battle.[60]

It took a long time, but the congressman from Sacramento had achieved something significant. He and his allies had effectively amended the U.S. Constitution. They had added a legal right of access to government information on behalf of every American citizen.

Despite the long years of frustration, the difficult negotiations with the Department of Justice, the forced House report language, and the threat of a presidential veto, Moss was gracious in his floor statement on the day the Freedom of Information Act was approved by the House of Representatives: "Let me emphasize today that government information problems did not start with President Lyndon Johnson. I hope, with his cooperation following our action here today, that they will be diminished. I am not so naïve as to believe they will cease to exist."

"I have read stories that President Johnson is opposed to this legislation. I have not been so informed and I would be doing a great disservice to the president and his able assistants if I failed to knowledge [sic] the excellent cooperation I have received from several of his associates in the White House."[61]

Moss was then in the prime of his career. He could have rested on his laurels. He could have continued to be the leading proponent of open government and for broadening the Freedom of Information Act. It was enough for most congressional careers. Not for John Moss.

*Sacramento's new congressman arrives in Washington, 1952. Credit: courtesy, California State University at Sacramento Archives.*

*The Moss family at home, circa 1960: first row, Jean and John; second row, Allison (left) and Jennifer. Credit: courtesy, California State University at Sacramento Archives.*

*Moss with Lyndon B. Johnson in 1960, before their disagreements over the war in Vietnam and the Freedom of Information Act. Credit: courtesy, California State University at Sacramento Archives.*

*Moss, left, on a legislative oversight trip to Danang, Vietnam, in 1970. The trip led to his opposition to the war and a rift with President Lyndon Johnson. Credit: courtesy, California State University at Sacramento Archives (United States Marine Corps Photo).*

# 6

# The Consumer
# Product Safety Act

## Consumer as Guinea Pig

In early 1965, a lawyer on the House Government Operations Committee staff received a telephone call from someone he did not know. The caller was working as a researcher somewhere in Washington. He was looking into the safety of automobiles. Not so much the "nut behind the wheel" idea—which was then popular—but the design of the vehicle, which he thought could cause a "second collision." This second collision—the driver and passengers hitting the windshield, steering wheel, or dashboard—was what the caller said was the major cause of death and injury in automobile crashes.[1]

This seemed like a worthwhile inquiry to Benny Kass. But what really caught his attention was what the caller said next. The caller was concerned that General Motors had assigned private detectives to trail him. He thought it was because he was investigating defects in GM cars, especially rollover accidents involving the new Chevrolet Corvair.

Kass told Moss about the call. The Moss subcommittee was, after ten years, still preoccupied with its seemingly endless investigation of government information and secrecy. Moss told Kass to refer the caller to Mike Pertschuk, who was Senator Warren Magnuson's chief consumer counsel. Although Pertschuk was new on the Magnuson staff and Moss knew of no organized effort to challenge GM or any other car company over the safety of their cars, Moss thought "Maggie," as the senator was known, and his consumer lawyer might be interested.[2]

"So we referred Ralph Nader to Mike Pertschuk. And the consumer revolution was launched," Kass said.[3]

In his book *Revolt Against Regulation*, Pertschuk says he first met Nader in the Senate cafeteria in the summer of 1965, probably after Nader's telephone call to Moss's subcommittee. They had coffee. At least Pertschuk did. Nader was too busy talking.

As part of Senator Magnuson's new interest in consumer protection, Pertschuk had been assigned to a modest piece of new legislation. It required the labeling of automobile tires with quality grades such as A, B, or C to allow consumers to judge their quality and safety. This was about six months before publication of Nader's book *Unsafe at Any Speed*, and eight months before the public revelation of General Motors's gumshoe efforts to intimidate or discredit him.[4]

After hearing Nader talk "with barely contained fury" about his work on the unsafe design of automobiles and the need for mandating safer cars by federal law, Pertschuk says he proceeded to lecture Nader on the realities of the legislative process. Pertschuk told Nader he could not possibly conceive of the Commerce Committee participating in a comprehensive legislative campaign against as powerful a political lobby as General Motors and the U.S. automobile industry.[5]

Two years later, the Magnuson committee and Moss's subcommittee, did just that.

* * *

Warren Magnuson served forty-four years in the United States Senate and House of Representatives, representing the voters of the state of Washington. In his last two decades, he also represented—in the broadest sense—the interests of American consumers. Magnuson became, in the opinion of some, "the most important consumer champion in America."[6]

He was not a consumer leader during his early years in the Senate. At first, he was known as a consummate insider, confidante of presidents, bearer of federal largess to his home state, and, at times, a playboy.[7] Elected to the Senate in 1944, Magnuson earned a reputation as a dashing bachelor. He liked his vodka and dated several attractive young women, including an aspiring Hollywood starlet named Toni Seven.[8]

He was chairman of the Senate Commerce Committee for twenty-four years, from 1955 to 1979. In the early years, it was a quiet, business-friendly committee. A member of the Senate Appropriations Committee, Magnuson focused on delivering federal money for health research at the University of Washington, public power projects on the Columbia River, and the development of the economically important fishing industry in his home state.

Magnuson's rise as a consumer champion was almost an accident. In his fourth Senate election campaign in 1962, he was a heavy favorite for an easy re-election. With a solid New Deal voting record, a powerful position advantageous to his home state, and a reputation as a Washington insider, Magnuson looked unbeatable. He had won in 1956 with over 61 percent of the vote. But looks could be deceiving.

In the 1962 election, Magnuson faced an unknown opponent, the Reverend Richard Christensen. Christensen was a handsome, spellbinding speaker, a Lutheran minister, and a dangerous conservative opponent. "Everybody underestimated Christensen," said Featherstone Reed, one of Magnuson's closest staff members.[9]

Christensen stirred an often alienated segment of America with an organization called Women on the War Path. He had big money from private power interests in the Pacific Northwest. He did not hesitate to suggest Magnuson belonged to "many communist fronts."[10]

Magnuson ultimately survived the challenge—by only forty-five thousand votes out of almost a million cast.[11] It was a demoralizing margin of victory for one of the most successful and powerful politicians in the state's history. Magnuson's chief of staff, Jerry Grinstein, recognized that if the senator was to win a fourth term, he would have to be "reinvented."

Magnuson's chairmanship of the Senate Commerce Committee had played a role in his near defeat in 1962. The image of an aging, shuffling, cigar-chomping deal-maker, who mostly lived in Washington, D.C.—not the other Washington—was hard to erase with the voters back home. Magnuson was viewed on Capitol Hill as an agent for business and commercial interests.[12]

The fact that Magnuson liked to play cards, drink, and was a stumbling speaker did not help. Magnuson's inability to pronounce names was legendary. He once introduced Olympic Committee Chairman Avery Brundage as "Mr. Average Brundy." He was known to call Lyndon Johnson's chief aide, Joseph Califano, "Joe Cauliflower." But Magnuson was also highly regarded by his Senate colleagues because he *always* kept his word, said his former counsel, Representative Norm Dicks.[13]

Grinstein was the opposite of Magnuson. He was a graduate of Yale University and Harvard Law School. He was also the son of the senator's doctor, who was a friend of some of Magnuson's biggest financial supporters. According to Grinstein, his idea to urge Maggie to sponsor consumer legislation came when he read an article in the *New Yorker* magazine around the time of Magnuson's narrow 1962 victory. The article commented favorably on *Consumer Reports* magazine for its testing of the quality and safety of sometimes shoddy consumer products.[14] According to Grinstein, polling at the time showed that consumer protection was virtually nonexistent as an issue among the voters of Washington. So, much of the credit for Magnuson's change in direction to consumer champion must go to Grinstein and to Mike Pertschuk—and to Magnuson's political sixth sense. Grinstein discussed the idea with the senator. He got a four-word response: "Sounds good to me." And the decision was made.[15]

The shift in direction revived a younger, populist Magnuson and dramatically changed the senator. It also changed the Senate. It turned Magnuson's final eighteen years in the Senate into his greatest years. He initiated and delivered one consumer bill after another from the Senate to the House of Representatives. There was legislation on fair packaging and labeling, deceptive advertising, generic drugs, poison prevention packaging, cigarette warning labels, automobile safety, product warranties, and the elimination of flammable fabrics from children's sleepwear. And Maggie did it while continuing his key role on the Senate Appropriations Committee and his leadership in the enactment of the Civil Rights Act of 1964.[16]

Magnuson was known as a master at delegating authority to his staff. But, as many Washington lobbyists found, Magnuson knew what his aides were up to. Going around his staff to the senator did not work well. Once in awhile, Magnuson would get tough with his staff. He once "grounded" top consumer counsel Lynn Sutcliffe, when Sutcliffe initiated an aggressive investigation of a group sponsoring advertisements favoring deregulation of natural gas prices.[17]

The Senate Commerce Committee staff became innovators and champions of consumer interests. Mike Pertschuk was Maggie's chief consumer counsel. Pertschuk had been a classmate of Grinstein's at Yale. "When I think of the public interest, I think of Ralph Nader, Mike Pertschuk, and Warren Magnuson," said former staff member Ed Sheets after Magnuson died in 1989.[18]

Pertschuk wrote that in the 1960s and 1970s there was "a rare, if not unique, concurrence of economic and political conditions" that fostered passage of consumer reforms.[19] He might have added that there was also a powerful, committed Senate staff and a committee chairman who backed them up.

Many of Magnuson's greatest achievements would not have been possible without John Moss. His Senate consumer legislation was being stalled or gutted in the House Commerce Committee.[20] Only the rise of John Moss, in 1967, to chair a subcommittee with jurisdiction over many of Magnuson's proposed consumer laws, opened the flood gates of consumer protection.

It is not true to suggest that without Moss there would have been no Magnuson as consumer champion. But it is true that, without Moss, Magnuson's record of consumer achievement would have been greatly diminished.

*　*　*

In 1966 Nader testified before Magnuson's committee about the General Motors private detectives that were tailing him. He also testified about rollovers and deaths in the Chevrolet Corvair. The press jumped all over the story. It made Ralph Nader a household name. "The rest is history," Kass said.[21]

Nader's testimony served to publicize the Senate committee's push for national automobile safety legislation, giving the government power to mandate safety standards for any part of a car, not just tires. It may seem shocking now, but fifty years ago no national automobile safety agency, safety law, or safety standards existed. Yet, the yearly death toll from car accidents was over fifty thousand people in 1966, with millions more severely injured. The economic and human cost was incalculable. Magnuson and his aggressive young staff began developing compelling evidence that automobiles were not designed safely enough.

The result of General Motors's public relations blunder, Nader's successful lawsuit against GM, and the evidence dug up by the Senate Commerce staff was that Congress passed, and Lyndon Johnson signed, new legislation: the National Motor Vehicle and Traffic Safety Act of 1966. It was a landmark law fueled by public anger. But it was nearly defeated and was significantly narrowed in the House Commerce Committee.

\* \* \*

In 1966, when the Freedom of Information Act finally was enacted, Moss had not yet assumed the chairmanship of the consumer subcommittee of the House Commerce Committee. In fact, there was *no* consumer subcommittee. The entity with jurisdiction over all consumer bills, including automobile and product safety, was then called the Commerce and Finance Subcommittee. Both it and the full Commerce Committee were dominated by business-friendly politicians and business interests. They were not particularly interested in consumer protection legislation.

There had been a few modest efforts at consumer legislation in both the House and the Senate, including amendments to the Flammable Fabrics Act triggered by reports of flaming children's "torch" sweaters. The resulting public outrage at the disfiguring burn injuries suffered by kids forced Congress to strengthen the law regulating the flammability of children's clothing. The Senate and the House had unanimously passed a seemingly minor law in 1968, which established a national study commission with a mandate to spend two years looking into whether there might be products other than automobiles and sweaters that were dangerous to users, and whether those products should be subject to some—as yet nonexistent—federal safety law.

Otherwise, the Senate committee under Magnuson's leadership, with Pertschuk as chief tactician, had passed significant consumer legislation, which was largely stalled in the House committee. The fate of the automobile safety bill is a good example of what happened to consumer protection bills in the House.

Columnist Drew Pearson, in an article that appeared in his column "Washington Merry-Go-Round," noted that, working quietly backstage, the automobile lobby had made amazing progress in the House Commerce Committee toward "gutting" the auto safety bill. Compared to the tougher Senate bill, what the House committee was reporting out, according to Pearson, was "milk and water" when it came to setting safety standards that the automobile industry must follow. Automobile lobbyists, according to Pearson, claimed to have "wrapped up" several members of the committee and were bragging that they had the "Staggers commerce committee all sewed up." [22]

Outnumbered pro-safety congressmen, including John Moss, were handicapped by the fact that the committee staff were, according to Pearson, "apathetic and seemed overly influenced by the auto dealers lobby." According to Pearson, the kindly chairman, Harley Staggers, was bewildered by the controversy and had not taken as strong a stand as had Senator Warren Magnuson. One can only imagine who was the source of such a scathing attack by one of the leading columnists of the day.

Ultimately, an automobile safety law was passed and was signed by President Johnson in 1966—a small part of the wave of Great Society legislation. But it was less than Magnuson, Moss, Nader, and consumer advocates wanted.

Whoever put the finger on Chairman Staggers and the lethargic House Commerce Committee majority, the Drew Pearson piece accurately described what was going on in the "people's house" while Maggie and Pertschuk were cranking out tough pro-consumer legislation in the Senate. The House became the graveyard of consumer bills.

Moss was almost powerless because he chaired neither the full Commerce Committee nor any of its subcommittees. He controlled only one vote—his own. Because subcommittee chairs were picked by seniority, Moss could not get the chairmanship of any subcommittee on commerce until 1967. By coincidence, that was just after he had won the long battle to get the Freedom of Information Act signed into law a year earlier.

It seems to have taken Moss a year or so to get his bearings. But by 1968, as chairman of the key consumer subcommittee in the House of Representatives, he was getting restless. Magnuson's work and Moss's own instincts suggested moving aggressively toward a new goal.

* * *

About that time, on a Sunday afternoon, a young Justice Department lawyer was sitting in Mike Pertschuk's living room in a row house in southwest Washington. He and Pertschuk were next-door neighbors. They were watching a football game when the Senate counsel unexpectedly turned and asked, "How would you like to be general counsel of a federal commission we are setting up?" The visitor was stunned. He had just two years under his belt in Washington, having moved south from living in New York City and working for a small law firm there. He had a wife and two young children. He had been hired as a trial lawyer, in the civil division of the Department of Justice, a relatively low-level job. He and Pertschuk were casual friends. They talked mostly about family and football, not politics. The young lawyer did not know much about what Pertschuk really did on Capitol Hill.

"What kind of commission?" he asked.

"It's going to be a commission to study the safety of household products," Pertschuk replied.

"You mean, like mops and brooms?"

"Well, actually," Pertschuk said, "we plan to rename it. The suggestion came from the Association of Home Appliance Manufacturers. We're going to call it the National Commission on Product Safety. Give it a little more sex appeal than household products."

"Well, I kind of like working in the civil division and I don't know anything about household product safety," the lawyer said. "It doesn't sound exactly like my kind of work."

"And it would pay around $25,000 a year," Pertschuk continued. That was roughly *twice* the salary the Justice Department lawyer was then feeding his family on.

That was it. With a wife and two kids, doubling one's salary is something that is hard to turn down. And the work sounded like it might at least be different. So the young attorney said he was interested.

Pertschuk said he would run it by the newly nominated chairman of the commission, a trial lawyer from New York City named Arnold Elkind, who would make the decicion. Elkind had not yet been confirmed by the Senate. The commission had no staff at all yet.

The visitor thought he had better study the somewhat obscure subject of household product safety. No promises were made. Pertschuk and his friend went back to watching the football game.

I was that young lawyer. I did not know it at the time, but the conversation that day changed my career—and my life.

* * *

A few weeks later, I walked into a small room in an aging office building on Sixteenth Street in the Northwest quadrant of Washington. The building was a bit wider than a tenement and six or eight stories tall. On one side was a nondescript office building; on the other side was the Gaslight Club, a renowned local watering hole. The only other person in the room was Arnold Elkind, the just-confirmed chairman of the now renamed National Commission on Product Safety. Elkind was a quiet, unassuming man—especially for a trial lawyer, a breed known for show-manship and ego. Elkind's selection as chairman of the commission was obviously orchestrated by Pertschuk, who perhaps saw in him some hidden ability to trigger public and congressional interest in consumer product safety legislation.

I was particularly uneasy that day. I knew nothing about Elkind and virtually nothing about the legislative process or consumer safety regulation. I had hurriedly studied the commission's mandate from Congress, noting it had large teeth—subpoena power—and the potentially broad effect of its recommendations. I crammed for the meeting just as if I was preparing for a law school examination. I tried to anticipate anything Elkind might quiz me on. The range of possible questions seemed limitless. I had not spoken to Mike Pertschuk about the job since our Sunday afternoon football conversation a few weeks earlier.

Elkind, a handsome, dark-haired man of medium build, was seated behind a tiny telephone table in the empty room. The commission had not yet received any money from Congress, so it did not have any other furniture, except a chair in front of the small table. After some small talk, which could hardly have enlightened him much, Elkind said, "So, I understand Senator Magnuson wants you to be the general counsel of the National Commission on Product Safety."

Stunned silence. I had thought I was going for an interview. It turned out to be a confirmation. I supposed it was Pertschuk's doing again.

The offer was accepted.

A letter filtered down from the attorney general to the deputy attorney general to the assistant attorney general for the civil division to the head of the general litigation section where I worked. The letter was on White House stationery. It directed that I be "detailed temporarily" as general counsel to the National Commission on Product Safety, pending appropriation of the commission's funds.

The furniture arrived a few weeks later. So did about twenty more staff members, including engineers, health and accident specialists, and more lawyers.

As I sat among the unopened boxes and newly arrived furniture at the office on Sixteenth Street and re-read the terms of the law establishing the study commission, I began to wonder whether any of the industries it affected had read it very closely. It was nothing less than a hunting license to investigate, publicize, and report to the president, the Congress, and most important—to the public—on any hazardous consumer product anywhere in the United States. As it turned out, there were quite a few. The safety of at least fifteen thousand largely unregulated consumer products was subject to the commission's hunting license.

* * *

The Joint Congressional Resolution establishing the National Commission on Product Safety was passed in November 1967 and promptly signed into law by President Lyndon Johnson, without much public notice. It may have been one of the last significant pieces of domestic legislation signed by LBJ before he was immersed, and ultimately submerged, in the turmoil of the Vietnam War. Nobody realized it at the time.

The law setting up the commission met no opposition in the Senate. Magnuson authored it, recruited the top Republican on the Senate Commerce Committee, Norris Cotton, of New Hampshire, to co-sponsor it, and saw to its easy approval by the committee and the Senate.

Staggers and Moss co-sponsored the study bill in the House, where it narrowly escaped a stunning defeat. Republican backbenchers, probably reacting to increased industry concern, revolted against their leadership on the Commerce Committee—which had not opposed the bill—and attacked the proposed study commission as "unnecessary government involvement in the marketplace."[23] The bill passed only when Speaker John McCormack left the Speaker's chair to cast a rare vote in support of the bill.

Most Washington insiders and business lobbyists understood that creating a study commission was a classic method of burying an issue, usually forever. Despite the close call in the House, the understanding was that the commission would blunt some of the automobile safety madness that Nader had stirred up, and its report would be filed and forgotten. It did not work out that way.

The National Commission on Product Safety was part of Pertschuk's and Magnuson's plan to build legitimacy for the concept of a new federal agency to oversee the safety of thousands of then unregulated consumer products. Shortly after the passage of the automobile safety law in 1966, the Senate Commerce Committee began receiving concerned letters from people who had been injured by something other than an automobile. There were plenty of them, but the Senate staff thought they were not enough to get public attention and generate real outrage.[24]

At the time, the major federal consumer safety agency was the Food and Drug Administration. Until Magnuson introduced his apparently innocuous study commission bill, the history of federal protection of consumers from unsafe products had been spotty at best. During the first part of that history, lasting until the 1950s, federal regulation was confined primarily to food and drugs under the Pure Food and Drugs Act of 1906. Its main purpose was to keep impure or adulterated foods and phony patent medicines out of the marketplace.[25] Other than food and drugs— and cosmetics after 1938—federal regulation prior to 1966 was based on a few specific laws generally reacting to passing public alarm over a specific hazard. These included legislation aimed at flammable children's clothing in 1953 and the Federal Hazardous Substances Labeling Act passed in 1960.[26] Federal protection of the consumer had been decidedly piecemeal before 1967. Warren Magnuson, Mike Pertschuk, and John Moss thought they had a better idea.

According to the Senate chief counsel, enacting automobile safety legislation with the "help" of General Motors private detectives was one thing. But, in 1967, the public was largely unaware of potential hazards relating to appliances, heaters, cribs, toys, chemicals, and other household products. Pertschuk and Magnuson believed a learning process was necessary. The injuries attributable to thousands of different consumer products were not documented enough to furnish a good basis for legislation. Nor was the economic cost. So they came up with the idea of an independent study commission as a way to "educate" the media and the public on an issue that was not yet politically ripe.

A commission looked like a good way to move things along. But they did not take any chances. The selection of the commissioners was made by the Senate Commerce Committee chair and his staff, perhaps with the concurrence of the Johnson White House. Arnold Elkind's life as a trial lawyer—suing corporations for injured consumers—was well-known, at least to the Senate staff. Whether anyone recognized that he also had an instinct for the jugular, remains unknown.

And, for reasons also unknown, I never had a real interview for the job as general counsel of the commission.

\* \* \*

Just to make sure that things went as planned, Pertschuk was named as one of the four Democratic commissioners—there were also three Republicans. Two of the Republican commissioners were officials of testing laboratories who were very aware of current safety problems in the design of consumer products. The third was Hugh Ray, vice president of Sears Roebuck, then the nation's leading retailer of household products.

For a member of the Senate staff, like Pertschuk, to be named a commissioner of a federal agency, even a temporary one, was unusual. Those jobs usually went as political rewards to some former or potential member of Congress, or someone with technical knowledge or a business interest in the issue. In hindsight, it is clear that Pertschuk and Magnuson were just making sure they could keep an eye on what the commission was up to.

The joint resolution directed the commission to conduct a "comprehensive" study and investigation of the adequacy of measures used to protect consumers against injuries from hazardous household products. It was a somewhat innocuous charter, but it was wide open. The word "investigation," rather than the more academic term "study," caught the eye of the eager young staff of the new commission. So, rather than statistics and studies, what the press and the public—and of course Congress—got from the commission was one long, memorable, tragic story of needless death and injury to ordinary people in America.

\* \* \*

The commission held nationwide hearings. It led off every hearing with an injured consumer and a story of suffering. The injury was always caused by a toy, chemical, appliance, or other household product that the commission believed could have been better designed to prevent the injury. In one case, at a Los Angeles hearing, the commission called as a witness a permanently paralyzed man in a wheel chair who had struck his head on the bottom of an unmarked, sloped swimming pool. The press cameras clicked.

There was testimony about everyday products, such as hot water vaporizers used to treat children's colds. The commission heard from the McCormack family, which bought a vaporizer advertized as tipproof, foolproof, and safe. It bore the "Good Housekeeping Seal of Approval" and Underwriters Laboratories seal. They placed it on a stool in their home and plugged it into a wall outlet. While it was steaming, their three-year-old daughter, Andrea, caught her leg in the electric cord. The vaporizer tipped over, spilling scalding water over Andrea. She spent five months in the hospital, endured a series of painful skin grafts, and bore scars for the rest of her life. The commission thought the product should have been better designed.[27]

Clancy Emert, a one-year-old toddler in Peoria, Illinois, swallowed about three tablespoons of Old English furniture polish during a few moments when his aunt left the bottle unguarded. The polish had a pleasant odor that a child might find attractive. The bottle did not have a safety cap or a warning on the label of the fatal risk of ingestion. The petroleum distillates from the polish collected in Clancy's lungs. He died forty hours later from chemical poisoning. Dr. Charles Edwards, commissioner of the FDA estimated that as many as a million children a year were injured by drinking harmful household chemicals.[28]

Small children were not the only victims of the products investigated by the commission. "I will be blind in one eye for the rest of my life because of a sudden explosion of a defective glass soda bottle," testified fourteen-year-old Sharon Jackson of Chicago. The Federal Trade Commission had studied the question of exploding glass bottles for three years before deciding to refer the matter to the Interstate Commerce Commission (ICC) for further study. The ICC concluded that the voluntary efforts of the bottling industry "were adequate," despite reports of five thousand to seven thousand injuries a year. The consumer commission recommended that improved quality control and design standards be mandated by the government, adding that soda bottles could be a hidden explosive danger to consumers.[29]

Miami Dolphins' star running back, Larry Csonka, testified that he had incurred a severe concussion when he was tackled in a game wearing a poorly designed football helmet. Csonka held up a better-designed helmet and urged enactment of a new safety law covering such equipment.

The National Commission on Product Safety also heard testimony about dangerous products that were part of the home itself, including glass doors, lead paint, and unvented gas heaters. One parent whose child survived a collision with a glass door made of plate glass testified, "I heard a crashing of glass and horrible screams. . . . I saw my son on his hands and knees . . . a mass of blood, a jagged piece of glass was pointed directly at his head." The boy survived, but the industry was forced to adopt new safety standards for shatter-proof glass doors and windows, even before Congress considered any legislation.[30]

Many newspapers sent reporters across the country to follow the hearings of the commission. The *Washington Post* sent Morton Mintz, one of its top investigative reporters. The hearings and final report received nationwide press coverage. Equally important, the *Post*, including Mintz's front section stories of injury and death, was required reading by members of Congress and their staffs each morning. By the time the commission's final report reached the Senate and the House in June 1970, its findings came as no surprise to the legislators.

* * *

John Moss became a member of the House Interstate and Foreign Commerce Committee (now the Energy and Commerce Committee) in 1956, after his tense conversation with Speaker Sam Rayburn. He had bluntly asked Rayburn for the job. But, for a decade since then, he had been focused mostly on government information and secrecy as a member of the Government Operations Committee. Moss did not have the necessary seniority on Commerce to obtain a subcommittee chairmanship. At the time, subcommittee chairs were always handed out by the chairman of the full committee in the strict order of a member's appointment to the committee. So, Moss could not become a subcommittee chairman of the House Commerce Committee until 1967. By that time, he ranked fifth in seniority on the thirty-three-member full committee, just ahead of his good friend John Dingell of Michigan who sat next to him in the committee's large, elegant, wood-paneled hearing room in the Rayburn House Office Building.

Moss was relegated to the least important subcommittee on Commerce—the Commerce and Finance Subcommittee. Other subcommittees were led by more senior Democrats and dealt with issues like transportation, communications, environment, health, and other prominent subjects. Commerce and Finance did not have anything like that kind of jurisdiction. It had the Commerce Department, the Census Bureau, weather, daylight savings time, and the incomprehensible—to most members—"securities and exchanges." In addition, it had a major hot potato: consumer legislation. Much of this legislation—sent over from Magnuson and the Senate Commerce Committee—had backed up in the House Commerce Committee like a logjam on Sacramento's American River in springtime.

\* \* \*

Harley Staggers, a Democrat from West Virginia, was chairman of the full House Commerce Committee. He had been a high school football coach before being elected to Congress. He had a unique way of running the full Commerce Committee with its sweeping jurisdiction over much of American business and the potential for making its members well-known and perhaps well-heeled. Staggers had only four professional staff members to support the legislative work of the thirty-three-member committee and its five subcommittees. The Senate Commerce Committee had a professional staff five times as large. Staggers controlled the referral of all legislation to subcommittees and gave permission—when he chose to—to hold hearings on specific legislation. He also chaired and controlled the full committee, which reviewed and often rewrote everything the subcommittees did. He managed all legislation ultimately reported by the committee to the House of Representatives. In 1967, the Commerce Committee was operating like a high school football team under the control of the head coach.

Even if a member could get Staggers to refer a bill from the full committee to a subcommittee, persuade the chairman to allow hearings to be held, and then to take the bill up in the full committee—if it was favorably reported by the subcommittee—there was another problem. All professional staff were hired and fired by Staggers. They did not answer to the priorities of the subcommittees or their chairmen. This meant that if anyone was going to tangle with big business over safety regulation of consumer products, warranties, deceptive advertising, class actions, no-fault insurance, toxic chemicals, or any of the other consumer bills Magnuson was pumping out of Senate Commerce, they would have to first get the permission of the often reluctant Staggers. If any staff member worked on such touchy issues without his permission, they risked being fired.

Moss, Dingell, and Representative Paul Rogers of Florida tried to induce Staggers to increase staff and place more authority in the subcommittees. The struggle is illustrative of what often goes on behind closed doors in Congress, and of Moss's strained relationship with Staggers—except that it is all preserved in writing. Apparently frustrated over the committee's slow pace—particularly on consumer bills—during the chairman's first two years, Moss wrote to Staggers, who was unaccountably back home in West Virginia. The lack of Staggers's presence in Washington was causing problems. In Moss's letter to Staggers, he wrote, "[the letter was] not the easiest I have ever written for many reasons, the most important being that I have a genuine affection for you and a strong desire to see you succeed and be . . . an outstanding chairman."[31] Moss went on to describe the lack of staff, the failure of the committee to proceed on major legislation, the lack of authority of the subcommittee chairs to consider bills, and the urgent problems facing the federal agencies within the committee's purview. Then Moss noted that Oren Harris, the previous chairman, had been around when the members needed him. The letter must have been like a red flag waved at a bull. It was met with silence at first.

A few days later, Moss, Dingell, and Rogers wrote a second letter asking for new committee rules giving the majority members of the committee control over staff and legislation—something that Staggers surely considered total rebellion.[32] He responded a day later to the three members. He was, he said, "not . . . the agent or a tool of some private interest opposed to the public good. . . . The captain of a ship runs the ship." Staggers said he based his operation of the committee "on procedures developed over nearly 200 years of experience. In this, they are like the moral law."[33] There was sure to be a further confrontation. Moss believed he was acting in the best interests of the Committee and public. He was not about to stop.

\* \* \*

An event in 1970 further illustrates Moss's problem after he ascended to the chairmanship of the Commerce and Finance Subcommittee. The National Commission on Product Safety filed its well-publicized report with the Congress and President Nixon in 1970, after more than two years of hearings that spotlighted repeated incidents of hazardous consumer products injuring and killing people. Under Elkind's direction, the commission had not focused as much on the number of injuries and deaths as it had on personal stories and headline-grabbing incidents. It did attempt to back up its recommendations with whatever data it could obtain. But the data were mostly estimates, including the commission's estimate of thirty thousand consumer deaths and one hundred and ten thousand permanent injuries each year "associated" with consumer products. The numbers would never have held up in a court of law.

The focus of the commission's investigation, and what the press picked up as it followed the commission around the country, were stories of glass doors that slashed consumers, color television sets that caught fire, unvented gas heaters that emitted fatal carbon monoxide fumes, bicycles without reflectors, chemicals that poisoned children, and one manufacturer's crib, which was designed so badly that the slats strangled one child per year for ten years.[34]

Despite this evidence of major safety problems, and despite a backlog of other consumer legislation, Moss did not have any staff under his direction to handle hearings, investigations, and the writing of draft bills. And, without staff, a chairman is largely powerless. Moss's and the other members' appeal to Staggers had been flatly rejected.

It took over a year of negotiations by Moss, Dingell (who chaired the Energy Subcommittee) and Paul Rogers (now chairman of the Health and Environment subcommittee) to finally pressure Staggers into awarding each subcommittee chairman a single staff member to handle all legislation referred to their subcommittees. But there was a kicker: the new staff member was to handle only "routine correspondence and similar things," and was to work out of the subcommittee chairs personal office, not with the committee staff. He or she was not officially a member of the committee staff authorized to plan hearings and draft legislation. It turned out to be a big handicap.

Moss and the other subcommittee chairmen promptly hired the counsels that Staggers had grudgingly authorized. As the National Commission on Product Safety ended its work, I became Moss's new special counsel.

One day, Rogers's newly appointed counsel Steve Lawton and I ventured into a legislative markup session of the full Commerce Committee, which was dealing with bills reported by their subcommittees. We sat in a row of chairs behind the Staggers staff members who were at a long table in front of the committee working on amendments from members and putting together the final text of the bills. This "invasion" of a "private" session of the committee was not appreciated by Staggers. He unceremoniously ordered both of us thrown out of the room and had the doors closed firmly behind us. To say that we were shocked is an understatement.

But Staggers had overreached. So embarrassed were the members of the committee at the humiliation of its staff that some of Staggers's closest political allies apologized to us for the incident.

The next day Moss told me, "Just come on in next time. It won't happen again." So we did. No one ever again raised any objection about the role of the new counsel to the subcommittees. We began working on planning hearings, drafting legislation, and on legislative markups of the subcommittees and the full committee. The logjam might be ready to break.

Moss was now the chair of what had now become the key House consumer subcommittee. By 1970, he had a staff of two. He also had a lot of big legislation to deal with. Among the bills waiting for action: the proposed Consumer Product Safety Act; consumer product warranty legislation; securities market reform; the controversial Federal Trade

Commission Improvements Act; national no-fault automobile insurance legislation, bills providing for class actions by injured consumers against manufacturers; a new round of automobile safety legislation; the proposed Toxic Substances Control Act; and, finally, a new kind of law designed to reduce the damageability of automobile parts—like bumpers and fenders—and thus lower the insurance premiums of buyers. It was a large agenda.

Moss summarized it all in a long letter, which the *New York Times* printed in full. He said that a series of "major issues" had arisen between the Nixon administration and the Democratic Congress. (He might have added that Nixon had the support of some Democrats.) Moss listed all the consumer bills. He said a clear pattern had emerged: the Congress—at least some of it—favored strong consumer bills; the Nixon administration supported "watered-down substitutes." Moss was not above using the press and public pressure to get what he wanted.[35] He did not mention that some of his Democratic "allies" in the House were unreliable votes on the pending consumer bills.

Moss had an additional problem in moving his ambitious agenda. Because of the narrow margin on the subcommittee between Democrats and Republicans, which reflected the close division of the parties in the House, he did not have real voting control of his own subcommittee. There were four Democrats and three Republicans on the Moss subcommittee. One of the Democrats was Bill Stuckey, a conservative businessman from Georgia, who often voted with the Republicans. So Moss was out-voted, understaffed, and faced a full committee chairman who was not pleased with the modest rebellion of his subcommittee chairs the previous year. If Moss was discouraged at the time, he did not show it. He and his allies repaid Staggers in spades a few years later.

* * *

The Senate acted first. It sent over to the House and to Moss's subcommittee a sweeping consumer product safety bill that not only would enact the tough legislation authored by the Product Safety Commission, but added the entire Food and Drug Administration (FDA) to the new independent safety agency. The industries affected and the Nixon administration were opposed to an independent agency.

To delay action in the Senate, opponents of the Magnuson bill had gotten it referred to both the Senate Labor and the Government Operations committees. Further review of the Product Safety Commission's recommendation followed, with Elliot Richardson, Nixon's secretary of Health, Education and Welfare (HEW), testifying in opposition to the Senate bill's provision creating an independent consumer safety agency.

Frank Carlucci, associate director of the Office of Management and Budget (OMB), also opposed the creation of an independent agency, saying that the secretary of Health, Education and Welfare would have a far better opportunity to consult with the president and bring important issues to his attention than would an independent agency. In addition, OMB was concerned that pulling the Food and Drug Administration out of HEW would fragment the existing regulatory establishment. Business also voiced its opposition to the Senate legislation. J. Edward Day, former postmaster general, said on behalf of the Electronics Industries Association (and just about everybody else in the business community) that the provision for a consumer safety advocate in the House and Senate bills would create a "high-level heckler and a backseat driver" for product safety activities.[36]

In the Senate Labor Committee, Magnuson's bill was also attacked by Richardson for taking the FDA out of the HEW and "drastically" reorganizing it. The Consumer Federation of America, Nader's Public Citizen organization, and the AFL-CIO were the main voices supporting the Magnuson bill.

Consumer Federation Director Erma Angevine thought reorganizing the FDA bureaucracy sounded good. She asserted that, hopefully, an independent agency, as proposed by the commission, would lessen the possibility of "political interference" with safety decisions, and called the FDA a captive of the food and drug industries. Her hopes were to be tested in the years ahead.

The Senate Government Operations Committee was never able to muster a quorum to report the bill and lost its jurisdiction thirty days later. The Labor Committee reported the bill to the Senate floor supporting Senator Magnuson's product safety bill with only minor amendments. The Senate passed the bill late in the ninety-second Congress on June 21, 1972—by a sixty-nine to ten roll-call vote. Amendments to keep the safety agency within the Department of Health, Education and Welfare and to strip the consumer agency of most of its enforcement power, which were backed by many business groups and by the Nixon White House, were defeated. It was hard to fight Magnuson in the Senate.

As usual, most of the opposition would come in the House of Representatives, particularly in the House Commerce Committee.

Moss, facing the united opposition of business leaders and the Nixon administration, as well as a sharply divided subcommittee, commenced hearings in February 1972. On the table was Moss's bill establishing an independent Consumer Product Safety Commission with a consumer safety advocate included, and implementing the other recommendations of the National Commission on Product Safety. Also before the subcommittee was the Nixon administration's bill, which would have placed the new agency within the sprawling department of Health, Education and Welfare; eliminated many enforcement powers; delegated much authority for setting safety standards to private industry; and, most important, eliminated the bill's consumer safety advocate.

Business witnesses, large and small, uniformly opposed the stronger legislation. The Association of Home Appliance Manufacturers—by now probably regretting its assistance to Magnuson in setting up the study commission four years before—supported the "concept" of the legislation, but called the Moss bill unnecessarily burdensome. The association said that any safety rule should be based on something called "proven need," and industry should be involved in the standard-setting process. It supported the Nixon bill. The Outdoor Power Equipment Institute, representing manufacturers of power lawn mowers and power tools, said that the government system of developing safety standards should be changed to "guarantee" fair treatment for all parties. The National Retail Federation said the administration bill offered a better approach for product safety. Other business witnesses echoed the cry for enactment of the Nixon bill, rather than the Moss-Magnuson legislation.[37]

The hearings went on for months as the clock wound down on the ninety-second Congress. The 1972 national elections neared. After the hearings, the subcommittee went into executive session to mark the bill up . . . or possibly to kill it.

Today, such markup sessions would be open to the public under the rules of the House, which were reformed after the Watergate scandal and Nixon's resignation. The fact that markups were not public then made it easier for lobbyists to write and deliver amendments that weakened legislation to committee members, and for members to offer them out of sight of the press and the public.

The probable outcome of the consumer product safety markup—a major battle of the consumer wars of the 1970s—remained very unclear. Moss and his main ally, liberal Congressman Bob Eckhardt, from Houston, Texas, needed one more vote to take the first step: report the consumer safety bill out of the subcommittee to the full committee.

During the hearings, the senior Republican on the subcommittee, James Broyhill, who came from the western part of North Carolina, had made what turned out to be an important comment about the bill his party was, in general, opposing. Broyhill had obviously read the report of the National Commission on Product Safety. At the first hearing, he said one could not fail to be impressed with the evidence of dangerous consumer products and personal injuries documented by the commission. He did not openly break with the Nixon administration and endorse the Moss bill. But Broyhill said he recognized that there was a basic "government responsibility" to ensure the safety of products sold to American consumers.

The statement was not very different from other general endorsements of the principle of the consumer's right to safety, which often were followed by opposition to the specifics of strong legislation. Broyhill's comment did not get to the nuts and bolts of the differences between the Nixon administration, the business community, and John Moss: Who would set safety standards? Who would enforce the law? And how? But Moss and his staff had noticed Broyhill's remark.

\* \* \*

Jim Broyhill was the senior Republican on Moss's subcommittee during the big years of the consumer revolution. He served in the House from 1963 until 1986, ultimately becoming the ranking Republican on the renamed Energy and Commerce Committee.[38]

He came from a well-known North Carolina family, the furniture-maker Broyhill Industries. He had worked there before entering politics. Broyhill became one of North Carolina's most popular congressmen. He had little difficulty winning elections, even in districts that had previously been controlled by Democrats.[39]

Broyhill was a conservative Republican, with an 88 percent approval rating from the American Conservative Union. He was a moderate on race issues, and later was appointed by Democratic Governor Jim Hunt to co-chair a statewide program to support a bond referendum for community colleges. He also chaired a business committee to implement welfare reform programs that promoted worker training and good jobs for welfare recipients.[40]

He was in a difficult position during the years of the consumer revolution. He faced a determined Moss, a liberal Senate majority, and a long list of legislation that worried his business-oriented supporters.

Broyhill was not by any definition a far-right conservative. He was often willing to negotiate with Moss. That was a major factor in the enactment of many consumer bills in the 1960s and 1970s. Later, Broyhill played a major role in bipartisan compromises over the Clean Air Act and natural gas price control legislation with John Dingell, who had, by then, risen to the chairmanship of the full House Commerce Committee.

Broyhill was always soft-spoken. He was the model of a North Carolina gentleman. According to Dingell, they disagreed on a lot of issues, but, "Broyhill wanted to see this place work."[41] He was called "one of the more creative parliamentary minds in Congress" by *Congressional Quarterly*.[42]

The North Carolinian rose to prominence among Republican legislators because of his legislative skills and his ability to forge agreements with the majority Democrats. In his last few years in the House of Representatives, he became one of the Reagan administration's favorite congressmen. "I am invited down to the White House all of the time," he told a home-state reporter in 1983, without boasting. "Either the Cabinet or White House people are in this office continually."[43]

The irony of Broyhill's constructive service in Congress and his willingness to compromise with Moss, Dingell, and the Democrats is that it probably cost him election to the United States Senate. He was appointed to the Senate in 1986 to fill a vacancy caused by the death of Republican Senator John East. When he stood for election, he was attacked in the Republican primary from the right by the Jessie Helms wing of the North Carolina Republican Party. He was charged with being a "turncoat" who voted for "Tip O'Neill's budget, the surrender of the Panama Canal, and a national holiday commemorating Martin Luther King's birthday."[44] After winning a bitter Republican primary election, Broyhill was narrowly defeated for the Senate by Democrat Terry Sanford.

In 1986, it was no longer acceptable in North Carolina Republican circles to be known as a congressman who reached agreements with the other party. The winds of political change ultimately swept Jim Broyhill from the Senate. His legislative imprint remains.

* * *

The days of markup dragged on, while the subcommittee debated the product safety bill well into the spring of 1972. On the eighth day of markup, a deadlock appeared certain. Democrat Bill Stuckey was siding with the Republicans in support of the Nixon administration bill. Moss remained determined to pass the pro-consumer legislation he had introduced. But he had only three votes. Counting Stuckey, Broyhill and the other Republicans had four. The House Commerce Committee looked, once again, like the graveyard of consumer protection legislation.

Moss and Broyhill sat next to each other up on the raised platform of hearing room 2322 in the Rayburn House Office Building. No press or members of the public were present. Several committee counsel sat below and opposite them at a long table, with the various versions of the bill and the proposed amendments spread out all over the place. Broyhill suddenly looked down and motioned for me to walk around the long table and come up the steps to the platform where the subcommittee members were seated. Heads turned. It felt like a very long walk.

"Tell the chairman," Broyhill said, "that we will trade him the consumer safety advocate for the independent agency."

Moss was sitting right next to Broyhill. Why Broyhill did not tell Moss himself, I never knew. Perhaps he wanted to be able to deny it. Perhaps it was Moss's stern demeanor that put him off. Whatever the reason, I walked about four feet to the right and whispered to Moss, "Mr. Broyhill says he will trade you the consumer safety advocate for the independent product safety commission in the bill." "Fine," said Moss, without looking at Broyhill and without any show of emotion. I walked the four feet back to Broyhill and told him it was a deal.

The bill was reported to the full Commerce Committee a few days later. After a long, unexplained delay in the Staggers's Commerce Committee, the Consumer Product Safety Act was sent to the House Rules Committee.

\* \* \*

The major opposition to the Consumer Product Safety bill now appeared to be blunted. Broyhill kept his agreement with Moss and supported the final compromise bill, although he must have been under intense pressure from the Nixon administration to block it. With what Moss thought was a tough pro-consumer bill reported out of the committee, the stage was set for the next act. Moss's staff prepared for final House floor action on the House-Senate conference report in June 1972.

Nothing happened.

The Rules Committee was charged with making a routine determination of when, and under what type of procedure, it would go to the House floor. But the Rules Committee, normally under the control of the Speaker, was, in those days, no rubber stamp. It maintained a tradition of independence and conservatism. The Rules Committee was chaired by William Colmer, a Mississippi Democrat, who did not see things the way Moss and his consumer allies did. The consumer product safety bill sat in Colmer's committee as the summer days and the final session of the ninety-second Congress slipped away. Nobody knew why.

About that time, I was talking with Joe Miller, a lobbyist for the Maytag Company. Maytag made washing machines and other high-end appliances that it probably did not think would be hurt much by the regulatory threat of the new consumer safety law. The company had an advertisement on television with a repair guy sitting in a rocking chair with nothing to do. Maytag thought it had a good name on Capitol Hill.

Miller, who was soft-spoken, slim, and gray-haired, had been a crusading journalist in his younger days. But the hours got long and the pay was low. So he took a job with Maytag.

We had formed a bond over time, mostly about horse racing. Miller had invited me to go with him to the horse races at Delaware Park. We had a fine time. In those days, taking a legislative counsel to lunch and the race track was considered ethically acceptable. It would be a serious violation today. The visit to the racetrack did not change Maytag's position or mine, but Miller and I became friends.

So, when we met in the hall of the Rayburn Building in late summer of 1972, I commented on the surprising delay in floor consideration of the

Consumer Product Safety Act, which was still stuck in the Rules Committee. Neither Moss nor I could understand it. Presumably, the Democratic
leadership of the House wanted the bill. "What was holding it up in the
Rules Committee?" I wondered out loud.

"Don't you know?" Miller asked. "The bill is as good as dead. The
Rules Committee will never report it. Most of the business interests in
town have talked to Colmer and other Rules Committee members, and
asked them to kill it," Miller said.

"Why?" I asked naïvely.

"Well, believe it or not, Rules was approached by Chief Justice (Warren) Burger," Miller said. "He told Colmer and his committee the bill
would overload the federal courts. That and the lobbying were enough
for Colmer to kill it."

William Colmer, chairman of the House Rules Committee, had served
forty years in the House and fourteen years on Rules. He was a conservative and no friend of consumer legislation. He represented a Mississippi
district that probably would have reelected him no matter what bill—or
other pinko-liberal plan—he had done away with.

I thanked Miller, turned on my heel, and walked (or maybe jogged) to
Moss's office. Moss picked up the telephone and called some reporters.
The next day the *New York Times* ran a story titled, "Burger Aide Linked
to Bid to Weaken Product Safety bill."[45] The *Times* reported that the
chief administrative officer of the United States Courts, accompanied by
lawyer-lobbyist Thomas G. Corcoran, known as "Tommy the Cork," had
approached the Speaker and the Rules Committee in an effort to kill the
bill, saying it would cause an increase in federal court cases.

Speaker Carl Albert was quoted as acknowledging that a man associated with "judicial administration" had come to see him recently with
Corcoran. The second visitor was identified as Roland F. Kirks, director
of the administrative office of the courts. Albert said the two men urged
him to remove consumer remedies from the bill and make some other
changes. Kirks said he was acting for Chief Justice Burger. The chief justice and Kirks both declined to comment.

Moss, who was not identified as the source of the story, was quoted
saying, "If this is true, it is a shocking and offensive intrusion by the chief
justice into the legislative process, bordering on judicial misconduct."[46]

A few days later, Drew Pearson's "Washington Merry-Go-Round"
column headlined a nationwide article: "Chief Justice Lobbies Against
Bill."[47] The story said that the chief justice had dispatched his aide to talk
with Speaker Carl Albert accompanied by one of Washington's most en-
gaging special pleaders, "Tommy the Cork." Tommy's clients were very
much opposed to the product safety bill. When Pearson's co-columnist
Jack Anderson called to ask Kirks whether he had indeed gone with
Corcoran to lobby against the product safety bill, Kirks hung up on him.

Tommy the Cork, as charming an Irishman as ever practiced the art of political persuasion, was happy to let it be known that he had taken the chief justice's deputy to see Speaker Albert. "Kirks asked me to take him to see the Speaker," he said. Corcoran had done most of the talking, as usual. He argued that the bill would clutter up the courts, and Kirks would just nod his head in agreement. Albert said that the leadership had not intervened with Rules and really did not want to weaken the bill. That was surprising, because the Speaker appoints members of the Rules Committee and usually controled it. The news story went all over the country.

Not long after, Chief Justice Burger broke his silence. He sent a letter to Albert, denying that he had intended to meddle in the consumer product safety legislation, and saying he was just calling attention to the impact that new laws, in general, can have on the federal courts. Moss pointed out that the usual way to do this is to appear before or write to a committee when it is considering the bill. So, Moss told the press that the chief justice's denial was "highly evasive," and accused Burger of "arrogant interference in the legislative process."[48]

If, as it has been said, sunlight is the best disinfectant, the heat Moss turned onto the Rules Committee and the chief justice was penicillin. The Rules Committee promptly sent the bill to the House floor, where it was heatedly debated. One significant amendment was added to the bill. It limited the consumer's right to sue in federal court for injuries from violations of safety rules issued by the new agency. Nonetheless, the Consumer Product Safety Act passed the House. And a lot of the credit must go to Joe Miller and Maytag.

Because of all the delays, the bill did not get to the White House until fall, in the last days of the ninety-second Congress. A presidential election loomed in November. It sat on President Nixon's desk until late October 1972. There was speculation that the president would let it die with a pocket veto. It was 1966 and LBJ all over again for John Moss.

But, despite his opposition to many of its provisions, in the end, Nixon signed the bill. It was, after all, a presidential election year. After opposing much of the bill for years, Nixon said it "answers a long-felt need," and added, "I am happy to give it my approval."[49]

The Consumer Product Safety Act—which the press called a "milestone" in advancing the rights of consumers—became law.[50] Like the Freedom of Information Act six years earlier, it had faced ferocious opposition from powerful interests and near death from a possible presidential veto. In 1966, Moss, Senator Edward Long, and an aggressive press corps had played a major role in gaining President Johnson's grudging approval. In 1972, Moss, Magnuson, and an honest lobbyist from Maytag tipped the balance in the public's favor.

# 7

# Reviving the Federal Trade Commission
## *The Magnuson-Moss Act*

Warranties have no political pizzazz. They may be phony or inscrutable. They may contain language that is meaningless gobbledygook to buyers of automobiles, mobile homes, appliances, or toys. They may give less to the buyer than they take away in the fine print.[1] But warranties—or the lack of them—do not injure, maim, or kill people. Back in the early 1960s, at the dawn of the consumer revolution, they usually remained in their fancy wrappings, unopened and unread by most buyers.

When John Moss and Warren Magnuson took up the consumer cause in that long-ago era, the convoluted wording of these gilt-edged papers was mostly intended by sellers to eliminate the rights of buyers—not to help them. Existing law in every state of the union, handed down over centuries by American courts, held that a product had to be "fit for the purpose" it was sold for, and thus not defective. In the words of many judges, it had to be of "merchantable quality." If it was not, the consumer could, at least in theory, obtain a refund or perhaps damages, if he or she had the fortitude to pursue the matter.

According to a series of studies in the 1960s and 1970s by the Federal Trade Commission, the Nixon administration, and even the home appliance industry, product warranties offered by manufacturers generally surrendered those existing consumer rights in exchange for very little in return. The FTC found that consumer complaints about nonperformance of automobile warranties topped the all-time list of consumer problems from the time the agency was first established in 1914.[2]

Most people did not really know much about warranties or care about them until something went wrong with the product. Legislation to make them more understandable, to preserve the buyer's existing legal rights, and give purchasers better remedies was first introduced jointly by Senators Magnuson and Carl Hayden of Arizona in 1967. Their bill sat around for years and went nowhere.

Mike Pertschuk, who had become Magnuson's consumer counsel in 1964, says the big "consumer protection" bill then pending in the Senate Commerce Committee was something called the "Fair Trade" law. That proposed legislation was actually written by manufacturers and handed to the committee. Its purpose was to override state laws banning something called "resale price maintenance." This was (and is) another name for price-fixing by brand-name manufacturers. It is a practice that prohibits retailers and dealers from dropping the price of a product below the manufacturer's "suggested" price. It thus precludes price competition in the same product, for example, General Electric washing machines, among GE dealers and retailers. In the view of many economists, this was and is a bad deal for buyers.[3] Pertschuk says the counsel handling the bill when he arrived on staff congratulated him for landing a choice job, one that would assure Pertschuk of a continuing supply of free, price-fixed products, from toasters to audio equipment, as a "perk."[4] It was all ethical in those days.

The Federal Trade Commission, the agency primarily responsible for protecting American consumers from all manner of marketplace fraud and deception, including deceptive warranties, was considered inept—if anybody considered it at all. "The Sleepy Old Lady of Pennsylvania Avenue," as it became known, focused most of its energy on trivial things like the labeling of wool products.[5] This was based on a law designed primarily to protect the wool industry against competition from synthetic fabrics, produced by other industries often at lower prices.[6]

The Federal Trade Commission was a small agency with a miniscule budget, as federal agencies go. It was created primarily to protect one business from another by preventing "unfair competition." Its constituencies were companies that made products like furs and textiles that did not like to see imitators mislabel their goods. Most consumers would have agreed that false labeling was worth eliminating—as long as the FTC did not ignore the bigger consumer rip-offs.

But the FTC was handicapped in most attempts at redressing consumer deception. It operated through an archaic system of individual trials against each seller that it claimed had deceived or defrauded one or more consumers. After a full trial, which could take years, if the commission could prove its case to an administrative law judge, it obtained what is called a "cease and desist order." In those days, nothing happened until after the long trial was over, and the FTC staff had proven a deceptive practice existed. At that point, the company was ordered to "go and sin no more." Only if it violated the cease and desist order could it be sued in an entirely new court proceeding—by the Department of Justice, not the FTC itself—for modest money penalties. These amounted to a maximum of $5,000 per violation, or slightly more if several violations were involved. It was a mere slap on the wrist for most companies, especially in the roaring consumer economy of postwar America. And any penalty hinged on the Department of Justice deciding that the case was worth prosecuting, often after an intense second round of lobbying by the defendant.

The commission was indeed a paper tiger. But it was the only tiger that oversaw consumer warranties, and supposedly all other types of consumer fraud and deception in the American marketplace.

John Moss in the House of Representatives and Warren Magnuson in the Senate labored for more than five years to convince Congress—and the public— that warranties were often a scam, and that the FTC needed a makeover. Moss and Magnuson wanted all warranties to be graded and labeled, such as "full" or "limited," so consumers could demand the better ones. It took persistence by Moss and Magnuson, and the economic crisis brought on by double-digit inflation in 1974, to finally bring Congress around to the idea that warranties could mean something to the average Joe.

Moss explained it in a floor speech supporting his bill: "Deceptive warranties that allow the sale of products that do not work cost consumers money. With inflation at 11.9 percent, consumers can ill afford to pay for products that do not work."[7]

Neither the press nor the public took much notice of these efforts. But business interests did. Their lobbyists in Washington—and there were a lot of them—were sensitive to the dangers of a law that could disrupt their way of doing business and force them to deliver on their promises.

Clearly, warranties were something that needed fixing, but Magnuson and Moss had a much bigger legislative goal in mind. They wanted to give the Federal Trade Commission real power to police the marketplace on behalf of consumers. They wanted the commission to be able to go to court promptly on behalf of large groups of financially damaged consumers, to stop all manner of deceptive practices, and to get damages or refunds for all of the people who were injured. In short, Moss and Magnuson wanted to make the FTC into a force for effective protection of consumers throughout the American economy. Consumers' recurrent problems with meaningless warranties gave them the hook they needed to achieve that end.

As Moss started work in the House on Magnuson's warranty-FTC bill, which the Senate had passed in 1970, almost every industry that might be touched by the bill, including those that produced and advertised consumer products from drugs to toys to television sets, disliked the thought of a tough warranty law, especially one without the escape clauses they were accustomed to. The idea of individual consumers having the ability to go to court—or worse, join with others in FTC class actions to enforce product performance claims—made producers shudder.

Even more distasteful was the possibility that the FTC might be given real power and a new mission.

One of the major changes that Magnuson originally sought to achieve was to give the FTC power to make "trade regulation rules" that could reduce misrepresentation and questionable practices on an industry-wide basis, rather than the existing way, which was one company or one advertisement at a time. Some of the things that concerned the sponsors and might be subject to such rules included the failure by funeral homes to disclose the comparative cost of caskets at the time a bereaved family needed to make funeral arrangements; the failure by used-car dealers to provide any warranty on used vehicles; the failure by mobile-home deal-ers to provide a warranty on mobile-home set-ups (an improper set-up often caused the home to buckle and break); and the failure by gasoline companies to post a listing on the pumps at gas stations of the octane rat-ing of gasoline.

The commission claimed it had the authority to set trade rules under its long-standing power to "prevent unfair and deceptive acts and prac-tices." But the courts were split on the issue, and the business community argued that only Congress could make such "laws." When Magnuson and Moss proposed giving the FTC explicit industrywide rule-making power, the idea was attacked by the Chamber of Commerce and almost every business lobby in the capital—and attacked effectively.

When the Magnuson-Moss Act finally passed, the FTC was granted rule-making powers. They were, however, so complex, confusing, and time-consuming that the agency basically gave up on trade regulation rules. It was definitely not a win for consumers.

On the other hand, the Magnuson-Moss bill was not just about rule-making. With its many provisions, the proposed Act was a large target at which its opponents took aim. "Maggie" and Moss had broad economic change in mind. Their opponents had the power, the lobbyists, and the dollars. But as it turned out, they could not kill it all.

Nancy Nord, who was then a lawyer at the Chamber of Commerce of the United States, predicted that the law's penalty and "consumer redress" provisions were going to cause "a lot of litigation between busi-nesses and the FTC." But, she said, "It was the best possible bill we could get." Nord later became acting chair of the Consumer Product Safety Commission under President George W. Bush. [8]

Whether the Magnuson-Moss Act was a major consumer victory at the height of the consumer protection revolution, or a disappointment that signaled the limits of the revolution, took years to become clear. And only some deft political maneuvering by the sponsors saved anything of the bill at all.

\* \* \*

To understand what Magnuson and Moss were dealing with in trying to rejuvenate the sleeping Federal Trade Commission, one must look back to the beginning of the agency and its evolution. The commission was created in 1914 on the recommendation of President Woodrow Wilson. It marked a high point in a long political battle to limit the role of monopolies and trusts in the national economy. It was a key achievement of Wilson and of President Theodore Roosevelt's progressive era in American politics—led by both Republicans and Democrats. Big business was feared by an America that remained primarily small town and rural.

The main function of the FTC originally was to define and outlaw unfair methods of business competition. It was designed to protect little businesses against unfair competition from bigger companies, such as small "mom and pop" grocery stores from the likes of A&P supermarkets. It was not intended to protect consumers directly, but primarily to limit business monopolies. Congress ultimately amended the original 1914 law more than twenty years later with the Wheeler-Lea Act, which enabled the agency to protect consumers directly against deception in the market-place. In doing so, Congress freed the FTC from having to base all of its actions on protecting competition. Wheeler-Lea directed the commission to prevent "unfair or deceptive practices" in commerce, generally. But even though the FTC had a mandate to protect consumers, it had, by the 1960s, become mostly an industry protection agency and not much else.

Then it ran into a firestorm. It all started with an unlikely report about the Federal Trade Commission by Ralph Nader and his team of youthful "Raiders."

The victor of the auto safety battle of 1966 did not just fade away after Congress enacted the new motor vehicle safety law. Nader had become a national figure, someone who could ignite a consumer revolution, provided there was some help from Congress. David Schmeltzer, a newly appointed government automobile safety lawyer, and later an official with the Consumer Product Safety Commission, remembered what it was like in a room when Nader testified. He said that Nader's obvious integrity and intensive research made him a media star. "He was like the Pied Piper. The press just followed him around. He was always good for a slashing, quotable remark. You could have heard a pin drop when he testified."[9]

The automobile safety crusader, fresh from his victory over Detroit in 1966, decided to recruit a student task force to study the Federal Trade Commission. The "Nader Report" on the FTC was actually written by three law students: Edward Cox, Robert Fellmeth, and John Schulz, who were recruited by Nader as members of the Raiders. They were more than critical of the slumbering federal agency.[10] Up front, the report was dedicated to "the nameless informed sources whose help made this book possible and to the long aggrieved American taxpayers and consumers who made it necessary."[11]

The Raiders found that the Federal Trade Commission had systematically failed to detect law violations, failed to establish enforcement priorities, failed to use its existing powers, limited though they might be, and failed to ask Congress for new authority to make its work more effective.

One story of the students charging around the FTC seeking evidence may have given rise to the commission's unflattering "sleepy old lady" nickname. The Raiders had scheduled an interview with one of the agency's top lawyers, a man reputed to be a bulldog of an attorney. When they arrived in his office, there was no one in the reception area to announce them, so they walked inside. There they found the lawyer fast asleep on a big leather couch with the daily newspaper covering his face. The image of that sleeping lawyer described in the report stayed in people's minds, particularly those on Capitol Hill who were supposed to be monitoring the agency's performance.

The strength of the Nader Report was that it cited specific examples of common consumer deception involving everyday products:

> The makers of Coke, Vanquish, Dristan, aspirins, sprays, gums, drinks, syrups, pills, and supplements, and all sorts of "combinations of ingredients" assure us that their products work magic on all varieties of ailments, real or anticipated. There is a marked resemblance to the "miraculous elixir" barkers of the 19th century. However, today's pitchmen pay $20 thousand to make each commercial and several hundred thousand dollars to present it, and they reel off their spiel to 30 to 60 million Americans at a crack. A 10-cent lie can pay for it all and more.[12]

Cigarette advertising was one of the Raider's prime targets. Although it has since been eliminated from television screens by consumer and government pressure, it was a major issue at the time: "Salem, Winston & Cool were among the top advertisers over this period, spending about 10 million dollars among them on TV over three months, trying to convince millions of people that death- and disease- dealing smoke is like fresh air, spring time, and cool mountain brooks."[13]

Nader, who wrote the preface to the report, knew how to sum up the frustration and failure of a promise to American consumers:

> On paper the FTC was the principal consumer protection agency of the federal government. As such, the Commission could have been an exciting and creative fomenter of consumer democracy. In reality, the "little old lady on Pennsylvania Avenue" was a self-parody of bureaucracy, fat with cronyism,

torpid through an inbreeding unusual even for Washington, manipulated by agents of commercial predators, and impervious to governmental and citizen monitoring.[14]

And to cap it off, the report pointed out that the FTC wasted money on trivial cases:

> between 1964 and 1968, the Commission obtained 562 cease and desist or consent orders. Of these, 286, or more than half, related to textiles, furs, and other matters involving claims regarding what country a product was manufactured in, or whether it was real wool. The balance dealt with the FTC's findings of deception, fraud, and unfairness in the entire American economy.[15]

Nader's FTC report, released in January 1969, was graphic enough to gain a lot of public attention. Later that year, the American Bar Association (ABA), its interest triggered by the Nader Report, commissioned a study of its own by a group of eminent lawyers and economists. The ABA study was under the chairmanship of a well-known Philadelphia attorney, Miles W. Kirkpatrick. The purpose of the study was to review the accuracy and findings of the Nader report. The ABA task force was considered by consumer types to be cautious and stodgy, and no one expected it to produce anything particularly newsworthy.

But the ABA group, shockingly, reached much the same conclusions about the FTC that Nader's team had. Its devastating bottom line was that the FTC had been preoccupied with "trivial matters" while "all but ignoring widespread retail consumer fraud."[16] Kirkpatrick was later appointed chairman of the Federal Trade Commission by President Nixon.

The Raider and American Bar Association reports—and the charisma of Ralph Nader—set the stage for improvement of the FTC. A relatively easy place to start was warranties.

There was some initial FTC action to work with. The FTC began an investigation to determine whether there were significant failures by automobile manufacturers in living up to their warranty promises. It is likely that Nader's testimony on automobile safety in the 1966 hearings before Congress on the new automobile safety bill, and press coverage of that issue, increased consumer warranty claims and expectations, particularly for automobiles.

The FTC's investigation results were issued in October 1968. They were highly critical of manufacturers and dealers for failing to live up to their promises to car buyers. In January 1969, a Nixon administration task force on appliance warranties and service reached similar conclusions. The Nixon administration report stopped short of recommending a new law. It said only that if substantial progress was not made by appliance manufacturers in promptly improving their warranty practices, legislation should be passed by Congress to require changes.

The problem with warranties, said the Nixon task force, was that "the majority of the major appliance warranties currently in use contain exemptions and exclusions, which are unfair to the purchaser and which are not necessary from the standpoint of protecting the manufacturer from unjustified claims of excessive liability."[17]

Twice in separate Congresses, the Senate passed consumer product warranty reform legislation, sponsored by Magnuson, only to have the bills die in the House Commerce Committee. The Senate Commerce Committee also reported a separate measure allowing financially damaged consumers to join to bring "class action" suits, but the full Senate did not take action on that potentially far-reaching bill. Business did not and still does not want class actions by groups of consumer plaintiffs, because of their huge potential cost.

In 1971, the Senate approved a bill that combined warranty protection and FTC improvements in a single package. That year President Nixon recommended a warranty-FTC bill in a major consumer message. Nixon's proposals were weaker than the measure approved by the Senate, but they put the issue on the political front burner. The House Commerce Committee again failed to take action, and the combined warranty-FTC bill died again at the end of the Ninety-second Congress. The House, and particularly the House Commerce Committee, remained the graveyard of consumer legislation.

For a third time, the Senate passed the warranty-FTC legislation in 1973. The bill was sponsored by Senator Magnuson and Senator Frank Moss of Utah, who was now chairman of a new consumer subcommittee, a part of Magnuson's committee.

* * *

John Moss had become chairman of the key House Commerce Subcommittee in 1967. His subcommittee had reported a couple of modest consumer bills, but nothing major could get past the full committee until 1972. The House Commerce Committee remained a hard road to travel for consumer legislation. Moss kept trying.

Then Moss, after serious in-fighting with his own committee chairman, but with the help of Republican Congressman Jim Broyhill, got the Consumer Product Safety bill through the Commerce Committee and the House in 1972. There was hope that the House logjam could be broken.

Moss turned to the long-dormant warranty-FTC bill as his next consumer priority. Behind Moss's effort lay a bitter, behind-the-scenes struggle with his own committee chairman, Democrat Harley Staggers.[18]

After a long delay and repeated requests to allow them to move forward with legislation, Moss and other committee members finally put enough pressure on Staggers. In September 1971, Moss got a grudging green light from the chairman to start what would prove to be a grueling four-year struggle to change both the FTC and the fairness of product warranties.

Moss opened the campaign for the FTC warranty improvements bill by noting that they were beginning hearings on legislation of "major importance to virtually all Americans." He said anyone who has ever purchased or intends to purchase an automobile, television set, refrigerator, stove, or other household appliance would be directly affected by the bill; anyone who has ever been deceived by a misleading advertisement or sales pitch would be intimately concerned with the consideration of FTC improvements.[19]

Moss's bill was quite similar to what Magnuson had reported from the Senate Commerce Committee. But Moss pointed out that the House and Senate legislation were very different from the Nixon administration's counterproposals. First, the administration bill did not give the Federal Trade Commission substantive rule-making authority. Second, it did not give the commission authority to order "consumer redress," that is, obtaining action to remedy injuries to consumers, such as refunding their money or replacing their property, or for the payment of damages caused by deceptive practices. Third, the administration's legislation did not provide for increased civil penalties, to replace the current wrist slap, when a company knowingly committed an unfair or deceptive act.[20] In addition, both the Senate and House bills contained authority for the FTC to go directly to court with its own lawyers to sue for consumer relief.

It helped that the administration had found it necessary to offer its own proposals. They were less than Moss wanted, but they did set the stage for an even more difficult battle than the one over the consumer product safety bill a year earlier.

Opposition to the legislation was intense. Former Kennedy administration postmaster general J. Edward Day led off as the voice of the Electronics Industries Association—and most of the U.S. business community—by pointing out that there would be competitive damage to American manufacturers if they were forced to give uniform warranties in a market where they were facing intense competition from imported products. Day said there were only a handful of consumer warranty complaints and no reason for the sweeping legislation that Moss proposed. He said that a national bill such as Moss and Magnuson's would hurt small companies and put unjustified pressure on all producers to offer a "full" warranty rather than be able to make reasonable business judgments about what the consumer needed or wanted.[21]

General Day, as he was known around town, emphasized import competition, inflation, and external forces that were clearly putting a damper on the consumer electronics business in America. He voiced concern over the broad powers the Federal Trade Commission would be given by the

Moss-Magnuson legislation. He predicted that lawsuits by consumers would flood the courts and that large attorney's fees could be awarded to any consumer who won a warranty case. Day asked the committee staff to attempt the daunting task of drafting a full warranty covering a color television set, one that would meet the requirements of the Moss bill and still be "usable" by the electronics industry.

Day was a grand figure, with the bearing of a former member of the Kennedy cabinet. Yet in Moss's mind, he was perhaps not sufficiently respectful of the subcommittee and its work. Moss, not a man known for the light touch as a chairman, did not treat Day gently.

"If I might interrupt at this point, Mr. Day," Moss said, as Day proposed his color TV warranty drafting challenge, "If you wish to supply a draft, you may do it yourself. The committee staff will not be instructed to prepare any such document."[22]

Day was not deterred by this put-down. Instead, he forged ahead with hard criticism of Moss's product. He suggested that the FTC improvements part of the bill, the real target of the business community, contained new powers for the agency that had repeatedly been rejected by congress as unsound. He said that giving the commission "unlimited authority to impose consumer redress" against manufacturers for deceptive acts would change the entire purpose of the agency and turn it into a consumer court. The FTC, he pointed out, had plenty of authority with its current power to issue the existing "go sin no more" orders.

Day also focused on the rule-making provisions of the legislation. Trade regulation rule-making, he testified, should be completely eliminated from the bill, unless the right to trial-type cross-examination was available to any industry facing a trade rule. He called the consumer redress provision and the rule-making provisions of the legislation "major departures" from current law.

Day and his clients attacked virtually all of Moss's proposals. Day told Moss that every section relating to strengthening the FTC should be split off into a separate bill and be subject to separate hearings at some undefined time in the future. He implied that such an extended review would prove that these provisions were not only unjustified, but unlawful as well.

Moss was not impressed by Day's legal wisdom. And Day might have overreached by somehow reminding Moss that he was not a lawyer, nor even a college graduate. Moss was not about to be lectured to by some high-priced, K Street barrister. As Nader later observed, it was probably a big advantage that Moss was not a lawyer. He did much more detailed preparation than most members of Congress.[23]

None of this hard-line opposition made Moss particularly pleasant that fall morning. The last thing he wanted was another delay. He thanked the witness and said he would reserve a place in the record for any further comments Day or anyone else had on the Magnuson-Moss bill. And he issued a warning to its opponents, many of them sitting before him that morning. In unusually stern tones, Moss assured Day, and all of the other industries there, that the FTC powers written into the bill had not been undertaken lightly. He and the subcommittee had considered them all in detail. He wanted them to know that he did not need a lawyer to know what was right—and he had plenty of lawyers working for him. Moss said, in effect, it was now or never for the business community to have its day in court. He did not want it to be claimed later that a full opportunity had not been given to them to make their case against his consumer bill.[24]

Moss's grilling of Day, supplemented by tough questioning from Representative Bob Eckhardt, the Texas trial lawyer, was illustrative of the struggle the subcommittee faced in moving a warranty-FTC bill forward. The points of attack were many and varied. At one point when an industry witness said that the legislation would actually cause companies to offer *fewer* warranties, Moss recalled his own experience years before as a small appliance dealer in Sacramento.

"I cannot conceive of any of your member firms giving up the warranties of the type they are now giving," he told them. "They are giving these warranties," he added, "because competition has forced them to, and I think they would continue to give . . . them because competition would continue to force them to. If they did not, their product would suffer in the marketplace."[25]

And Moss, in 1971, added a bit of prophetic advice for the electronics and other industries that might be facing stiff competition from imported products:

> I think part of our problem is not only imports. Part of our problem is a failure to have quality control on many of the things we produce domestically. It has led to deterioration of confidence by American consumers in those products. I think there is much to be gained here by the members of your association, if they were to sharpen up their quality control and pay more attention to the warranties that they do put out.[26]

Moss's ally Eckhardt emphasized that warranties that covered defective parts only (and not labor)—a common practice then and now—were essentially a scam. He put it this way: "Mr. Chairman, I'm inclined to think that the labor to repair a product is the senior factor in the cost and, therefore, giving a parts-only warranty is misleading."[27]

Moss wound up the hearings saying he wished that some of the individual companies would show up under their own names, rather than "hiding behind the trade associations," to criticize the legislation. He recalled that with other legislation there had been similar dire warnings that the bills would "drive prices out of sight and destroy the industry."[28]

Then he pointed out that the industries involved seemed to be vigorous enough. In fact, sales of color television sets were way up, even with the new product safety law now in force. Whatever injury was faced by the manufacturers surely would not be due to the actions of Congress in increasing consumer rights.

From 1971 to 1973, the Moss-Eckhardt debate with industry representatives in the subcommittee continued through twelve long days of hearings and innumerable meetings. Nobody seemed ready to change his mind. Once the hearings were over, Moss and his subcommittee spent days in markup in an attempt to write a bill that might get passed. Eckhardt succeeded in carving out a major consumer victory during the markup. It centered on his belief that over time, individual rights of consumers to sue in court would be as important as effective federal regulation.

Eckhardt was a typical individualistic Texan. He wore a big wide-brimmed hat and droopy bow tie, rode his bicycle to his office in the Longworth House Office Building, and believed in self-help. So he took a look at the warranty section of the bill, allowing a lot of potentially small-potatoes claims, and did his best to incorporate the concept of consumer "class actions" into the bill.

Then, as now, class actions represented a potentially powerful group weapon for consumers. But they can be abused and have always been highly controversial. Class actions allow a group of injured consumers to band together on behalf of themselves and anybody else who might be injured by the same deceptive practice to bring a class suit for the combined damages and for attorney's fees as well. Plaintiff's lawyers love them. Defendants hate them. Legislation to make it easier to bring such cases in federal courts for consumer claims had been introduced in Congress. It never stood a chance of passage.

Initially, the Magnuson-Moss bill did not include a class action provision but did allow individual consumers to sue for a deceptive warranty or failure to perform promised service. But the individual claims were mostly small, and few lawyers could afford to touch them. Eckhardt, who in private life had represented injured plaintiffs, was determined to squeeze into the bill some kind of class action provision for deceptive warranties.

While the bill was still locked in subcommittee markup, Eckhardt sat down at the end of the row of subcommittee members with a black felt-tipped pen and scribbled away on a big copy of Moss's legislation. Moss had already inserted in his bill a class action right. But with that provision, it did not stand a chance of getting out of the House Commerce Committee. Moss probably knew it was doomed. Eckhardt had his own ideas. With pen in hand, he began drafting a compromise. He suggested that there should be at least one hundred injured consumers before the case could be heard in federal court. And he added that the damages would have to total at least $10,000 with at least $25 for each claimant. The section provided that class actions could be brought in state as well as federal courts. Eckhardt's idea was novel. Moss thought it was too damned complicated and would weaken the bill.

At one point Moss leaned over to the legislative counsel sitting next to him and said with rising frustration, "Would you please go down there and take the pen away from that Congressman." Eckhardt probably did not hear Moss and, as the legislative counsel in the seat next to Moss, I was too stunned to react. But Eckhardt would not be deterred. He kept negotiating with Moss, Broyhill, and the Republicans and finally got his limited class action section grudgingly adopted by the subcommittee. Moss even voted for it.[29]

With the limitations the Texan had written, the provision was viewed as harmless by most industries and was buried in the final bill. It has proven over time not to be "harmless." Some lawyers now actually advertise that they will represent consumers injured by mass-product warranty claims involving automobiles or other expensive products. Consumers gained something more, and unsuspected at the time, from the Texan's stubborn persistence. Some attorneys specialize in individual warranty lawsuits—mostly meritorious ones, since they are entitled to legal fees only if they win.[30]

After all the talk and repeated attempts to vote out the bill in the subcommittee, it appeared deadlocked between supporters and opponents, just as the consumer product safety bill had been two years before. Twice, Magnuson's bill had been passed by the Senate and then died in the House Commerce Committee. In 1974, a third and perhaps final death sentence appeared likely.

Moss needed something to jump-start the bill and break the deadlock. Two big developments provided that jolt. The first was created by Moss himself. The Nixon administration had issued its Task Force report on appliance warranties in 1969, the one that was critical of existing industry practices, and had suggested that federal legislation might be needed if voluntary steps were not taken by producers to remedy existing warranty practices. This was surprising for a business-oriented administration, but such was the power of consumerism at the time. What had happened to warranties, Moss wondered, in the five years since the Nixon report?

Moss directed his staff to conduct a new warranty investigation. The staff surveyed two hundred warranties issued by fifty-one major American companies. The results, released by Moss in a 1973 report, were devastating. The study found "no significant improvement" between 1969 and the date the report was released in 1974:

> Today's consumer product warranties are replete with limitations on manufacturers' obligations. Any actions taken to clean up these guarantees during the past five years appear to have had minimal results. These certificates, often marked "WARRANTY," in most cases serve primarily to limit obligations otherwise owed to the buyer as a matter of law.[31]

The subcommittee report undermined claims that warranty performance might have improved or that warranties were not misleading. The ensuing press coverage of the report embarrassed the bill's opponents.

The second boost came from Federal Trade Commission Chairman Lewis Engman, who was a recent Nixon appointee. Engman, who may have surprised the president by his commitment to the commission's mission to promote competition and protect consumer interests, became concerned that the Moss subcommittee had drafted a bill that would give industry too much cross-examination potential in the rule-making process. Engman worried aloud about the long delays such big trials might cause. There was, he concluded, *too much* due process, a conclusion that stood in sharp contrast to the position of Day and the electronics industry.

Engman, surely no liberal, was a strong supporter of the commission's mission, but, when it came to rule-making, he thought he could do better in the courts than in Congress. He came before the Moss subcommittee in 1974 and said he had reevaluated the provision and decided that, while the commission favored the Moss bill, the rule-making section could unnecessarily jeopardize rapid passage of other essential, but less controversial, provisions of the package. Engman said the commission would oppose any statutory rule-making provision that gave it less flexibility than he believed it had under the existing law, which was almost total flexibility.

Engman based his position on a single Court of Appeals decision supporting his point of view that the FTC already had rule-making authority without restrictions. It took a lot of nerve for Engman to take such a position, in opposition to the Nixon administration, which had just appointed him chairman.

But Engman also had stepped on Moss's sometimes sensitive toes. His reversal and request to drop the rule-making provision from the bill surprised Moss and undermined a key section of his bill. Engman had not followed what Moss believed was the requisite congressional courtesy of telling a chairman, in this case Moss, in advance that he was about to surrender a major part of prized legislation. There is no question that the rule-making idea worried the business community and made it *the* prime target of the bill's opponents. But crossing Moss was not a good idea. And, just as in the case of the Eckhardt amendment, Moss remained optimistic that he could get a good bill out of the committee and Congress.

So, while Moss wanted the strongest bill he could get, Engman's flip-flop gave him an opening for negotiations. He began talking with Jim Broyhill, the ranking Republican on the subcommittee, regarding inclusion of a limited right of cross examination in the bill. This was what industry really wanted and the FTC feared. Moss and Broyhill reached an agreement: cross examination only on material issues of fact, not policy or small issues. Only time would tell who was right.

While the new rule-making section with limited cross-examination rights gave consumer groups much less than they wanted, the deal allowed the bill to get out of the subcommittee. It still included effective provisions regarding consumer warranties and other FTC powers, such as getting refunds for consumers. While Moss and his staff initially thought that Engman's retreat had undermined a strong bill, the successful negotiations with Broyhill and the Republicans made enactment of the bill in some form at least a possibility.

As the cherry blossoms bloomed near the Rayburn House Office Building in the spring of 1974, the Magnuson-Moss bill still faced an uncertain future in the House of Representatives. As usual, Moss did not have enough pro-consumer votes to get the bill out of the full House Commerce Committee. Opponents of the legislation represented virtually every industry that had testified and many that had not. Its only supporters were a few citizen groups, such as Public Citizen and the Consumer Federation of America, and some unions, including the AFL-CIO represented by its diminutive, feisty consumer labor lobbyist, Evelyn Dubrow.

Despite intense lobbying against it, the bill was reported favorably by the Moss subcommittee to the full House Commerce Committee. All the Democrats, and most of the Republicans, went along with the Moss-Broyhill-Eckhardt compromises on class actions and rule-making and voted in favor of the bill. But yet another battle was to follow.

Over Moss's protests, the bill took a hard hit in full committee. All Republicans and some Democrats voted to strip one of the remaining enforcement powers, the "consumer redress" provision, from the legislation, further weakening the bill. Chairman Staggers, usually a reliable pro-consumer vote, was surprisingly absent from the full committee markup when the damage was done. Moss then turned and attacked his own weakened bill as passed by the committee and promised he would find a way to strengthen it.[32]

In May 1974, the *Washington Post* reported that the full House Commerce Committee had voted out a compromise bill. The *Post* opined,

The House Commerce Committee voted out a bill that gives to the consumer with one hand and takes away with the other. Although it establishes minimum federal standards for warranties on consumer products and a limited opportunity for class action suits for breach of warranties, the bill also restricts the Trade Commission's existing consumer protection powers.[33]

The now weakened Magnuson-Moss bill slipped through the House of Representatives, as its industry opponents breathed a sigh of relief. It went on to conference with Magnuson's tougher Senate version, still containing the class action provision that Eckhardt had written, and the power of the FTC to represent itself in federal court. Other than that, the bill as passed by the House was a faint shadow of what Moss originally intended.

After a conference between the Senate and the House on the different versions, the bill came back to the House for final approval. The Ninety-third Congress was nearly at an end. It was late in December 1974. The House remained in session until almost Christmas that year. One of the reasons was the fate of the warranty-FTC bill. Another was emergency legislation dealing with the gasoline shortage caused by the Arab oil boycott. To say that consumer worry and anger were running high as the year came to a close is an understatement.

The conference report came before the House just before Christmas. Surprisingly, it passed with only modest protests from opponents. Perhaps they decided to join in the glad tidings of the season. Perhaps they just wanted to go home for Christmas. The final bill was not everything the two legislators or consumer leaders had wanted. But Magnuson and Moss had one last surprise for their supporters.

For once, time had been on the side of the little guys. The "consumer redress" provision Moss had fought so hard for in committee had been slipped back into the final version of the bill in the conference committee. The bill's opponents lacked the votes to knock it out of the conference agreement or to kill the entire bill on Christmas Eve. The Moss-Broyhill compromise had worked. Magnuson called the final bill "a Christmas present for the American consumer."[34]

Gerald Ford, now president after the resignation of Richard Nixon, was facing a difficult re-election fight in two years. He signed the legislation in the first week of January 1975.

Consumers had won a major victory in the Magnuson-Moss Act. After three tries, Moss had finally pushed the bill through the House. Magnuson had bounced it back from the conference committee even stronger. And a weakened President Ford signed it.

* * *

In the decades that followed, the FTC reawakened. The Magnuson-Moss Act caused something of a breakthrough in consumer warranty protection. According to one analyst, it affected a major change in the purchase and sale of consumer goods and has emerged as the dominant legal regulation of consumer product warranties in the United States.[35] It led to a wave of "lemon laws" in almost every state, which focus specifically on purchases of new automobiles. Triggered by the federal law, they go a step beyond it, giving new car buyers the same relief as a "full" warranty, which is voluntary under the Magnuson-Moss Act. The buyer can get a new car when the original one does not function properly after several attempts at repair.[36]

The Moss-Broyhill agreement both establishing and limiting the FTC's power to issue industrywide trade regulation rules did not fare as well. The agency has largely given up on rule-making, a major Magnuson-Moss goal, because of the complex, delaying cross examination the law allows.[37] But the consumer redress provision has had a major impact. According to the American Bar Association report, fraud and deception were rampant in the marketplace in 1969. By 2007, using the Magnuson-Moss consumer redress provision, the FTC obtained orders requiring vendors who had deceived or defrauded consumers to pay over $240 million in remedies in a single year, mostly in refunds to consumers. In 2007, the leading consumer complaints were identity theft, misleading catalog sales, and Internet fraud. The product warranty problems of the 1960s had faded with the changed economy and a new sense of mission for the FTC.

Over time, the Act has had a positive effect both on warranty practices of manufacturers and on the ability of the Federal Trade Commission to obtain refunds and other remedies for groups of defrauded consumers. FTC Commissioner Steven Nye said at the time the law was signed that it "didn't sound very sexy but was of monumental importance."[38] Jodie Bernstein, former director of the FTC's Bureau of Consumer Protection, gave two graphic examples of the law's impact on the consumer. After its enactment and the publication of FTC rules regulating warranty practices, the number of consumer warranty complaints received by the FTC went down, and industries set up consumer arbitration panels to resolve disputes before the government could even get involved.

She recalled a groundbreaking case under the Act concerning a product called Doan's pills. They were advertised by the manufacturer to cure backaches. The FTC thought that Doan's pills were no different than aspirin. Using medical testimony, they convinced a federal court, using the Magnuson-Moss Act, to require the company to run expensive, corrective television advertising telling viewers the true facts. It was powerful medicine from the "new" FTC.[39]

A Library of Congress report summarizes the transformation of the Federal Trade Commission after 1973:

> From this low point in the FTC's history, the agency was able to make a truly remarkable turnaround; during the first few years of the 1970s, it was transformed from an apparently weak agency on the verge of collapse into an aggressive one with extraordinary clout. The transformation was a result of new leadership, the rendering of a decision by a federal court holding

that the Federal Trade Commission Act empowered the Commission to issue substantive rules, and lastly the granting of far-reaching powers under the Magnuson-Moss Federal Trade Commission Improvements Act (P.L. 93–637).[40]

The agency was rejuvenated. It became, sometimes even during the tenure of conservative presidents, a force in the marketplace on behalf of the buying public. And if it should ever push the limits of its authority, as Moss had always urged, it could be an even more important consumer guardian.

Magnuson, together with Mike Pertschuk and his entrepreneurial Senate staff, must receive much of the credit for initiating the law now known as the Magnuson-Moss Act.[41] Magnuson started that fight on behalf of consumers. John Moss finished it. Without Moss there would have been no law.

The Californian was forced to challenge his own committee chairman, initiate his own investigation of deceptive warranty practices, and cajole enough votes out of a collection of liberal Democrats and moderate Republicans to force the bill through a reluctant House of Representatives. Only a member of Congress at the peak of his powers, with a deep commitment, acting during an era of high public awareness, could have achieved such a result.

One former official of the Federal Trade Commission said the impact of the law "reverberates today."[42] Another, asked to recall Moss and his efforts on behalf of the American consumer, said, after long reflection, "I cannot conceive of there being anyone like him today."[43]

The tenacious Moss, backed as always by the progressive voters of Sacramento, could now point to a primary role in the enactment of the Freedom of Information Act, the Consumer Product Safety Act, and the Magnuson-Moss Warranty-Federal Trade Commission Improvements Act. He was sixty-four years old and could have kicked back and called it a career. In fact, he was just getting started.

# 8

# Investor Protection

## *Breaking Wall Street's Monopoly*

Wall Street was in freefall. The New York Stock Exchange (NYSE), which in eight years had tripled its trading volume, lost 35 percent of its value in one year. One hundred and sixty brokerage firms, mostly New York Stock Exchange members, were bankrupted or forced to liquidate.[1] Thousands of investors who had accounts with the failed firms lost their money. Investments in securities held in "street name" (meaning the stock was held in the broker's, not the buyer's, name) or in cash were wiped out, along with the firms that held them.[2] It was as bad as the infamous Bernard Madoff swindle of 2008, except that in 1969 when Wall Street unraveled, it was all perfectly legal.

In the aftermath of the crash, Moss and Senator Ed Muskie sought to do something to protect small investors. It was not easy. Neither of them could claim any popularity points with the securities industry. Muskie was defeated in the presidential primaries of 1972. He did not have much Wall Street support in his failed campaign. Moss found that some small financial players, such as the American Stock Exchange, supported the securities market reforms he and Muskie wanted. Still, when Moss addressed a securities industry gathering after the crisis had ebbed and the changes were in effect, James Needham, chairman of the New York Stock Exchange, approached him to tell him that he did not appreciate the federal assistance the securities industry had received. "You are the greatest disaster to hit the securities industry since Franklin Roosevelt," Needham told Moss, who responded, "Thank you, Jim. That is a great compliment."[3]

\* \* \*

115

There were many reasons for the 1969 stock market crash: a get-rich-quick, "go-go" market frenzy by both investors and brokers; the huge growth in the number of small, unsophisticated investors; insider trading abuses by brokers; and lack of effective regulatory oversight by the Securities and Exchange Commission (SEC).

The problem for individual investors was simpler. National banks had been insured against failure by the Federal Deposit Insurance Corporation since the enactment of the New Deal bank legislation of 1934. But stockbrokerage firms, often holding just as much wealth for individual investors in cash and securities, were largely uninsured. Stocks deposited by customers with brokers and "free" cash balances from dividends or deposits were wholly at risk of loss if a firm failed.

One obvious reason: stockbrokers were allowed to use their customers' stock and cash as if it were the companies' money. They could and did pledge it for firm loans. They could and did count it as an asset or "net capital" of the firm to meet the vague, voluntary industry guidelines of the day. Thus, they risked their customers' investment money in their own businesses.

There was no state or federal regulation of an investment firm's financial stability, its management capacity, or its qualifications to be in the securities business. When investment firm loans were called in, in the economic upheaval that followed the 1969 stock market drop, a lot of money belonging to small investors was used to pay off their stockbroker's loans.

The markets were not totally unprepared for problems. In 1964, five years before the crash, a New York Stock Exchange insurance fund had been created in response to the bankruptcy of Ira Haupt & Co., a big Wall Street firm. It was designed to reimburse customers who lost money through a brokerage's failure. But the fund was small compared to the huge risk involved, and, in the 1969 crash, it was soon exhausted. Nor did the fund cover nonmember firms, such as those trading in the over-the-counter market, or firms that had withdrawn from, or been suspended by, the New York Stock Exchange. This meant that some of the most troubled firms were not covered. The so-called insurance fund was voluntary; the Exchange could deny coverage for many reasons.

Ultimately, the Exchange paid out $140 million in reimbursement to customers of some of the bankrupt or liquidated firms during the crisis. But total losses to customers, creditors, and shareholders were many times greater.[4] Clearly, there was no real safety net, no federal deposit insurance or government guarantee of funds or securities deposited with a brokerage firm. As the market unraveled, the little investors, rather than the more sophisticated institutional investors, bore the brunt of the debacle.

\* \* \*

Just as the financial crisis hit Wall Street and the U.S. economy, John Moss took over the chairmanship of the Commerce and Finance Subcommittee of the House Commerce Committee. Moss had, until then, been chairman of the Government Information Subcommittee of the House Government Operations Committee, which had been his vehicle for gaining enactment of the Freedom of Information Act. Now he was faced with a choice: he could stay on as chair of the nationally prominent Government Information Subcommittee or move over to a subcommittee of the House Commerce Committee. He moved—the politically riskier of the choices.

The Commerce and Finance Subcommittee had jurisdiction over things like product labeling, newsprint, tourism, weather, time, consumer bills, and the virtually forgotten—and little-understood—"securities and exchanges." Moss had never evinced any particular interest in the financial markets. He had no background in finance, except as a small businessman. He elected, nonetheless, to switch to the Commerce and Finance Subcommittee in 1967, primarily because of its consumer jurisdiction and, because of the senority system, it was the only commerce subcommittee he could get.

The stock market crash of 1969 almost immediately pulled Moss into the financial world. Despite his lack of experience, the issue was tailor-made for him. Ordinary people were getting hurt in the stock market. The press reported that people were losing the money they had put aside to send their children to college or to use for retirement. Helen Rosenblatt, a widow who was financing her son Adam's medical school education through dividends she received from a New York brokerage firm, suddenly found that her dividend checks stopped coming. "It is all I have. . . . I have the feeling of being left high and dry," she said.[5] Jack Parker, who had just retired from a modestly successful corporate career, found his life savings of $225,000 in cash and stocks, which he had invested with his broker, were gone. "I am hurting and I am burning," he said.[6]

Behind the stories of Mrs. Rosenblatt, Mr. Parker, and many others lay both excessive speculation and a breakdown by Wall Street firms in keeping pace with the rapidly increasing numbers of large and small investors entering the stock market. The "Street" had hyped and promoted the huge growth in investment in the market by small investors. They did it through mass advertisements urging people to buy stocks, by hiring thousands of additional stockbroker-salesmen to push stocks to almost anyone who could come up with a few dollars, and by opening new offices in cities and towns across the United States. Stock exchange trading volume skyrocketed. So did investor risk.

The primary victims of the era's speculation, incompetence, and greed were the new, small investors.

Hurd Baruch was special counsel to the Securities and Exchange Commission. He later wrote that the 30 million shareholders who, by 1970, were at risk in the American securities markets, were consumers, just like the buyers of appliances, cars, or houses. The situation reminded Baruch of the great market crash of 1929:

> Four decades ago, our national economy was brought to the verge of collapse as the result of excessive speculation fostered and engaged in by the members of the brokerage community. In an effort to restore investor confidence . . . Congress enacted six major statutes between 1933 and 1940 that effected sweeping reforms in the securities markets. . . . These laws, substantially unchanged for the past thirty years, despite major transformations in financial institutions and practices, proved unable to forestall the speculative orgy during the late 1960s or to protect customers and industry members alike during the inevitable aftermath.[7]

It was clear to Moss that "our only hope . . . for stemming the crisis of investor confidence" was fundamental change in the operation of the securities markets. Absent that, investor-consumers would remain largely unprotected from securities firms' bankruptcies, excessive speculation, and crime.[8]

The combination of uninsured customer stock and cash, coupled with the huge increase in the number of investors, suggested to one *New York Times* columnist that, with major firms teetering on the brink of insolvency, investors might feel more confident "stitching their stock certificates into a mattress rather than leaving them with a broker in 'street name.'"[9] The writer noted that the New York Stock Exchange refused to assume responsibility for yet another major failure, that of First Devonshire Company, which had pledged its customers' securities for debts of $4.3 million. Devonshire did not have the money to repay that debt. Many of its customers faced the loss of their entire investment.

Then, Goodbody & Company, one of the nation's largest brokerage firms, badly undercapitalized like many Wall Street firms at the time, was forced into liquidation holding $33.6 million of uninsured customers' cash. That collapse exhausted the New York Stock Exchange's insurance fund. Investors now were on their own in a turbulent, plunging market.

The 1969 market crisis was reminiscent of the "tulip mania" that struck Holland during the "Golden Age" of the seventeenth century. At the peak of tulip mania in 1637, speculation in tulip bulb contracts caused the price to skyrocket to ten times the annual income of a skilled Dutch craftsman. When the wild speculation in the newly introduced flowers ended a year later, investors in tulip bulbs were ruined by falling prices. Dutch commerce suffered a severe shock. It took decades to recover. It was the first, and classic, example of a speculative economic bubble that burst, at great cost to individual investors and to a nation's economy.[10]

The Wall Street crisis of the late 1960s was another bubble of expanded volume and excessive speculation. So-called glamour stocks sold at one hundred times their projected earnings, while stocks of established corporations could be had for as little as seventeen times earnings.[11] The predictable downturn hurt not only investors, but public confidence in the stock market itself. Wall Street became a street of despair. The financial crisis was becoming a national crisis.

Posh Wall Street watering holes, such as Eberlin's and Delmonico's, high-end restaurants where brokers and financial analysts had been wining and dining for decades, found their business had dropped 20 percent in six weeks. At Eberlin's, sales at the bar took the first hit, according to George Piscina, the manager. Receipts were off "because some men, instead of having three or four drinks, [were] only having one or two." A small drugstore three blocks from the New York Stock Exchange was also hurting. Its sales of tickets for the New York State lottery were way down, the owner complained.[12]

It was not just harm to little people and to the economy that piqued John Moss's interest in the securities markets (although that probably would have been more than enough); it was also the history of securities regulation, or rather nonregulation, that bothered him. While Moss's Subcommittee on Commerce and Finance had exclusive responsibility in the House for legislation relating to the securities markets, there had been very little securities regulation by Congress or the SEC since the wave of New Deal legislation enacted in the aftermath of the 1929 stock market crash.

The liberal Congresses of the 1930s had enacted groundbreaking legislation to protect investors. There was the Securities Exchange Act in 1934, which prohibited misrepresentation in the sale of securities, and the Securities Act in 1933, which required extensive disclosure, in the form of long and often incomprehensible prospectuses designed to tell individual investors exactly what they were getting when they bought a stock. But over the prosperous decades of the 1940s, 1950s, and early 1960s, Wall Street was largely self-regulated, primarily by the New York Stock Exchange. The SEC was effectively directed by law, and expected in practice, to take a back seat. It was the industry's drive to increase its business and the collapse in the1960s of its insurance fund and self-regulatory structure that ultimately forced Congress and Moss to get deeply involved.

* * *

There was another reason. It started in Maine and in the Senate. In 1969, Senator Edmund Muskie was not only a leading Senator; he was running, in a subdued but determined manner, for president of the United States.

Muskie had been the surprise Democratic nominee for vice president in 1968. The Humphrey-Muskie ticket lost one of the closest elections in U.S. history to former Vice President Richard Nixon and his running mate Spiro Agnew, the governor of Maryland. But Muskie had caught people's attention. Because of his integrity, the *New York Times* said he stood out among all the "clever, confused, cunning, and cynical men" in the race.[13]

He was the obvious and likely choice of the Democratic Party for the presidential nomination in the 1972 election. Almost out of nowhere, Muskie appeared to be a new national leader. His years of quiet service in the Senate, and as governor of a small state, had not fully prepared him for a national presidential race. Now, the failing securities markets and the national financial crisis suddenly made his membership on the Senate Banking Committee important.

The Maine Democrat was one of fifteen members of the Senate Banking Committee, which had jurisdiction over securities markets and investor protection. Until 1969 he had shown little interest in financial issues. His primary legislative interest was protection of the environment. John Sparkman of Alabama was the chairman of the committee and normally would have been expected to take the lead on a major new financial bill. There was no obvious reason why Muskie should have led the fight; particularly, because the issue would inevitably involve a struggle with powerful Wall Street financial interests. But Muskie's star was rising in 1969. He was looking for big issues. Investor protection, in the face of the rapidly growing financial crisis, certainly qualified.

Not surprisingly then, in 1969 he took the lead in sponsoring Senate legislation to address the growing securities market crisis. He introduced a bill to create a Federal Broker-Dealer Insurance Corporation in June of that year. He made a perfect partner for Moss in the fight to enhance investor protection.

\* \* \*

When Moss became chairman of the Commerce and Finance Subcommittee in 1967, three words, "securities and exchanges," gave it jurisdiction over the engine of American commerce. Those three words did not appear to mean much, until disaster struck Wall Street. When the stock market dropped, and brokerage firms went into bankruptcy, the hot potato landed on Moss's desk. He and Muskie reacted to the crisis and to the ensuing panic. But not without determined opposition from the industry they sought to help.

Moss, as chairman of the only House subcommittee with jurisdiction over the securities markets, believed he must address the looming threat, particularly to individual investors, with new legislation. The Muskie-Moss bill was designed to establish something like the Federal Deposit Insurance Corporation, which had insured bank deposits for decades, to provide that cash and securities left with brokers by individual investors would be backed by a federal guarantee. This Securities Investor Protection Corporation would, the lawmakers believed, bring consumer protection to the securities markets.[14] But Wall Street was used to regulating itself. It did not like the idea of any federal interference. The Muskie-Moss "SIPC" legislation was fought by the New York Stock Exchange and the securities industry.[15]

Creating an insurance program guaranteed by the federal government for individual investors, not necessarily big investors, was important to Moss and Muskie. The big investors were thought to be sophisticated enough to take care of themselves.

A federal insurance law Moss and Muskie reasoned. They believed the law would enhance public confidence in the market system itself. But that was not the way Wall Street saw it. According to Senator Edward Brooke, the Massachusetts Republican who was a strong supporter of the proposed law, the legislation was "opposed strenuously from the beginning" by the New York Stock Exchange and the securities industry.[16]

The securities industry feared further federal involvement in the securities markets and, ultimately, control. But as the crisis became worse, public pressure forced representatives of the industry to modify their opposition somewhat. They continued, nonetheless to oppose key provisions of the law and attempted to tailor the Moss-Muskie bill for their own financial benefit.[17]

In July 1970, at the height of the financial meltdown on the Street, New York Stock Exchange president, Robert Haack, misled the Senate and House congressional committees about the scope of the crisis: "Of the more than 600 member firms of the Exchange, two are now in 'net capital' violation," he told them. "There are no other member firms of the Exchange in violation of the net capital rules."[18]

At that moment, in fact, there were ten additional firms threatened with imminent bankruptcy, not including the huge Hayden Stone, whose exposure to loss, including investors' money and stock, was $53 million. According to the SEC's Hurd Baruch, at the time that the New York Stock Exchange was reassuring Congress that things were not very bad, the question was not whether Hayden Stone was still alive, but rather how to divide up the carcass and how much it would cost investors.

When hearings started in the Senate, Muskie observed with displeasure, "We were continually frustrated in our efforts to decide precisely what steps should be taken immediately . . . because of a devastating lack of precise information from the industry."[19]

The report of the House Commerce and Finance Subcommittee, based on Moss's hearings, completely contradicted the NYSE's optimism:

Unfortunately . . . this year, three members or former members of the New York Stock Exchange have been forced to go into bankruptcy or to commence liquidation proceedings . . . the exchange has not undertaken to protect the customers of the firms. . . . In refusing to do so, the exchange has cited the voluntary nature of the trust fund and the apparent exhaustion of the money available . . . customers of those firms must face the specter of not only inevitable delay in receiving their funds and securities, but also the possibility of never receiving all to which they are entitled.[20]

In addition to attempting to lull Congress into inaction, preserve its role of self-regulation, and defer legislation, the New York Stock Exchange had a fallback position. If there was going to be a federal guarantee of deposits, through the proposed Securities Investor Protection Corporation (SIPC), the exchange and the securities industry wanted to dominate the management of the new agency. The government would be guaranteeing up to $1 billion in stocks and cash; the Street wanted to control how and when it was paid out. And while the thrust of the Muskie-Moss bill was to protect only small, individual investors, Wall Street managed to slip provisions into the bill that allowed brokerage company debts to be covered at public expense.[21]

An additional problem for Moss had arisen within the committee. Although he had a huge financial crisis on his hands, he had virtually no subcommittee staff, and a reluctant, perhaps intimidated, full committee chairman, in Harley Staggers. Compared to Moss, Muskie had a cakewalk in the Senate.

Staggers, for example, decided that an industry-dominated board of directors for SIPC would be the right way to go, because the industry members would be more alert to what was going on and, thus, minimize taxpayer exposure. Staggers asserted, "Men who pay money into the fund are going to watch over that fund. . . . It takes a crook to catch a crook."[22] But he failed to note that the fund was insured by the taxpayers, and much of the capital of the member firms actually belonged to their customers.

Emanuel Celler, Moss's old friend from the days of the Freedom of Information Act fight in 1966 and the chairman of the House Judiciary Committee, argued against Staggers: "If we do not have more public directors of (SIPC) . . . it would be very much like setting a cat to watch a bird in a cage."[23] After all, Celler and Moss reasoned, the real risk was being assumed by the taxpayers.

There was very little debate over whether there was a need for a new "bird cage" at all. Congress could have considered an obviouse alternative. Why not give the authority to insure small investor accounts and to monitor the qualifications of securities firms directly to the Securities and Exchange Commission, which had been created in 1934 supposedly to do just that?

This was a debate Moss would have wanted to have. But the SEC, as regulator, was not in favor with Congress in 1970. The securities industry had the power and the votes in Congress. Moss was forced to follow the federal insurance model to have any hope of getting any bill at all out of the House. Whatever the answer to the question, "Why have a SIPC at all to bail out badly run brokerage firms?" the issue was mostly forgotten over the years. At least it was forgotten until the market crash and the bank and corporate bailouts by the government thirty-eight years later in 2008.

But in 1970, one thing was certain. Wall Street was about to get public backing to guarantee much of its business and hopefully give the public confidence in the securities markets. It already had access to billions of dollars in investors' deposited securities and to "free" cash balances. Stagger's comment about crooks watching their own money more carefully was an indication of confusion in Congress over whose money was really at risk.

Moss was faced with an additional problem in pushing federal insurance legislation through the House. He had a subcommittee with a majority of members who were supportive of, and in many cases financially indebted to, the interests of Wall Street. There also was a tradition of self-regulation of the financial markets going back to the days of the New Deal. The Securities and Exchange Commission was largely created as a back-up to self-regulation by the NYSE. So the Exchange pushed back vigorously against federal intervention in what its members believed was their exclusive business. The attack focused not so much on the insurance guarantee part of the SIPC, but on the authority of the SEC and the new insurance corporation—SIPC—to investigate and regulate how customers' money would be used and managed in the future. It could be the camel's nose under the tent. And that made Wall Street extremely wary of the Moss-Muskie bill.

The stunning decline in stock prices, a 35 percent fall in the Dow Jones Industrial Average between 1969 and 1970, and the collapse or bankruptcy of so many Wall Street firms finally forced the Street to go along with Muskie and Moss on the idea of federal insurance. But they did not do it without a fight over control of the Securities Investor Protection Corporation and the degree of regulatory authority that would be given to the SEC over industry activities.

Staggers seemed hesitant to move forward with the challenging task of dealing with Wall Street and the financial markets. Moss was forced into the unusual position of publicly pressuring his own chairman to get the securities insurance hearings moving.

In March 1970, Eileen Shanahan of the *New York Times* reported on a letter Moss handed to her, one that he had sent to Staggers. It urged Staggers to move forward immediately on the SIPC bill; it was their "only hope of stemming the crisis of investor confidence."[24] This sort of exchange usually occurs behind closed doors. The fact that Moss felt he had to send

Staggers a public message just to get the bill moving says a lot about the power of the securities industry and about the tense Staggers-Moss relationship.

When Staggers finally relented and told Moss to go ahead, Moss's subcommittee held combative hearings in June and July of 1970. Moss received some help from a Nixon appointee, Hammer Budge, the chairman of the SEC. Budge said that he did not think investors should "assume that their securities and money in the hands of brokers and dealers were adequately safeguarded" in the event a firm suffered severe financial reverses. There was little question, according to Budge, that some form of comprehensive insurance system was needed. Budge would not, however, endorse a government insurance fund. But Budge did want to give the SEC authority to regulate the use of customer securities and cash balances, and the power to compel the stock exchange and other self-regulatory organizations to adopt new rules to improve the financial stability of brokerage firms. The exchange and the securities industry did not think that kind of power was necessary for the SEC. They fought back with every weapon they had.[25]

Moss challenged the New York Stock Exchange repeatedly over its inadequate insurance fund and its failure to cover some firms while insuring others. In an effort to generate support for a strong bill, he publicly asked the Exchange why it had arranged a bailout of a favored firm, Goodbody & Co., while "cutting others and their customers adrift."[26]

Ultimately, with Wall Street near panic, Moss was able to get an investor insurance bill out of the House. It authorized an assessment on all stock brokerage firms of 1 percent of their gross revenues for the SIPC insurance fund. The fund would be backed up by a $1 billion federal guarantee. That was real money in those days. And the industry contribution to the fund, required by Moss in the House bill, was twice the amount provided in the Senate bill.[27]

Both the House and the Senate authorized $50,000 in insurance for each investor's securities account. Moss fought, but lost, a battle to require that the $50,000 coverage extend to customers' free cash balances as well. The cash balance coverage was reduced to $20,000 in the conference committee.

The conference committee also took a major step forward in strengthening SEC regulation over the financial responsibility and operations of brokers and dealers by giving the SEC discretionary rule-making authority over firm practices. This allowed it to bypass existing Exchange guidelines, at least when the SEC thought it was necessary.

* * *

With the support of the SEC and a worried administration, the Securities Investor Protection Act was signed by president Nixon in 1970. The bill was a watershed in enhanced protection for consumers of securities. But it left some major questions unanswered.

What amount of risk were the taxpayers taking in agreeing, through Congress, to insure brokerage accounts? What were safe financial practices for companies in the securities industry? What should be the minimum amount of "net capital" that brokerage firms had to maintain so they would not be subject to financial collapse in the next market downturn? Could capital investment be withdrawn by firms, as it had been in 1969, when things got bad? Could institutional investors, like pension funds, become members of the stock exchange and thus dominate market trading and prices? Most important, would the commission rates charged by brokers to customers, on even small transactions, remain fixed by the New York Stock Exchange, or would there be competition among brokers to offer lower rates to the investing public?

Moss and Muskie had pushed through a new law to give federal insurance protection to small investors. But the law left much of the basic self-regulating structure of the securities industry and its monopolistic rate-fixing practices intact. The House and Senate sponsors promised to conduct a full investigation of the operation of the securities markets, hopefully to avoid another bubble, another mania, and yet another investor crisis in the future.

The Securities Investor Protection Act turned out to be the opening wedge in a battle for more far-reaching change in the securities markets. The bill crafted by Muskie and Moss meant that Congress was putting the United States Treasury behind American stockbrokers, dealers, and, most important of all, investors. While the primary purpose of the law was to protect the small investor, the result was that the government was buying into the securities business. Exactly what was this industry that the public was guaranteeing, and what were its problems? Congress, belatedly, wanted to know what it was getting into.

So, Staggers and Moss, the key committee and subcommittee chairs, pledged, on the House floor, that immediately after the insurance bill passed, they would conduct a broad inquiry into the causes of the market problems of the late 1960s and possible solutions. The camel's nose was definitely under the tent. Moss, whether he liked it or not, was riding the camel. The little known "securities and exchanges" jurisdiction of his subcommittee was about to become front-page news.

\* \* \*

In 1970, Harvey Rowen was a staff attorney in the General Counsel's office at the Securities and Exchange Commission, having worked his way through UCLA and the University of California law school at Berkeley.

As a young man, he had worked at odd jobs, like delivering Christmas mail, ushering at the Los Angeles Greek Theater, and clerking at a local drug store. He was the first person in his family to go to college.

Rowen had been on staff at the SEC for three years when, in 1970, he was assigned to a group of lawyers and economists and directed to complete a study on the increasing impact of large institutional investors on the securities markets.

Shortly after that, he read in the *Washington Post* that Moss's subcommittee was initiating a study of the securities markets. Rowen did not know Moss or anyone who did. On an impulse, he sent his résumé and a letter to Moss, pointing out his recent work on the SEC institutional investor study, which he thought might at least be somewhat related to what Moss was doing. He did not really have much hope of a response. Congressional committees, he knew, got a lot of letters like his. The senders rarely received anything but a polite rejection.

A few days later, the young SEC lawyer got a call to come over to the Rayburn House Office Building for an interview, not with a staff member, but with Moss himself. At the time, there were not many people in Washington who had any experience at all in the functioning of the securities markets. So Rowen at least had some useful experience, even if he did not have the usual political pull necessary to land a coveted staff job. Moss and Rowen talked for a while, perhaps thirty minutes. Rowen thought it was not a great interview, the kind where you feel an instant connection. But then Moss asked the young lawyer to go see Harley Staggers for a second interview.

Harley Staggers came from the little town of Keyser, West Virginia. Rowen said Staggers "knew nothing at all about securities." He was a graduate of a small Virginia college and had become the football coach at Potomac State College in Keyser. It was a railroad town, and Staggers, according to Rowen, was "a railroad man." He probably would have worked for the railroad, as some of his family had, if he had not decided to run for election to Congress. "I went to see Staggers. And it was the strangest interview I've ever had in my career," Rowen said. As he recalled that interview years later, it went something like this:

Rowen: "Mr. Chairman, how are you?"
Staggers: "Very good. Sit down. So tell me, where do you live?"
Rowen: "Silver Spring, Maryland."
Staggers: "Thank you very much. We'll be in touch."

Rowen says he left the interview absolutely certain he was not going to be hired. "I have never heard of a job interview where you are only asked one question and have gotten the job. And I certainly didn't live in Keyser, West Virginia." But Rowen got a call the next day from Moss's office. When could he start work on the study of the securities industry? [28]

To some extent, it would be, Rowen thought, a continuation of the SEC institutional investor study he had been working on at the SEC. The job, however, turned out to involve much more than he had ever thought it would.

"It took two years of hard work," he said, "to complete a sweeping study of the securities industry and to draft a report." Working at Moss's direction and closely with two subcommittee Republicans (Congressmen James Broyhill, the senior minority member, and John McCollister of Nebraska), they managed to get the unanimous approval from the often-divided subcommittee. Then, another surprise. Instead of just releasing the report like so many others, the staff was told by Moss to prepare a bill, which would actually implement the recommendations of the report.[29] The bill they wrote turned out to be a complete stock market restructuring. It would not be easy to get the members to agree on something so radical, Rowen thought.

Eventually it became obvious to the staff that Moss had a major goal in mind: to break the monopoly of the New York Stock Exchange and force price competition into the citadel of American capitalism. Moss believed that regulated competition, not monopoly, was in the best interests of investors. When Moss dropped the bill into the House hopper in January 1973, it had, after a lot more negotiating, all the subcommittee members as co-sponsors—a rare example of bipartisanship on a controversial issue. The securities industry study that Moss and Staggers had promised had gone, because of Moss, from being "an academic exercise, to a political dog fight."[30]

The Senate had undertaken a similar review of the securities industry. Just as in the first battle for investor protection, the Securities Investor Protection Act, Moss had an important ally in the Senate. Ed Muskie had moved on, down the long road toward the presidential nomination and to defeat in the primaries in the snows of New Hampshire.

* * *

The Senate securities industry review would be led by Senator Harrison "Pete" Williams, chairman of the newly created Securities Subcommittee of the Senate Banking Committee. Williams was starting his third term in the Senate in 1970 and had an admirable legislative record, in occupational safety among other things, but not in financial legislation. But Williams was the third-ranking Democrat on the banking committee, and it fell to him to lead the Senate subcommittee charged with reviewing and perhaps reforming the stock market. It was a risky undertaking for a Senator from New Jersey, many of whose constituents worked just across the Hudson River in the securities business.

Williams was a good Senate partner for Moss. Both were willing to deal with the issue of the erratic history of U.S. financial regulation. Both believed government must play a larger role. Both surely knew what a battle they were getting into.

The New Deal investor protection laws relied primarily on full disclosure of information related to stocks that were offered to the public, and to a prohibition of fraud and misrepresentation in the sale of securities to the public. The Securities and Exchange Commission was set up as the main federal securities oversight agency. But the New Deal, consistent with its overall Depression recovery policy of reforming American industry through government-industry cooperation, left regulation of the day-to-day operation of the stock market primarily under the control of the securities industry. That meant the New York Stock Exchange. Self-regulation by NYSE rules, largely rubber-stamped by the SEC, remained the standard in 1970.

The securities markets were and are extraordinarily complex. Why they crashed in 1929, or 1969—or for that matter in 2008—was not obvious, nor was a remedy an easy thing for Moss and Williams to devise. The markets, and perhaps Congress, were dominated by the financial power and the prestige of the New York Stock Exchange and the industry. If there were systemic problems, postwar prosperity had tended to obscure them.

The House Commerce Committee's study of the securities industry started with hearings chaired by Moss in 1971. Few members of the subcommittee bothered to attend, other than Moss, Broyhill, and, occasionally, McCollister. The subcommittee's work on the study and legislation lasted four years. The New York Stock Exchange did its best to slow things down and avoid legislation. Moss, always the populist or progressive or both, did his best to ensure that the NYSE monopoly would be broken, the power of the SEC increased, and small investors protected.[31] Staggers did not get involved much after approving Rowen, preferring to let Moss take the heat. And there was heat.

What Moss found upon commencing the investigation was that the stock market was functioning badly. Hundreds of brokers had gone out of business during the previous four years. Securities were being lost or stolen daily. Small and large investors alike could not get access to their money. It was called a "back office problem," but, in fact, it represented the near total breakdown of self-regulation.

There were two underlying issues. First, the monopoly control that the New York Stock Exchange had over everything that went on in the securities business in the United States tended to restrict modernization and protect its most inefficient members. Second, this industry, at the core of American free enterprise, was engaged in price-fixing.[32]

There was a long list of major problems in the securities industry that Moss's investigation uncovered:

- The amount of commissions charged to investors for the purchase of securities was fixed by the New York Stock Exchange and was not competitive.
- The powers of the SEC to regulate stockbrokers and the Exchange were limited. For example, the amount of net capital that a brokerage firm needed to invest and maintain in order to be in the business was inadequate. It was controlled by Exchange regulations and not by the SEC.
- A New York Stock Exchange Rule—394—prohibited any of its members from trading securities on any other exchange, such as the Pacific Coast Exchange or the over-the-counter market, further limiting investor options and increasing costs to investors.
- There was no authority, in government or elsewhere, to require development of a national market system, which had been recommended by the SEC study. Such a system could integrate all securities markets into one electronic system, so that an investor or broker could see and obtain the best price and commission rates at which to buy or sell securities.

Moss set out to change things. Absent the market crash of 1968–1970, he surely would have failed. But the support of the Ford administration, after Nixon's resignation in 1974, and that of the monopoly-conscious Department of Justice and the SEC, helped. With steady cooperation from Pete Williams's committee in the Senate, Moss succeeded in affecting the most sweeping investor protections since the New Deal.

It was not an easy struggle—or a sure thing. Moss was criticized for being stubborn and unwilling to compromise. Some of his colleagues, such as James Broyhill, the ranking Republican on the subcommittee, found him unwilling to bend much.[33]

After twenty-three years of legislative warfare, Moss was perhaps getting weary. Most of the detailed negotiation was done by the securities staff, Rowen and Charles Curtis, who was counsel to the full Commerce Committee, and by subcommittee members, Broyhill, Eckhardt, and Mc-Collister. But Moss knew what he wanted: to protect the small investor and to permanently break the monopoly of the New York Stock Exchange. And he had the final say on every provision of the bill.[34]

One staff member who knew Moss at the time said, "He's an incredibly unpolitical animal for a man who spent most of his adult life in politics. If he thinks he's right on the issue, he will never focus on the politics of it. I was really sorry he didn't have just a little more give in him."[35]

In 1974, after four years of investigation, negotiation, and combat, Moss got out of the Commerce Committee what he considered was a strong bill reforming the stock market and protecting small investors. The Senate moved a similar bill under the direction of Pete Williams and his counsel, Alton Harris. It had the SEC's quiet support. The Ford administration appeared lukewarm to the bill but did not oppose it outright. Prospects for Moss and stock market reform looked promising.

But Moss's bill never made it out of the House Rules Committee. So powerful was the New York Stock Exchange that, after four years of work by Congress, the Exchange was able to successfully lobby the relatively uninformed Rules Committee at the last minute, behind closed doors, to kill the bill. That blocked House consideration of the securities amendments. It was exactly what the National Association of Manufacturers and other business organizations had done three years earlier to the Consumer Product Safety Act. Moss's Securities Act died at the end of the Ninety-third Congress. The Exchange and its allies in the industry had apparently succeeded in avoiding reform and, as it turned out, in shooting themselves in their collective feet.

Moss and his friend and ally Bob Eckhardt were furious. They had been blindsided by the industry and the Rules Committee. The usually cool Eckhardt hurled his jacket across the room, smashing it against the Rayburn office window. Moss fumed with silent anger.

Moss went public again. He accused reform opponents of killing a bill that was good for the investor and the markets. In an interview with the *Washington Post*, Moss said he knew the New York Stock Exchange and the Securities Industries Association were responsible for blocking the work of four years—in a couple of weeks of secret lobbying. He said he would start all over again as soon as the Ninety-fourth Congress convened. He promised action on a new bill. He warned the securities industry not to expect any concessions this time around.

Among the most important provisions Moss sought were those that gave the SEC clear authority to end fixed-brokerage commission rates and to create a national stock market system. Moss reminded Wall Street: "Bears make money. Bulls make money. But pigs make nothing." He said the opponents had been "piggish," and stated, "I believe that they will come to regret it."[36] He was right.

In the spring of 1975, under intense pressure from both the House and the Senate committees and the Department of Justice, the SEC ordered the NYSE and all other exchanges to approve one of Moss's primary goals—competitive commission rates. That breakthrough ended the logjam, and the Moss-Williams bill passed a few weeks later loaded with more investor protection provisions and enforcement powers for the SEC. President Ford signed the Securities Act Amendments in June 1975.

James Needham, the NYSE chairman, was forced to do an about-face and applaud a result he had blocked a few months before.[37]

\* \* \*

The Securities Amendments of 1975, the culmination of four years of work by the Moss and Williams subcommittees, paved the way for the integration of existing securities markets into a national market system. It did not spell out the exact shape of that system, but delegated power to the Securities and Exchange Commission to ensure (1) that competitive rates would remain in effect permanently, (2) that the New York Stock Exchange monopoly would be broken, and (3) that a national market system involving all stock exchanges would be created. The measure, over the fierce objections of the securities industry, significantly expanded the oversight powers of the SEC over the stock market, brokers, and dealers.

The new law functioned effectively for many years. Brokerage commission rates became competitive and remain so. The small investor can now search for a low-budget broker or one that charges more for additional services. By SEC rule, mandated by the new law, stockbrokers can now trade on any exchange or on the over-the-counter market on behalf of their customers.

The SEC gained enhanced powers to regulate the "net capital" that brokers must maintain, and to review and revise the rules of the stock exchanges. A transparent, integrated national market was created under SEC oversight. It broke the monopoly—but not the political power—of the New York Stock Exchange.

The Exchange did succeed in blocking Moss's effort to abolish the sale of stock exchange seats and open exchange membership to all brokers large and small. It also succeeded in eliminating an immediate revocation of Rule 394, which forced Exchange members to do business only on the New York Stock Exchange. But the legislation gave the SEC power to force these changes over time, and that is what happened. "It was," said Rowen, "the most sweeping securities law since the passage of the original Securities Exchange Act in 1934. It rewrote American securities law affecting the markets."[38] Its provisions remain law to this day.

Despite claims by the securities industry that the Moss-Williams amendments would undermine its existence and erode its profitability, the opposite has proved true. The markets have continued to grow. The number of securities investors skyrocketed to over 130 million people by 2008. The U.S. exchanges, now supplemented by the NASDAQ electronic market, remain the leading securities exchanges worldwide.

One might ask, however, why the enhanced powers given to the SEC by the Moss-Williams amendments did not prevent the market crash of 2008. Rowen, Moss's securities counsel who lived through both eras, sees it this way:

> The SEC used its authority over the exchanges effectively over the years. Obviously, effectiveness changes with the makeup of the commission. The

years 2001 to 2008 were not a good time for the SEC. They were not vigilant. The White House could well have said, "You don't need new laws." All the laws were already on the books. But you did need somebody to enforce those laws, and that was the problem. It's all about regulatory will and consumer protection in the securities arena. Moss was dedicated to making sure that the little guy was treated right, that his government was taking care of him. That did not happen in those years.[39]

Harvey Pitt, former Securities and Exchange chairman under President George W. Bush, concurred with Rowen's assessment of the reasons for the 2008 melt down. He said it was a function of "a regulatory system that had broken down and of legislation in 1999 that had denied the SEC authority to regulate derivatives and allowed banks to get into risky investments." Pitt who held senior positions at the SEC during the years of Moss's fight to reform the financial markets, added that people often "throw around superlatives" about public figures. Moss, he said, was, in fact, "unique and larger than life" in his impact on the financial markets.[40]

In the decades since the enactment of the Moss-Williams securities amendments, small investors, retirees, pension funds, and even banks have learned that the best legislation is not self-enforcing. "You can pass a law, but you cannot make the SEC enforce it," said Rowen, referring to the historic, billion-dollar Madoff swindle and the market meltdown of 2008.

Self-interest may never be absent from the securities markets or any free market. Moss fought a monumental battle to balance the scales of commerce to protect the small investor. Perhaps he and Williams should have fought harder to protect the securities industry from itself.

*Moss at his desk in the Rayburn House Office Building at the prime of his congressional career, circa 1975. Credit: courtesy, California State University at Sacramento Archives.*

A member of the Joint Congressional Committee on Atomic Energy, Moss visited Lawrence Livermore Laboratory's nuclear research facility in 1975 with Jerry Wymore (second from right), his long-time political adviser. Credit: courtesy, California State University at Sacramento Archives (by Merkle Press).

Moss reporting by radio from Washington to the voters back home, in the 1960s. The brace is for a neck ailment that plagued him throughout his career. Credit: courtesy, California State University at Sacramento Archives.

A few of the millions of consumer products recalled for safety hazards under the Consumer Product Safety Act, sponsored by Moss and signed by President Nixon in 1972. Credit: courtesy, U.S. Consumer Product Safety Commission.

# 9

# Cars, Chemicals, and Arab Oil

## *Changing Times*

The consumer revolution was running out of gas. The Arab oil boycott became a weapon against the United States in 1973. It did much more than create long lines of cars at gasoline stations. It threw the nation into a deep recession, followed by double-digit inflation. Pocketbook issues became more important to the American people—and to their elected representatives—than consumer protection.

The Arab nations, including most members of the Organization of Petroleum Exporting Countries (OPEC),[1] initiated the oil boycott in October 1973 to retaliate against the United States for its decision to resupply the Israeli military during the Yom Kippur War with Egypt, Syria and most of the Arab nations. The boycott was very effective. While there was domestically produced U.S. crude oil and its by-products, gasoline and home heating oil, only about half of the country's needs could be satisfied. Within weeks, the energy-dependent American economy suffered an "oil price shock" and massive dislocation. Gasoline prices increased fourfold at the pump.[2] Unemployment rose by 2.5 million people to over 8 percent, the highest rate since the Great Depression. Double-digit inflation soon followed, reaching an extraordinary 13 percent. The economic turmoil lasted into the next decade. Among other things, it resulted in sharply higher prices for food, fuel, housing, and other basic consumer goods.[3]

The stock market reflected the oil price shock. Between January 1973 and December 1974, the Dow Jones Industrial Average lost 45 percent of its value. It was the seventh-worst bear market in its history. The nation did not reach the same market levels, in real terms, until August 1993, more than twenty years after the 1973–1974 crash.[4] High inflation and unemployment continued through the last year of the Ford administration in 1976 and throughout the Carter administration, which shuddered to a halt in 1980.

There were other currents of change simultaneously affecting the nation. None of them were helpful to the consumer revolution. The Vietnam War and a generation of young American protestors—some of them shot at and killed by National Guard troops—were seared into Americans' minds and shook their trust in government.

That trust was further shaken by the Watergate scandal. It forced the resignation of President Richard Nixon in August 1974. Nixon was under threat of a federal indictment for his role in directing the break-in of the Democratic National Committee's offices at the Watergate complex in Washington. The investigation of the Watergate break-in revealed unsavory things about how the U.S. government could function—or malfunction. It did not seem to matter to the voters which party was in charge. Confidence in government was falling fast.

In reaction to the Watergate scandal, Democratic candidates swept the 1974 and 1976 congressional elections. They gained large majorities in both the House and the Senate. A weakened president, former Vice President, House Speaker, and Freedom of Information Act advocate, Gerald R. Ford, moved into the oval office. But large Democratic majorities in Congress could not overcome the economic conditions of the country and a growing public determination to reduce the size and impact of government. Consumer protection programs, including Moss's and Magnuson's—proposed and already enacted—were prime targets.

The shift soon became very clear to lawmakers in Congress. In one of the great reversals of American history, the tide of public opinion—the public that had so forcefully backed new consumer protection laws and tougher enforcement of existing laws—turned around. With Watergate and the oil embargo in the background, there was a decided shift away from support for consumer programs. Business lobbying groups capitalized on the new public mood. Between 1974 and 1980, the country started down a long antigovernment road.

Long before presidential candidate Ronald Reagan told the American public that government "was the problem, not the answer," and that if he was elected president he would "get the government off our backs," business opponents of consumer protection sensed the change in public mood and fueled it. Their response to consumerism can be traced through intense battles over three major Moss-Magnuson consumer proposals. They each started at the peak of the consumer tide and met widely different fates as the popularity of consumer protection wound down. They included

- an attempt to reduce the costs to owners of automobiles from damage caused by collisions;
- an effort to require motor vehicle manufacturers to pay owners for the cost of repairing unsafe automobiles and to risk sharply increased penalties for failing to immediately report safety defects to the federal government; and
- a bill to limit the amount of toxic substances used in consumer products.

\* \* \*

## THE MOTOR VEHICLE
## INFORMATION AND COST SAVINGS ACT

The year was 1972. Consumer protection remained a powerful force on Capitol Hill. President Richard Nixon was concerned about the Watergate break-in, as yet undiscovered, but lurking in the background. Nixon, attempting to end Lyndon Johnson's failed war in Vietnam, was especially sensitive to public opinion. His administration was not anxious to oppose consumer protection. Anything with the word "consumer" in the title was considered very carefully. The White House issued a consumer protection message incorporating a "Buyer's Bill of Rights," which sounded very much like a consumer advocate's wish list.[5]

The economy was still strong in 1972. The Arab oil boycott and the Middle East war were a year away. And Ralph Nader's name had political punch.

Riding the coattails of the 1966 automobile safety law and the widely reported hearings of the National Commission on Product Safety, political leaders in the Senate and the House began to look beyond consumer safety to the economic effects of automobile crashes.

Magnuson and Moss were aided in this effort by a new organization, the Insurance Institute for Highway Safety. It was established and funded by the insurance industry in an effort to demonstrate its support for a goal that seemed to serve both consumer and industry interests. If payouts in automobile property damage accidents could be reduced—if bumpers, for example, were stronger—there would be less damage to the car and, therefore, fewer and smaller claims. This, in turn, would help reduce insurance premiums for owners—a major potential consumer benefit. It was further acknowledgment of the political clout of consumer protection. In addition, there was potential economic benefit for the insurance industry. It would be able to sell more policies, and the time lag between the receipt of customers' premiums and the need to pay out lower claim costs would enhance profits.

Whatever the motivation, much of the insurance industry, led by State Farm Insurance Company, lined up with Magnuson and Moss in support of the proposed automobile damage reduction law. The impact of the Insurance Institute for Highway Safety was immense. It was headed by Dr. William Haddon, a respected graduate of the Massachusetts Institute of Technology and Lyndon Johnson's first administrator of the new National Highway Traffic Safety Administration. The Institute represented, and still represents, a major public interest commitment by much of the insurance industry.

At congressional hearings, Haddon testified in support of automobile damage reduction. He showed color films of automobile crash testing done at great expense by the Institute. The difference in the cost of repairing different cars, depending upon the make and model owned by the consumer, was shocking. And was seemingly inexplicable.

In five-mile-per-hour front-barrier crash tests that Haddon ran, a Chevrolet Impala cost $153.75 to repair. In the same five-mile-per-hour front-barrier crash test, a Ford Galaxy cost almost three times as much to fix at $402.10. When multiplied over the car crash universe, that was real money with significant potential for savings to the consumer.

There were similar results in the testing of both large sedans and smaller models. All showed that the capability existed to build a bumper, as well as other car parts, that could resist a five-mile-per-hour crash without much damage to anything other than the bumper. The result, thought the sponsors, would be less money paid out by the insurance companies and ultimately less paid by consumers in insurance premiums.[6]

Seeking to use the same wave of public indignation that had triggered the enactment of the new automobile safety law six years earlier, a broad alliance of consumer advocates, and much of the insurance industry, supported enactment of new legislation establishing federal minimum construction standards for automobile crash resistance.

Advocates of the law thought General Motors, Ford, Chrysler, and their then-small foreign competitors, such as Honda and Toyota, had the technology to do it. When he signed the automobile safety law in 1966, President Johnson had said so in ringing terms:

> The automobile industry has been one of our nation's most inventive industries. I hope, and I believe, that its skill and imagination will be able to build in more safety without building on more cost . . . safety is no luxury item; no optional extra. It must be a normal cost of doing business.[7]

Johnson pointed out that, over Labor Day weekend that year, twenty-nine American servicemen had died in Vietnam, but shockingly so had 614 other Americans in automobile accidents here at home. Johnson urged the nation to cure the "disease" of highway accidents, which until then the country had tolerated.[8]

Proving the powerful impact of the name "Nader," the *New York Times* ran a statement by the consumer advocate side-by-side with the president's words that day. Still angry at Detroit, Nader wrote,

> The humane technology needed to bring safer automobiles to the public will require not just the spur of government action, but the operation stimulus of industry conscience. Hefty doses of safety research and development by auto companies in vibrant competition will do wonders for highway safety.[9]

Evidence that federal safety standards could be effective also came from the impact of the new motor vehicle safety law. It seemed to be working. In 1972, opening House hearings on the automobile damage ability legislation, Moss looked back with some pride at that earlier success: "We are now beginning to see real proof," he said, "that this legislative effort is producing returns. While the death toll has not been reduced in an absolute sense, there is direct evidence that safety standards . . . have saved lives, and that the trends of death and serious injury have been turned around."[10]

Moss was on target. He could not know it in 1972, but in succeeding years, the rate of motor vehicle deaths and injuries would drop dramatically. It stood at 5.5 deaths for each 100 million miles driven in 1966, when the automobile safety law was passed. By 2007, it had dropped to 1.36 deaths. In absolute terms, fatalities on the nation's highways were about 50,800 in 1966, 41,000 in 2007, and 37,000 in 2008, despite there being many more cars on the roads and many more miles driven.[11] The motor vehicle safety law, including the increased use of seat belts and the regulatory mandate of passive restraints, which the law required, remains one of the great success stories of the consumer decade. And in 1972, it raised this question: If technology, triggered by government safety standards and recalls of defective cars, could reduce deaths and injuries, could it not also save consumers money? In the Senate, Warren Magnuson and Senator Philip Hart and, in the House, John Moss, thought it could.

* * *

One of the key players in moving this idea forward was not a congressman or a Senator at all. Don Randall was a newly appointed member of Hart's Senate Antitrust and Monopoly Subcommittee staff in 1966. Randall was a soft-talking Georgia boy, born in the little town of Lyons in central Georgia, one of six children. His father, F. C., died when Randall was in high school. A local banker in Vidalia, Pete Brice, helped Randall pay his way through college and law school. With the Korean War on, he volunteered in the Army Signal Corps as a 2nd lieutenant. When he was discharged in 1962, he faced a large choice. Griffin Bell, later attorney general of the United States, was a well-known judge of the United States Court of Appeals in Atlanta. Bell offered Randall a prized clerkship with the court. Such a job has been the making of many a lawyer's career.

But Randall also had applied for a job at the Federal Trade Commission's small field office in New Orleans. For a single guy, he said, New Orleans looked a lot better than Atlanta. So he packed his car, sent his regrets to Judge Bell, and headed for The Big Easy.

When he arrived at the commission's New Orleans office, he was assigned to a new investigation. It was not one focused on New Orleans or the southeast region, but was a major national inquiry. The commission had become concerned with monopolization of the U.S. automobile market by the major automobile manufacturers. They had most of the new car market, and they seemed to be moving in lock step into the parts industry.

The FTC was not a particularly tough antitrust cop in those years. But someone apparently thought that GM, Ford, and Chrysler, which were dominating the parts distribution market, might be overcharging small auto parts dealers and repair shops while giving price discounts to their large competitors. This would be a violation of the rarely enforced Robinson-Patman antitrust law in the form of price discrimination between purchasers in the same market. The FTC's Bureau of Competition was at least willing to open an investigation and designated New Orleans to be the lead office.

Randall was hooked. It was a small-business investigation that could also involve harm to buyers of automobile parts. The small parts dealers and repair shops were facing large competitors and could not get comparable prices out of the parts manufacturers. Congress had promised them a better deal when it passed the Robinson-Patman Act thirty years before.

Randall's investigation on behalf of the FTC took him all over the United States and lasted two years. It ultimately demonstrated to the commissioners that the small dealers were indeed getting a bad deal. The New Orleans office recommended action by the FTC against price discrimination, resulting in a decision in favor of the small dealers. Randall even got the FTC to change its policy and approve the use of dealer-buying cooperatives by the small parts dealers.

In Washington, Charlie Bangert headed up the overall FTC investigation. He was supportive of Randall's work, which caused the telephones to ring at the FTC and on Capitol Hill. So when Bangert moved up to the staff of the Senate Antitrust and Monopoly Subcommittee, he called Randall and invited him to come up to Washington and work for the Senate and Senator Philip Hart. "He is from car country—Michigan," Bangert told Randall, "but he is very strong on competition."[12]

Don Randall started packing. He gave his notice to the Federal Trade Commission, loaded up his old car, and headed north. On the way, he stopped in Vidalia and went to see the local banker Pete Brice. Randall had a final check for Brice to reimburse him for the years of college and law school bills he had volunteered to pay. It had taken Randall eleven years to save the money. Now he held the last check in his hand. Brice refused the money: "Your success is all the repayment I will ever need. Do a good job in Washington."

"I never would have been able to go to college or to law school without help from that small town banker," Randall said. "It is a lesson I never forgot."[13]

\* \* \*

Once in Washington, Randall became the chief staff council for the proposed Motor Vehicle Information and Cost Savings Act for Senator Hart. He was supported by testing data generated by Haddon's Insurance Institute for Highway Safety and by insurance companies. Hart and Magnuson in the Senate, and Moss in the House, proposed a law that had four parts.

First, the federal government would issue minimum automobile damageability standards for cars sold in the United States. The cars would have to be built to withstand low-speed collisions with a minimum amount of costly property damage.

The manufacturing industry thought this was a terrible idea. They said they knew what the car-buying public wanted, and did not need a bunch of bureaucrats designing their products. The federal government they charged, wanted them to build Sherman tanks. Building their case, they convinced some large insurers to oppose the Moss-Hart-Magnuson bill.

The second part of the bill required comparative damageability testing by the Department of Transportation (DOT), which would then be made available to consumers in showrooms before they bought a car. Understandable "crash ratings" was the general idea. Consumers could then compare a Toyota with a Ford in terms of how much they would pay if they got into a property damage collision. The issue was both safety and economics. The goal was saving both consumer lives and money.

Title III of the bill provided for a demonstration project of periodic state testing of car owner's vehicles for safety components, such as brakes, lights, and windshield wipers. It was not entirely clear then, or now, whether the public would accept periodic safety testing of their cars. It could prove costly to a car owner if a car did not pass and required repairs. On the other hand, if a car's brakes were inadequate, its tires bald, or the shock absorbers caused it to be unstable, the results could and can be deadly.

The final part of the proposed legislation involved adding federal penalties for rolling odometers back, a common practice at the time by some car dealers.

In January of 1971, Hart and his staff met to discuss the senator's priorities.

When Randall mentioned the automobile damageability bill as a first choice, Hart said, "You know, Don, I am from the biggest automobile producing state in the country."

"Yes, sir.

"And I am supported by the automobile workers unions. If I lose, you lose."

"Yes, sir."

Hart hesitated.

"Well, if you still think this is that important, go on ahead with it," he said.

As he recalled this conversation many years later, Randall said, "He was a brave senator."[14]

* * *

In the Senate, the bill came under the jurisdiction of Magnuson's Commerce Committee, so Magnuson and Hart co-sponsored it. In the House, Moss, as usual, was the lead sponsor and the primary target of the opposition. Randall staffed the bill through the Senate without much trouble. Then he came over to help Moss's staff pull off something similar in the House. It would not prove to be an easy task.

Moss still had a closely divided subcommittee made up of four Democrats and three Republicans when he took up the bill in 1972. He offered the Senate-passed legislation. Federal damage prevention standards were the heart of the Senate bill. It had passed the Senate eighty-four to nine the year before. The insurance industry estimated that the bill would save at least $1 billion annually in repair costs, based solely on a five-mile-per-hour bumper requirement, or more if other damage prevention standards were included. The three Republicans on Moss's subcommittee sided with the car companies. If one Democrat yielded to pressure from the industry, or more likely from his local Chevy or Ford dealer, and switched sides, Moss's damageability bill would be dead. And that is exactly what happened.

The automobile industry and some insurance companies opposed anything but a comparative information bill. The industry feared the potential for increased costs and predicted an adverse effect on design creativity. The subcommittee proceeded to cut the heart out of Moss's bill.

An amendment by Representative John McCollister of Nebraska, backed by the Motor Vehicle Manufacturers Association, proposed a requirement that the Department of Transportation only provide in dealer showrooms an "index" comparing the damageability of one model versus others, but no standards requiring actual construction of less damageable cars. The comparative data would be largely useless, because it would be based on past performance, not on pre-market tests of the new models then on sale. The McCollister amendment passed, four to three.

Moss was angry. He said the bill "could now . . . not even be called consumer protection legislation." He promised to fight to restore his original proposal in the full Commerce Committee.[15]

Moss tried to put the damage standards provision back in the legislation, but the industry smelled blood. The House Commerce Committee was not known as the "graveyard of consumer legislation" for nothing. It was not like the Senate, where the bill had passed easily. In the full committee, the result was even worse than in the subcommittee. Instead of broadening the bill to parallel the Senate measure, the full committee first defeated Moss's proposal to strengthen it by a surprisingly large vote of twenty-three to fifteen. Almost all the Republicans and some Democrats voted "no." Then, to rub salt in Moss's wounds, the committee went further: it voted twenty to eighteen to kill the bill completely and send it back to the subcommittee.

Moss refused to quit. He knew that four of the five Democrats inexplicably"absent" during the key committee vote were supposed to be supporters of the bill. If they could manage to be there, the bill would pass. Moss said that if he failed to win a reconsideration vote, "it is a dead issue for this session."

He was not reticent in placing the blame for killing the bill. "The automobile manufacturers have decreed the death of this bill. By doing so, they have shown continuing cynicism toward any program that would reduce the shockingly high cost of repairing automobiles. Their activity has been contemptuous of the public interest."[16]

Among the committee members who took a walk on Moss's bill were four Republicans and five supposedly "liberal" Democrats. Among them were Chairman Harley Staggers of West Virginia and three committee members: John Murphy and Bertram Podell of New York and Ralph Metcalfe of Chicago. The voters of their districts might have been shocked if they had known of their stunning absence. But the power of the automobile industry, even at the height of the consumer revolution, was evident.

Moss fought on, turning to the press once more. Newspapers jumped on the story of a backroom industry-politician deal covered up as unavoidable absence. The story caught people's attention. It made some congressmen think twice about the voters back home. After all, it was an election year. A compromise was reached late that night. The subcommittee would report a narrower bill, including damageability standards, but limiting them solely to damage that could be reduced by stronger bumpers. No particular speed would be specified in the bill, but it was understood that the Department of Transportation would set the front bumper standard at five miles per hour, the rear impact at 2.5 mph.

The compromise was reported out of Moss's subcommittee. It passed both the full committee and the House of Representatives without much debate. It was less than the Senate had initially passed and less than Moss wanted. But it did include the front and rear bumper requirements, authority for the Department of Transportation to publish comparative car repair data, and a pilot program for state periodic motor vehicle inspections.

Moss said something was better than nothing: "Sometimes you fight, sometimes you have to compromise. You have to learn the difference."[17] The Senate-House conferees adopted the House bill. The legislation was signed by President Nixon in September 1972.

Over time, the Moss-Hart-Magnuson damageability legislation has proven moderately successful in making the public, manufacturers, and insurers more sensitive to the quality and durability of automobiles. It also is said to have been a major factor in reducing the economic cost of automobile accidents. Insurers now rate cars by make and model for purposes of setting premiums. Car manufacturers now consult with insurers regarding which models are more or less vulnerable to damage in crashes.[18]

Five-mile-per-hour front bumpers remained the law until the years of the Reagan administration. Then the American car companies complained to the Reagan White House that foreign competition was hurting them. They asked that two standards, the passive restraint (air bag) and the five-mile-per-hour bumper standards, be repealed. The bumper standard was then reduced to 2.5 miles per hour and narrowed only to protection of "safety components." State Farm Insurance Company and several consumer organizations filed suit to save both standards. The Supreme Court reversed the Reagan administration decision only on the passive restraint rule, upholding the reduction in the bumper standard.[19]

Some insurance premiums for some models are lower now than they otherwise would have been without the law. The Department of Transportation and the Insurance Institute for Highway Safety regularly publish and, in the case of DOT distribute, to dealers comparative automobile crashworthiness data. *Consumer Reports* and the national consumer organization, Center for Auto Safety also publish damage reports.[20] Periodic motor vehicle safety inspection was adopted by about half of the states, but the demonstration project ended without triggering a truly national program. Perhaps the reason that periodic inspection was not adopted by all fifty states is because consumers do not like having to take their cars in for inspection and pay for mandated safety repairs. However, because of the bill, it is a federal crime to "spin" the odometer of a motor vehicle.

* * *

## THE MOTOR VEHICLE AND SCHOOL BUS SAFETY ACT

Another challenge facing Moss in the mid-1970s was the effectiveness of the Motor Vehicle Safety Act of 1966. A May 1973 report by Magnuson's

Senate Commerce Committee spelled out both the success and failure of the new safety law.[21] Since its enactment in 1966, over 36 million motor vehicles had been recalled because of the presence of a safety-related defect in the car. That was a lot of potentially dangerous vehicles that were no longer a threat on the highways. However, the committee emphasized that only 75 percent of the automobiles subject to safety recalls were actually returned for correction. Either the owners never received the recall notification letters from the manufacturers or something else was preventing people from getting the defects fixed.

The Senate report said that a major part of the problem was the failure of the motor vehicle industry to live up to its promise (not explicitly written into the original law) to pay for the repair of safety-related defects. A House report a year later, written by the Moss subcommittee, reached similar conclusions.[22] It found there had been more than fifteen hundred motor vehicle recall campaigns involving 45 million automobiles at that time. Each had involved a safety defect as determined by the Department of Transportation, most agreed to by the manufacturer. Nevertheless, many people were not responding to announced recalls.

Both the House and the Senate emphasized that there was no legal requirement that a manufacturer actually pay for a repair ordered by the Department of Transportation. The Senate noted that during the months prior to the issuance of its 1973 report, there were two notable cases in which the "manufacturer's promise of reimbursement has been breached."[23]

In 1971 the National Highway Traffic Safety Administration found that the heaters on all 1960 through 1968 Chevrolet Corvairs contained a safety-related defect. The heaters leaked poisonous fumes into the passenger compartment, threatening to asphyxiate the driver and passengers. There were 680,000 Chevrolet Corvairs involved. But General Motors required each owner to bear the cost of the heater repair, approximately $150 to $200 a vehicle. There was no warranty that the repair would last and no reimbursement from General Motors.

A year later, in November 1972, the senate committee spotted a second breach of the manufacturer's promise, this one involving Volkswagen. The windshield wiper system on all 1949 to 1969 VWs was found to be defective. A screw could loosen without warning, causing failure of the wiper system. If this occurred in rain or snow, the visibility of the driver could be impaired. Although Volkswagen sent notification letters to all known owners, the company had the names and addresses of only 220,000 of the 3.7 million VW owners. Volkswagen compounded the problem by refusing to absorb the repair cost.

Both the Senate and the House quickly passed legislation, known as the Motor Vehicle and School Bus Safety Act of 1974, to require the manufacturers to pay for any safety recall ordered by the Department of

Transportation. In addition, the Moss-Magnuson legislation doubled the civil penalties for violations of federal safety standards and for failure to comply with recall orders from a maximum $400,000 to $800,000 for each violation, with every car representing a separate violation.[24]

Moss also added a requirement that the Department of Transportation issue special school bus safety standards for at least eight separate parts of school buses made for the U.S. market. Reports from the National Transportation Safety Board had led him to conclude that these "yellow tin cans" tended to collapse on impact and were not strong enough to protect the 19 million children who rode in them on any given school morning.

When the new safety bill left the House, it included yet another surprise for manufacturers. Moss was still steaming over the industry's treatment of his automobile damage reduction bill. He also was concerned about long delays in getting cars with safety defects fixed. It did not cost a manufacturer anything, except lawyer's fees, to endlessly negotiate with the DOT or appeal a safety recall order to the courts. While the appeal went on, the defective cars stayed on the road.

So Moss wrote a provision into the House bill that an order of the secretary of transportation triggering a safety recall required *immediate* compliance. Failure to comply with the order could be appealed by the manufacturer to the courts. The penalties, civil fines for noncompliance with the DOT order, would, however, start accumulating from the day of the order.

While the legislation gave manufacturers their day in court, Moss had inserted a major risk factor for car makers. If they lost in the courts, they paid fines from the date of the original order. And the conferees, led by Moss and Magnuson, also directed that an order of the secretary finding a safety defect must be upheld, unless the court determined that failure to notify consumers was "reasonable," and, even more important, that the manufacturer could establish it was "likely" to prove that there was no defect. The shift in the law toward greater respect for the safety orders of the government was clear. Defying an order by the secretary of transportation became a potentially costly business for automobile manufacturers.

Joan Claybrook, who served as president of the consumer group Public Citizen for twenty years, later said Moss was "very effective in totally rewriting and strengthening the recall powers of the agency in the 1974 safety bill." She recalled that even Moss's ally, Bob Eckhardt, suggested giving the manufacturers more "due process" through a trial-type hearing before a recall could be ordered.[25] Moss was more concerned about consumer safety and delaying the recall. He overrode his ally's objections and refused to weaken the bill.

Moss disagreed with Claybrook sometimes. When she became administrator of the automobile safety agency during the Carter administration, they clashed over Moss's release of an allegedly confidential Firestone tire safety survey and also over the use of human cadavers in the agency's automobile crash-testing program. Years later, Claybrook recalled the battle over the cadavers and found perhaps a gentler side of Moss because of his opposition to their use in testing the crashworthiness of cars. "I suppose he had moral objections or thought people should be allowed to rest in peace after they died," she said.[26]

The automobile makers appealed the Moss-Magnuson safety law to the courts in an effort to have it declared unconstitutional. They said it denied them due process. They lost. The United States Court of Appeals for the District of Columbia held that their appeal rights had not been taken away but only limited in the interests of public safety.[27] In recent years, manufacturers have tended to comply with DOT recall orders rather than sue. Very few recalls or penalty cases concerning motor vehicles wind up in court now.[28] In light of the powers given the secretary of transportation and the National Highway and Traffic Safety Administration by the Moss-Magnuson law, it is difficult to understand the ineffectiveness and delay of the agency in dealing with the massive and potentially fatal Toyota acceleration incidents between 2000 and 2010.[29]

The consumer victory that Moss and Magnuson achieved in the Motor Vehicle and School Bus Safety Act came at a price. The Department of Transportation had required that, starting in 1974, all cars be equipped with seat belt ignition systems that would prevent the car from starting unless the seat belt was buckled, the so-called "ignition interlock." The department was attempting to cut down on the high rate of traffic fatalities and the very low usage, less than 50 percent, of passenger car seat belts. It was also attempting to delay or avoid a fight over the requirement of airbags, or passive restraints—something the industry vehemently opposed.

The regulation was overkill. People would get in their car, and the engine would not start. Or they would put a grocery bag on the seat next to them, fail to buckle the grocery bag's seat belt, and the engine would not start. Or the family dog would hop up on the front seat, and the engine would not start. Even dedicated consumer advocates like Representative Edith Green of Oregon decided it was too much: "After the federal government has advised me that my chance of survival in an accident is better if I fasten my seat belt," she said, "then I think the federal government has no right to intrude any further."[30]

Representative Lewis Wyman, a Republican from New Hampshire and later the state's attorney general, was more aggressive in his attack on the regulation. He said the feds were becoming "big brother," and that the provision that required buckling up was extraordinary, unfounded, and unreasonable. Representative Jim Collins, a Republican from Texas and a member of Moss's committee, supported Wyman saying, the buzzer system that went along with the seat belt interlock was "something carried over from the Chinese torture system."[31]

Wyman moved to add a provision to Moss's bill killing the ignition interlock. Moss fought the amendment on the House floor. He relied on the president of General Motors, Edward M. Cole, who urged finding a way to protect drivers who neglected to buckle their seat belts and protect themselves. Moss cited an insurance industry statement urging that Congress use something more than "volunteerism" to cut down on the rapidly escalating costs of injuries in car accidents. Yet volunteerism was what the public seemed to want.

Moss offered a substitute amendment, making the ignition interlock and a buzzer warning device only an *option* for the consumer. The inconvenience factor and faith in deregulation overwhelmed consumer advocates that year. The result was a defeat for the Moss substitute for Wyman's amendment by an overwhelming vote of 339 to forty-nine.[32]

Thirty-five years later the ignition interlock fight is ancient history. All that remains of the ignition interlock is the eight second warning buzzer to remind drivers to buckle up—all that the car industry would agree to. But the driving public does buckle up more now and seems quite satisfied with mandatory passive restraints, or air bags, now required by federal motor vehicle safety law in all cars.

* * *

## THE TOXIC SUBSTANCES CONTROL ACT

The consumer-environmental challenge of the 1970s decade was the Toxic Substances Control Act. It still is. The proposed law represented the opening round of an enduring battle to rid the environment and consumer products of harmful chemicals that continues today.

The proposed Toxic Substances Control Act was originally introduced by Moss in 1972 when he was chairman of the Commerce and Finance Subcommittee. By the time it passed four years later, the chairman of the subcommittee was Moss's Texas ally, Bob Eckhardt. What Eckhardt, Moss, and Magnuson, along with Senators Vance Hartke, John Tunney, and Phil Hart, pushed through the Congress was a much compromised bill. Buried in the legislation, and not completely obvious even to supporters, were several "poison pills." These procedural roadblocks would, in the future, severely cripple federal regulation of toxic substances. But it was the best the legislators could do in 1976.

The main issue that deadlocked the House and Senate from 1972 through 1976 was the question of requiring pre-market testing of new chemicals sold in the United States. The chemical industry was opposed. Extensive government testing requirements would increase their costs and hurt smaller chemical manufacturers the most, they said. The industry lobbied vigorously against the initial Senate and House bills in 1972 and 1973. Moss, as chairman of the House Subcommittee on Commerce and Finance, had the jurisdiction and held long days of hearings on the legislation. He favored the Senate bill with broad powers to require pre-market testing for the new Environmental Protection Agency, newly created in 1970. But there was no way such a pre-market testing mandate could be pushed through the House Commerce Committee. Enough Republicans and moderate Democrats were convinced by the chemical industry's arguments to make the Senate's pre-market testing requirements too big a pill to swallow.

The concept of a Toxic Substances Control Act was based on a report by the newly established Council on Environmental Quality. Its chairman was Russell Train, the Republican administrator of the Environmental Protection Agency under President Ford. Train supported tough toxic substances legislation, somewhat in contrast to the Ford administration. He testified that the country could not afford to wait to deal with the growing problem of chemical pollution. Train acknowledged that his superiors in the Ford administration had doubts about the pre-market testing provisions of the Moss-Senate bill. Administration officials supported the chemical industry position, which would limit government authority over testing of new and existing chemicals to those chemicals that had demonstrated a serious problem. But Train said he hoped that President Ford would sign a bill involving pretesting anyway, and he was critical of the chemical industry for trying to cripple the bill. The only real "crippling" going on, Train said, was the kind the legislation would try to prevent: the crippling of many Americans every year who contract cancer or other diseases after exposure to hazardous chemicals.[33]

The current events that drove the toxic substances proposal were accidents involving exposure to two of the thousands of new chemicals that entered the environment each year. As Congress began considering the proposal of the Council on Environmental Quality, reports appeared of the poisoning of workers at a Hopewell, Virginia, chemical factory. Kepone, a carcinogenic insecticide was released into the waters of the James River while the factory was producing a pesticide under contract to Allied Chemical. Twenty-eight employees were hospitalized for Kepone poisoning.

About the same time, PCBs, or polychlorinated byfills, which were used by General Electric as an adhesive, an insulating oil, and for caulking, were found in large amounts in the Hudson River near Troy, New York. PCBs are a probable human carcinogen and may also cause nerve and brain disorders in children. The risk was obvious. It frightened people. Ogden R. Reed, the New York State environmental commissioner, ordered the Hudson closed to fishing because of the PCB contamination.

The James River remains polluted today. More than forty years later, the Hudson is still one of the largest Superfund clean-up sites in the nation.

"We are literally surrounded by a man-made chemical environment," said the report of the Senate Commerce Committee supporting the toxic substances law. "We continually wear, wash with, inhale, and ingest a multitude of chemical substances."[34] PCBs offered just one example of the risk. The substances, which were widely used at the time, were known to be highly toxic. Medical research linked PCBs to tumors, skin lesions, and genetic disorders, but there was a lack of clear-cut legal authority to regulate and restrict their use.

Moss tried to get a toxics bill out of his subcommittee, something similar to the Senate version. He held hearings in 1972 and called Train, as well as other environmental experts, to testify.[35] Moss said that the legislation before the subcommittee recognized that insufficient authority existed to regulate toxic chemical substances that threatened human health and the environment. He said legislative action was required to achieve adequate protection from the new and dangerous substances that were being continuously developed. He promised to push for effective legislation protecting the public and the environment from irreparable injury.[36]

Train led off the hearings and was the star witness. He pointed out that industrial chemical production had been increasing since 1967 at an extraordinarily rapid rate. He cited the danger of PCBs as an illustration of the potential human health hazard of toxic chemicals in wide use.

Train stopped, however, at fully endorsing the pre-market clearance requirements of the Senate bill. He was clearly under pressure from the Ford administration. Yes, he saw the hazard. Yes, he wanted legislation. But he hesitated over the primary tool for verifying the safety of chemical substances before consumers and the environment became subject to their impact.

The House and Senate deadlocked on the legislation for four years. The most divisive issue was, who had the burden of proving that a chemical was safe—the manufacturer or the government? Magnuson's Senate bill required that the industry demonstrate safety before it marketed a new substance in any substantial quantity—a "precautionary" approach. The best the House committee could produce was a bill that was much easier on the industry. It required only limited pre-market testing in cases where the EPA could show, based on whatever evidence it could locate, that a chemical posed a "likely substantial danger to health for the environment." A head count by Moss of the subcommittee and of the full House Commerce Committee showed that antiregulation votes outweighed votes supporting the Moss bill. A strong proposed bill could not reach the House floor.

Despite Moss's best efforts to get a House bill comparable to the Senate legislation, a coalition of Republicans and conservative Democrats blocked the Toxic Substances Control Act from moving to the House floor in 1972. Moss, as leader of the coalition supporting the bill, refused to accept any of the proposed compromises. The bill deadlocked in the Ninety-second Congress.

* * *

When the Ninety-third Congress commenced in 1973, Moss still had the same narrowly divided subcommittee of five Democrats and four Republicans. He faced the loss of conservative Democratic votes, now mostly known as "Blue Dogs," regarding most expansions of federal protection for consumers, particularly the proposed Toxic Substances Control Act.

There was now a new member of Moss's subcommittee. Republican Samuel Young narrowly won election to Congress in 1972 from a newly drawn suburban Illinois district centered in Evanston, north of Chicago. It was an affluent district, but it included a number of moderate and liberal voters. It was closely divided between Democrats and Republicans. Young's opponent was Abner Mikva, a legislator who had first been elected to Congress in 1968. He had been redistricted out of his urban Chicago congressional district in the reapportionment of 1970.

Moss liked Mikva. He had a glittering résumé. He had clerked for United States Supreme Court Justice Sherman Minton after graduating at the top of his class from the University of Chicago Law School. He had served as a member of the Illinois legislature for ten years before finally getting the Daley machine to go along with his congressional nomination and getting elected to Congress in 1968. He was a liberal member and a supporter of civil rights, environmental, and consumer legislation. He was not on the Commerce Committee, but Moss had noticed him.

Mikva lost his re-election fight to Sam Young in the new suburban Illinois district by a few hundred votes. It was a cliff-hanger election. It resulted in Young's ascension to the House of Representatives and Mikva's retirement from Congress.

Young had been a Republican stalwart for twenty-two years. Starting in 1951, he attended every Republican state convention as a delegate. He was smart and had worked as a lawyer with the Securities and Exchange Commission office in Chicago. He was appointed by the governor as Securities Commissioner of Illinois in 1953 and served two years. He moved up to assistant secretary of state for two more years. He seemed well qualified for Congress.[37] The Republican House leadership had obviously considered Young's securities law experience and political savvy in selecting him to be a member of the House Commerce Committee.

Moss was never a warm and friendly congressman. He had few close friends in Congress, except for John Dingell, the Michigan Democrat who sat next to him in full committee. But even his opponents agreed that he was unfailingly courteous to other members. He did show anger at times. He would hammer his gavel at hearings, but mostly when he thought a witness was not telling his subcommittee the truth, or shading it a bit.

Moss stayed away from the personal in his comments regarding another member's position on an issue. He did not show animosity toward other members of his subcommittee when they disagreed with him. The closest he came was when he thought Republican Norman Lent of New York was "badgering" a witness. Moss asked Lent to please stop. To which the New Yorker replied, "Mr. Chairman, why should I stop? Your counsel, Mr. Lemov, badgers witnesses all the time."

In general, Moss believed in the old political adage, "It is possible to disagree without being disagreeable." But he had his limits when his goals were being thwarted, as an incident with Sam Young in 1973 suggests.

Moss had a heavy legislative schedule that year, as the new Congress started. He had pushed through the Consumer Product Safety Act and the Motor Vehicle Information and Cost Savings Act in the previous Congress. He had initiated a sweeping investigation of investor protection and competition in the securities industry in 1970. Pending before his subcommittee in 1973 were the Warranty-Federal Trade Commission Improvements bill, the Motor Vehicle and School Bus Safety bill, and the National No-Fault Insurance bill. Toxic Substances Control was also on the list.

Toxic substances were not "number one" on Moss's list, because no one at the time fully recognized the pervasive nature of chemicals and their impact on people and the environment. The wide use of asbestos, cadmium, PCBs, phthalates, and such, and their effect on brain function and disease, had not yet become obvious. Toxic substances legislation seemed like a good idea to Moss and his staff. It would force the government at least to take a hard look—hopefully via mandated industry pre-market testing—at what sorts of chemicals were going into consumer products and the environment before they were put there. But it did not seem to be an urgent problem. It seems sad now, that when there might have been the power to act, we were not able to grasp the full scope of the long-term health threat involved.

Moss was not willing to significantly weaken his toxic substances bill in order to force a conference with the stronger Senate bill. That was what had caused the deadlock in 1972. He just dug in his heels and decided to wait until he could get a strong bill out of the House.

When Sam Young showed up on his subcommittee in 1973, the issue of toxic substances was coming around for the second time. Young had little chemical or environmental background, other than spending two years in the 1950s as financial vice president and treasurer of a hospital supply company. That was not surprising. No one else on the subcommittee was much of a chemical expert either. It was more a matter of where your instincts led you and whether you were listening to academia or the chemical industry.

Moss's second toxics bill was scheduled for markup in April 1973. Young took the lead in opposing the bill. He offered repeated amendments to limit EPA's power to control toxics or to weaken other provisions of the bill. One of Young's amendments limited EPA's authority to obtain data about various types of chemicals. Another would have made it harder to obtain civil penalities against companies violating the proposed law.[38] Young's amendments sometimes carried because conservative Democrats would vote against Moss's position favoring stronger legislation.

Congressional committee and subcommittee consideration of legislation, since the founding of the Republic, had been done in "executive session"; that is, in private. It was a matter of tradition and of the rules of the House. There were no members of the press in the room when bills were "marked up" or voted on. No members of the public could attend. The only people watching the deliberations of the subcommittee members on the Toxic Substances Control bill in 1974 were members of the Democratic and Republican staffs and a single clerk from the committee recording the votes on each of the amendments. And, one by one, in Moss's opinion, Young's amendments were gutting his legislation.

Moss turned to his subcommittee counsel who that day sat next to him on the raised platform at the front of the small locked committee room on the second floor of the Rayburn House Office Building. "Are you keeping track of the amendments Representative Young is offering?"

"Yes, Mr. Chairman."

"Do you have copies of the amendments Representative Young has offered?"

"Yes, Mr. Chairman."

"They sound like they were written by the chemical industry. Why don't you give them to the Chicago newspapers?"

Soon after the contentious markup ended in yet another deadlook, but before the 1974 elections the *Chicago Sun-Times* published several articles that were critical of Young's effort to weaken the Toxic Substances Control Act.[39]

Sometime after the subcommittee battle Young stormed into the tiny, windowless office of the subcommittee staff and stood directly in front of Moss's counsel. "Do you have any idea who has been telling the newspapers about the proceedings and votes of the subcommittee in the markup?" he demanded to know.

"I don't have the slightest idea," replied the counsel—who happened to be me. "Why don't you ask the chairman?"

An angry Young stormed out of my office. He did not pursue the issue, which seemed to be a violation of House rules, with Moss or with anyone else.

In the next congressional election in November 1974, Abner Mikva rebounded from defeat and ousted Young from Congress. The election again was close, with Mikva winning by only two thousand five hundred votes out of about one hundred fifty thousand cast. In 1976 Mikva won again, and then by a few hundred votes in 1978. He went on to compile a record of support for environmental, civil rights, and consumer issues over the years. Eventually, he served as a judge on the United States Court of Appeals and as White House Counsel to President Bill Clinton. Looking back, he said, "I consider the legislative process the most fascinating human experience that I've ever had."[40]

Moss was not particularly proud of what he did to Sam Young. He never talked again about the incident. He liked to treat fellow members with respect. But it was clear he saw no reason why the actions of a committee or a member of Congress should be shielded from public view, especially when he believed the member was weakening a bill that Moss cared about. It mirrored his fight for openness in government in the Freedom of Information Act a decade earlier.

Sam Young faded from the scene. The Toxic Substances Control Act deadlocked once again in 1974 between the House and Senate proposals. It was revived for another fierce legislative struggle in the succeeding Ninety-fourth Congress in 1976. The *Washington Post* summarized the problem over toxic chemicals as the battle neared a climax:

> As experts learn more about environmental hazards to health, several basic points have become obvious. The first is how many afflictions can be traced to toxic substances such as kepone, vinyl chloride, asbestos, and PCBs. National Cancer Institute studies have found very high rates of various cancers in 139 counties around the country where chemical production facilities are concentrated.[41]

And the threat was widespread. According to the U.S. General Accounting Office, today there are over eighty thousand commercial chemicals on the U.S. market. In 1976, there were sixty-two thousand such chemicals. The flood of new substances in products that consumers buy, touch, eat, and come in contact with overwhelmed existing government facilities and laws, then and now.

With Moss moving to chair the Oversight and Investigations Subcommittee, it fell to his ally, Bob Eckhardt, to try to reach agreement with opponents of the bill in the spring of 1976. The bill became a faint shadow of what had been proposed by Magnuson's committee four years before. Press reports on the actions of the Commerce Committee indicate ambivalence from just about everybody. Linda Billings, representing the Sierra Club, commented, "We are not likely to see a very adequate response by the EPA under the legislation." Billings predicted that the measure left too much to the agency's discretion and lacked a specific timetable for actions against dangerous chemicals. The chemical industry, on the other hand, felt better about the bill, concluding it did not fully approve of the House committee compromise, but "it was the best result that could be achieved." Moss and five other members of the Commerce Committee thought it was not. They filed a sharp dissenting opinion in the House report.[42] It proved prophetic.

The dissenting views, written by Moss, charged that his own committee's bill was a "dramatic concession of the public interest to private commercial concerns." The bottom line "is that lives, not short-term profits, are at risk during whatever time is required for the EPA to act."[43] Moss and the other dissenters predicted that requiring a court action by the EPA before a new chemical substance could be banned, and requiring a court order even where the hazard was immediate and dangerous was a shocking loss to the public. They criticized the time-consuming and cumbersome administrative and court requirements that the new law imposed on the EPA.[44]

The dissenters appear to have foreseen the embedded problems of the flawed Toxic Substances Control Act. In the thirty-three years since it was passed, the burden on the EPA to establish that a chemical is dangerous has been so high that the agency has issued regulations requiring pre-market testing for only two hundred out of the more than eighty thousand chemicals currently in use in the country. It has managed completely to ban only five hazardous chemicals in that same period.[45]

The weakened Toxic Substances Control Act did establish broad federal responsibility to eliminate dangerous chemicals from the environment and from consumer products. But the law is so flawed that, by 2009, a new Congress and a new president appeared poised to completely rewrite the Act and to re-fight the battle over one of the last laws that came out of the fading consumer revolution.[46]

\* \* \*

Bob Eckhardt made a valiant effort to negotiate a strong bill with Jim Broyhill and John McCollister, the two Republicans on the committee most familiar with the legislation. He wanted to produce a law that would protect the public against emerging chemical hazards. What he finally got was imperfect legislation. The substantial evidence criteria imposed on the EPA has tied its hands. For example, in 1991, after ten years of regulatory proceedings, EPA thought it had enough evidence to regulate and ban the carcinogen asbestos from commercial use. But when the case, involving forty-five thousand pages of EPA documents, finally got to the U.S. Fifth Circuit Court of Appeals in New Orleans, the court threw out the EPA's entire asbestos regulation. It said the EPA had not met its burden of proof under the law. The Toxic Substances Control Act is loaded with similar procedural landmines. The chemical industry knew, and environmentalists foresaw, that they would make effective regulation almost impossible.

In 1976, Moss left the chairmanship of the Commerce and Finance Subcommittee. Moss's departure came as a shock to a lot of people. He had achieved a stunning record of consumer protection legislation over eight years. Included were passage of the Consumer Product Safety Act, the Magnuson-Moss Federal Trade Commission Improvements Act, the Motor Vehicle and School Bus Safety Amendments, the Motor Vehicle Information and Cost Savings Act, the Securities Amendments of 1975, the Securities Investor Protection Act, and more. Why did Moss give up the chairmanship of the key consumer subcommittee at a time when at least two major consumer bills, the Toxic Substances Control Act and the National No-Fault Motor Vehicle Insurance Act, remained to be dealt with?

* * *

Moss elected to challenge full committee chairman, Harley Staggers, for the chairmanship of the largest subcommittee of the Commerce Committee in 1976. That subcommittee, Oversight and Investigations, could investigate and report to the House and the public on any issue within the broad scope of the committee's jurisdiction. It was not limited to the scope of Moss's former subcommittee, but included things such as health, energy, the environment, and communications. It was, as Moss knew, a license to review consumer problems in almost all of U.S. commerce—and how people were being affected. It was traditionally chaired by the chairman of the full Commerce Committee. In this case that meant Moss's sometime adversary, sometime friend, Harley Staggers.

Why did Moss seek a new jurisdiction with no legislative, but more investigative, power? The answer may lie in the public mood, which Moss sensed was becoming weary of legislation and government regulation. He saw a wave of antigovernment feeling and calls for deregulation from members of his own party as well as Republicans. They posed the most direct threat to his progressive goals. His staff was totally surprised. They, myself included, had missed the signals.

By taking control of Oversight and Investigations, Moss enabled himself and other members to seize public attention. The subcommittee became, for a time, the most powerful investigative arm of Congress. It could, and did, directly challenge the deregulation fervor and defend the gains that had been made over the previous decade.

Moss had had some experience in aggressive congressional oversight in the past. When he was chairman of the Government Operations subcommittee on Foreign Operations and Government Information in the early 1960s, he had traveled to Vietnam to lead an investigation of allegations of waste and the conduct of the war generally. The visit and the investigation made him an early opponent of the Vietnam War.

When he returned from Vietnam, according to Jim Nelligan, a staff member and later a Republican member of Congress, he was sick and had to be hospitalized. Word leaked out to the Johnson administration that Moss was about to release a report that was highly critical of the war. The president came to visit him at Bethesda Naval Hospital. He asked Moss not to release the report, saying it would harm national security. Moss said he could not do that. So, according to Nelligan, the White House somehow got the Government Operations Committee leadership to fire Moss's entire staff in order to kill the report. The discharges were ultimately reversed, and the critical report was published. But according to Jean Moss (and Nelligan), Moss was never invited to the LBJ White House again. "The invitations," Jean said, "stopped coming."[47]

Moss's willingness to oppose both the Johnson administration and the House Democratic leadership over the Vietnam War had come up again soon after President Johnson reluctantly signed the Freedom of Information Act in 1964.

The House held a night session to vote on the Defense Authorization bill to fund the war. Although antiwar fervor had not yet gripped the country, Robert Leggett, a California Democratic, announced he would vote against further Vietnam funding, angering the powerful chairman of the Armed Services committee, Mendel Rivers of Mississippi. Rivers stood before the House and accused Leggett of acting in a manner that was "unpatriotic and a betrayal of the troops." Moss did not have to get involved in this debate and risk the wrath of Rivers and the House leadership. He was not a member of the Armed Service committee.

Nonetheless, as a member of Moss's staff who was watching that night recalled: "Moss took the floor. He pointed his finger at Rivers who was sitting about thirty feet from him. He was angry." Moss said that Rivers's charges were "an outrageous personal attack on a member of the House." He demanded that Rivers retract the slur. After a hurried conference between Rivers and House Speaker John McCormack, Rivers rose, apologized, and withdrew the offending statement.[48]

The scene was reminiscent of Moss's challenge to the speaker of the California assembly over the conduct of lobbyists many years before. Moss's temper showed in both instances, as did his moral compass.

But by 1976 Moss may have been getting weary. Or perhaps he wanted to see the oversight subcommittee take a more assertive role. His friend

John Dingell said the reason for Moss's move and the interparty scrap that it caused was that "Harley just wouldn't do anything with that big subcommittee staff."[49]

Moss won the chairmanship of the oversight subcommittee by one vote, after a marathon session of seven ballots. As chairman of the Oversight and Investigations Subcommittee, he went from the offense, mostly to defense. He produced a widely read multivolume analysis of the successes, and some failures, of economic and safety regulation. His reports enumerated ways in which federal agencies could be more cost-effective and ways in which they had failed to protect the public adequately. Moss conducted broad-ranging hearings on everything from the excessive cost of natural gas to consumers to health care. Moss wanted a national health insurance program. His oversight hearings documented the costs and dangers of unnecessary surgery by doctors and other problems with health care in America. They resulted in significant changes in Medicare reimbursement rules, but not the national health insurance law Moss wanted.[50]

He met with President Ford at the White House. They agreed to disagree on additional methods of improving or reducing federal regulation. Moss held hearings and generated enormous press coverage on the benefits of regulation, as well as its burdens. It cannot be said that he and his subcommittee allies, many of them known as the "Watergate babies," elected in the wake of Nixon's resignation and the Watergate scandal, did not repeatedly warn the public about what was happening as consumer protection initiatives ground to a halt.[51]

Years later, the *Washington Post* said Moss had "reinvented" congressional oversight. Whether Moss's warnings would be heeded, and what the results of his decision to leave the House consumer subcommittee would be, remained to be determined over many years.

The fight to unseat Staggers as chair of the powerful oversight committee was not pleasant. It relegated the senior West Virginian to a largely symbolic role for the balance of his congressional career. Moss's campaign manager was his friend and ally, John Dingell. Staggers, bitter in defeat, swore he would never retire and allow Moss to become chairman of the full committee. He was true to his word. Moss never became chairman of the Commerce Committee or any other full committee. What else Moss might have accomplished for consumers and the public as chairman will never be known. "If Moss had lasted another ten years, Detroit might have been saved," observed Ralph Nader. "After he left, Congress gave the motor vehicle industry everything they wanted. It was like giving too much candy to a kid."[52]

Only after Moss retired in 1978 did Staggers retire. That gave John Dingell the chairmanship of the full Commerce Committee. He served as chairman for twenty-nine years. Over all those years Dingell never forgot the long-departed Moss. "The only mistake John Moss ever made," he said, "was retiring too soon."[53]

# 10

# Consumer Protection
# in Retreat

*Two Crushing Defeats*

"This will never happen again," said Bill Chapman, General Motors's chief lobbyist on the House side of Congress. Chapman, a big, burly man with a surprisingly gentle personality, and Moss's counsel, were talking in the hallway of the Longworth House Office Building. The year was 1974. Chapman was referring to the wave of consumer legislation that Moss and his allies had managed to push through Congress in the preceding four years. He had been sent in to build up the GM team, which had been taking a beating in legislative battles in both the House and the Senate. Chapman's statement was made in his usual friendly way, even though GM was opposing almost everything Moss was trying to do. It was Chapman's—and GM's—reading of the future.

As we stood in the hallway talking, two years had passed since President Richard Nixon had signed the Motor Vehicle Information and Cost Savings Act, a Moss-Magnuson law designed to reduce the cost of automobile collision repairs to consumers. It was only a few weeks after Nixon's successor, Gerald Ford, had signed the even tougher Motor Vehicle and School Bus Safety Act in October 1974—over GM's protests.

Magnuson and Moss had launched this second automobile safety bill a year before to close a loophole in the 1966 motor vehicle safety law. That loophole allowed manufacturers to avoid paying for safety repairs. Moss had strengthened the House bill, not only requiring that motor vehicle manufacturers pay for safety repairs, but also giving the Department of Transportation powerful new enforcement authority to force recalls and police compliance with the growing number of new motor vehicle safety standards.

161

Moss had dropped his surprise enforcement amendment into the safety bill after the House hearings on the bill were over. It was not exactly cricket, but there was not much the manufacturers could do about it—except attempt to defeat the entire bill, which is what they did. Moss thought the Department of Transportation, which regulated automobile recalls through the National Highway Traffic Safety Administration was a toothless tiger. He was determined to give it teeth, even if it meant angering the Detroit giants—General Motors, Chrysler, and Ford. At that time, they were among the largest and most profitable companies in the nation.

General Motors and its allies in the vast U.S. motor vehicle industry had not been able to muster the votes to defeat either of Moss's two motor vehicle bills in the House.

On that day in 1974, it did not seem to me that the consumer protection coalition was in any trouble. It was riding high. I just laughed at Chapman's "never again" remark and did not respond to his prediction of doom. Never is a long time, I thought.

In 1972, two years before our conversation, consumer protection appeared to be an unstoppable force for change. The *Wall Street Journal's* editorial page—surely the voice of a large segment of the American business community—conceded that for years the consumer had been "poorly represented in Washington." The *Journal* noted that "the consumer wheel" had become "one of the squeakiest in D.C. . . . one that requires a shot of lubrication." One lubricant would be the Consumer Product Safety Act, enacted later that year. But the *Journal* did not dismiss out of hand another idea: the proposed Consumer Protection Agency (CPA). The *Journal* called the combined impact of the two laws, one enacted and one pending, a "federal charter for consumerism."[1]

Consumer groups saw the CPA as guaranteeing them a place at the bargaining table on issues such as food safety, drug prices, automobile safety, and competition. It was a key piece of legislation for them, potentially the crowning moment of the consumer revolution.

Not surprisingly, many business groups were negative. They thought the CPA would be a federal troublemaker. The National Association of Manufacturers went as far as to say that the proposed Consumer Protection Agency would "terrorize" American industry. Still, in 1972, when the CPA was just beginning its long journey through the legislative process, a large segment of American business could scarcely miss the public's message. Some of the business community seemed prepared to cooperate with Congress in the enactment of reasonable consumer legislation.[2]

The moderate approach to the consumer movement voiced by the *Journal* may have reflected the rising tide of consumer awareness in the country. But that assessment did not prevail within the business community at large as the consumer wave moved into the mid-1970s.

Instead of conceding that a Consumer Protection Agency could be reasonable and that some other consumer legislation might be unavoidable, American business—under the banner of the National Association of Manufacturers (NAM), the Chamber of Commerce of the United States, and the newly created Business Roundtable—organized an aggressive counterattack. The NAM, the Roundtable, and the Chamber used intense one-on-one lobbying of members of Congress, big campaign contributions, and think-tank reports (often funded with tax-deductible corporate dollars) to take issue with the drive for a CPA.

GM's Chapman had been dead right. What happened in the decade of the consumer revolution would never—in my lifetime—happen again. The consumer era was fitfully drawing to a close.

The end of the consumer decade can be traced to 1978. Two major legislative defeats signaled that the American public had changed its priorities and that an antigovernment era was beginning. They were proposed no-fault automobile insurance legislation and the Consumer Protection Agency.

\* \* \*

After Moss elected to move on to become chairman of the Commerce Committee's Oversight and Investigations Subcommittee, next in line to be chairman of the Consumer Subcommittee was Congressman Lionel Van Deerlin, a San Diego Democrat and former newspaper reporter. Two major pieces of legislation were pending before the Consumer Subcommittee when Van Deerlin took over. One was the Toxic Substances Control Act, which Moss had tried unsuccessfully to get passed for four years. The other was a national No-Fault Automobile Insurance bill, which Magnuson and Moss had been sponsoring since at least 1970.[3]

As with so many of the other consumer bills, experts were needed on the congressional staff to work on no-fault and the CPA—a necessity in dealing with complex, high-stakes issues.

In staffing up his subcommittee, Van Deerlin hired, among others, Peter Kinzler. Kinzler had worked for five years for Congressman Thomas "Lud" Ashley, the powerful Ohio Democrat, who rose to be chairman of the Housing Subcommittee of the House Banking Committee and chairman of the House Budget Committee. Kinzler tired of the Banking Committee work and moved on to become an attorney in the consumer protection division of the Federal Trade Commission in Washington.

When he got the call from Van Deerlin, Kinzler was ready to return to Capitol Hill. It can be a place that is hard to stay away from. Kinzler thought he would probably be working on Federal Trade Commission-type consumer issues, such as deceptive advertising, which was his specialty. He had no idea he was about to become a leading national expert on automobile insurance.

It happened quite by accident. Kinzler and the other new subcommittee counsel, Janie Kinney, essentially flipped a coin to decide who would staff which bill. Kinney won and picked toxic substances. By default, Kinzler got no-fault. It turned out to be a challenging experience and a roller-coaster ride that lasted twenty-three years.[4]

The no-fault insurance bill had a stormy history by the time Kinzler arrived on Van Deerlin's staff. The idea of "no-fault" type automobile insurance was the brainchild of professors Robert Keeton of Harvard, and Jeffrey O'Connell of the University of Virginia. They wrote a book in the mid-1960s that was highly critical of the lawsuit, or "tort" system, as the method of compensating people injured in automobile accidents.[5] Keeton and O'Connell thought the system was expensive and unfair. It paid out big money to a few people and almost nothing to most accident victims. Lawyers' fees took a big chunk of most payments. Getting paid took a long time.

Keeton and O'Connell recommended a new approach: payment of all the expenses of an accident—medical bills, lost income, and other *direct* economic costs—by the injured party's own insurance company. Payment would not depend on who was at fault; there would be no need for lawsuits. But there would be a ban on recovery for *indirect* costs, primarily "pain and suffering," except in very serious cases of death or permanent injury. According to supporters, a no-fault system would save as much as 10 percent annually in premiums for consumers and give them better insurance coverage as well.

The tort system, however, was—and is—a sacred cow to much of the American legal community.

Michael Dukakis was a student of Bob Keeton at Harvard. Dukakis, who eventually became governor of Massachusetts and presidential nominee of the Democratic Party, started his political career by getting elected to the Massachusetts legislature. There, he led a four-year battle to enact a state no-fault insurance system. In 1971, it became the first no-fault law in the United States and gave momentum to the idea of a national law.

Even before that, there had been some modest congressional activity. In 1968, when John Moss was just getting his feet wet as chair of the Commerce and Finance Subcommittee, he was the principal House sponsor of Public Law 90–313. This obscure piece of legislation provided for a little-noticed two-year study of the motor vehicle accident compensation system by the Department of Transportation. It produced twenty-three special reports and a dynamic final volume that was made public in 1971 by President Nixon's Secretary of Transportation, John Volpe.

Moss read the study and was convinced that it "established once and for all that our motor vehicle accident compensation system should be based on universal, compulsory, first-party insurance, for all motor vehicle owners—no-fault motor vehicle insurance."[6] At hearings on no-fault before his subcommittee, Moss said there were only two questions that remained after the Department of Transportation's exhaustive work: Should the federal government assume the initiative in requiring no-fault motor vehicle insurance, or should this be left to the states? What should be the time frame for the transition to a no-fault system?[7]

Quite a few legislators, many lawyers, and the American Bar Association thought that Moss had left out a key question: should the right to sue for personal injury damages—and attorney's fees—be limited at all?

Ultimately, the answers to these questions would determine the fate of the Moss-Magnuson no-fault insurance bills.

House and Senate supporters organized simultaneously in 1971 to press for early passage of legislation reforming the automobile insurance system. Congress was controlled by Democrats who appeared, at first, supportive. But many of them were lawyers or knew lawyers back home. Most lawyers did not like the no-fault idea at all.

The position of the Nixon administration on no-fault insurance was unusual. As a young law student at Duke, Nixon had written a law review article that was critical of the tort system as a method of compensating accident victims. When Democratic congressional leaders floated the concept of no-fault in 1971, the Nixon administration did not oppose it outright. The White House took the position that it favored no-fault, but it should be done on a state-by-state basis.[8]

Jim Broyhill, the ranking Republican on Moss's subcommittee, told a congressional staff member that the administration position was "a complete cop-out." The states would never act, he said, because of the power of the insurance industry and the desire of the state insurance commissions to maintain their traditional control over insurance.[9] Broyhill might have mentioned another problem: the Association of Trial Lawyers of America, representing plaintiffs' lawyers, had formed a rare and powerful alliance with the American Bar Association and defendants' lawyers, to preserve the right to sue.

When President Ford replaced the departed Nixon, a major internal White House struggle ensued over what to do about the no-fault proposal. The new Secretary of Transportation, William Coleman, a solid administrator, was not quite up to speed on the pros and cons of the no-fault insurance legislation. When Coleman met at the White House with Ford's staff, Tom Korologos, the chief White House political advisor, was very concerned about a challenge to Ford in the 1976 Republican primary elections from Ronald Reagan. The White House believed Reagan would challenge Ford from the right and would adamantly oppose federal no-fault insurance. That argument carried the day, and the Ford administration did not support no-fault legislation.

In fact, according to Kinzler, but unknown to no-fault supporters at the time, candidate Ronald Reagan had written a letter saying that a no-fault insurance plan for automobile owners was "a great idea," adding that "the states will never do it."[10] Unfortunately, Reagan's letter did not surface until it was too late to make any difference.

The idea of the Magnuson-Moss no-fault bill was pretty simple. The average lawyer charges his client about one-third of any money recovered for personal injuries and property damage in an auto accident. The defense lawyer, funded with insurance company dollars, also must be paid. It is easy to see why as much as 50 percent of the insurance payout in successful cases is spent on things other than compensating the victims. Magnuson, Moss, Senator Phil Hart, and others thought that a system that would pay directly for all medical expenses, lost wages, and related damages—regardless of who was at fault—would be better. Without the intervention of contingent-fee lawyers and lawsuits, the system could be run much more efficiently.

Kinzler, who served as counsel to the Commerce and Finance Subcommittee under Van Deerlin and the two other chairmen who succeeded John Moss, explained it this way: "Benefits under a no-fault system were estimated at the time to be about $150,000 for each injured person, mostly in medical expenses and lost income. Because there would be no lawsuits or legal fees, except in a few cases, the insurance premiums paid by all drivers could be reduced at least ten percent. And payment would be fast, rather than after a long lawsuit."[11] It sounded like a very good idea—unless you were a personal injury or defendant's lawyer.

The bill's sponsors did not count on the fact that America's trial lawyers and the American Bar Association would fight so vigorously to preserve the existing lawsuit system. Kinzler estimated that lawyers—mostly the Association of Trial Lawyers of America—outspent the pro-no-fault coalition by as much as *one hundred to one*. Part of the insurance industry, including the giant insurer Allstate, fearing a federal takeover of the insurance business, joined in opposing the no-fault bill. Kinzler remembered that Lynn Sutcliffe, who had departed as counsel to Magnuson's Senate Commerce Committee and gone into private law practice, was hired as lead counsel by the pro-no-fault coalition for an annual fee of $250,000. That had to be weighed against lobbying and legal fees of "millions of dollars" spent by the insurance industry and trial lawyers in an effort to kill the bill. "When you add in the political contributions they made, it was several million annually," said Kinzler. "We were just outmonied."[12]

Kinzler said the labor unions were supportive of the bill, but that "Nader took a pass."[13] Why? Nader may just have had a negative attitude toward insurance companies. Perhaps he did not trust them to run the system. And, it must be added, Nader's public interest organizations received substantial financial support from individual members of the plaintiff's trial bar.

Whatever the reason, the supporters of no-fault were left with a coalition consisting of part of the consumer movement, part of the insurance industry—and not much money. There is also evidence that, by the time the bill surfaced during President Jimmy Carter's tenure, the president was supportive, but his administration was ineffective in its lobbying efforts. "We never saw Brock Adams, the Secretary of Transportation," Kinzler said. [14]

Moss sponsored the original no-fault bill, H.R. 10, in 1971, along with John Dingell and other Democrats. But Moss was unable to get a quorum in his subcommittee to mark up the legislation. He was stymied.[15] In late 1974, a frustrated Moss wrote a letter to President Gerald Ford to request Ford's backing for the national no-fault bill. He linked his request to Ford's priority: the problem of inflation. Moss pointed out that no-fault would save consumers $1.5 billion a year. He said if Ford would support the bill, it could be passed in that Congress.[16] He never got an answer. Although Moss held fifteen days of hearings between 1971 and 1974, he could not move the bill out of his Commerce and Finance subcommittee to the full House Commerce Committee.

Over in the Senate, Magnuson won an important victory in May 1974 when the Senate narrowly voted, fifty-three to forty-two, to enact a national no-fault system. The Senate action reversed its 1972 stance when it had recommitted a similar bill to the Judiciary Committee where it had died. After that, all of the pending no-fault bills were narrowed by their sponsors to offer the states an opportunity to pass their own legislation, imposing a minimum federal standard only if the states failed to act after a period of several years. It was a futile effort to compromise with opponents.

Back in the House, pressure was intense, particularly on Democratic members, to oppose no-fault legislation. Kinzler met with Al Gore, then a second-term congressman who was on the Commerce Committee. Gore said he had received an awful lot of letters from trial lawyers in Tennessee who supported him personally and financially. They urged him to vote against the bill. He said it was going to be a very tough vote for him. But Gore voted in favor of no-fault when it got to the full committee.

Congressman Tim Wirth, of Colorado, later under secretary of state for global affairs in the Clinton administration, told Kinzler he had been "offered big money if he voted against the bill." He asked Kinzler—possibly in jest—what he should do. Kinzler remembers saying, "There are few things that violate the federal law applicable to bribery in the legislative process, but this is one of them."[17] Spencer Rich, a reporter for the *Washington Post,* spent six hours trying to call Wirth to ask how he would vote. There was agreement within the committee staff that if Rich had ever gotten through, and Wirth had talked to the *Washington Post*, some people would have gone to jail.

Wirth never talked to the newspapers about the pending legislation. But he submitted a "yes" proxy vote in favor of the bill when it finally came before the full committee.

By 1978, Van Deerlin was succeeded as chair of the subcommittee by Bob Eckhardt. Both men were the chief sponsors of the House no-fault insurance legislation after Moss left, but Moss continued to co-sponsor the bill. In 1978, Moss signed a joint letter to the members of the full committee urging them to support the measure when it came to a vote. But he did not testify at full committee hearings on the legislation, as did some other co-sponsors.

Why did Moss fail to testify in support of the no-fault legislation he had originated seven years before? Was he signaling policy reservations? Is it possible he was too deeply involved in legislative oversight? As chairman of the Oversight and Investigations Subcommittee, he compiled an extraordinarily detailed record of the success—and sometimes the failure—of the federal regulatory process in protecting consumers. Why not come forward again on no-fault?

Moss saw the handwriting on the wall in 1976. The legislation had been defeated in the Senate that year. The chances that Eckhardt could revive it in the House were not great. And the bill was causing a huge split in the Democratic Party in Congress.

Trial lawyers have long been major financial supporters of the Democrats. Republican leaders have generally sought to limit or eliminate personal injury lawsuits. Democrats have tended to support the right to a jury trial in injury cases. That was, and remains, a basic difference in political approach between the two parties. Moss, who sometimes was accused of being too stubborn, this time may have been acting as pure politician. Was it worth another bloodletting when the public mood seemed to be turning against federal regulation? Was it worth the potentially divisive impact on the party?

Moss was sitting in his office one day in 1974, going over the subcommittee's jammed legislative schedule with me. When no-fault came up, Moss said, "I don't think we are going to be able to get that one." As his subcommittee counsel, I was surprised and asked him why he felt that way about a bill that had been one of his priorities. "It's just not going to make it," Moss said. He never explained further. He surely would not have caved in to the Democratic leadership. He would not have backed off under threats from his own supporters. He had proved that time and again over the years. He sometimes returned the financial contributions of people who opposed his position. Perhaps Moss had just counted the votes.

Although he continued to support the idea of no-fault automobile insurance, Moss may have decided that his final battle would not be for any particular piece of legislation. Rather, Moss seemed bent on defending the public from what he saw as the disaster of deregulation. In his final four years as a member of Congress, Moss became the leader of a battle different from no-fault or other new legislation—the battle to stop the nation from turning away from government regulation of abuses in the marketplace and from consumer protection generally. Kinzler says Moss remained "a stern and unbending advocate of laws to protect average people. Movements need leaders. Moss was that leader. He made it possible for others to make the compromises."[18]

The no-fault bill, with Bob Eckhardt risking a lot of his own political support, came to the Commerce Committee with the backing of the Carter administration in February 1978. Moss and Staggers both supported it, along with Al Gore and Tim Wirth. But conservative Democrats switched sides and joined almost all the Republicans in voting against the bill. The no-fault legislation was narrowly defeated in committee votes twenty-two to twenty. That was its swan song. Congress had killed it, despite its potential savings to automobile owners.

No-fault was not revived until 1998, and then only as a purely optional insurance choice for car owners. Kinzler, then a lawyer in private practice, continued to work on getting it passed. But no-fault was defeated again, even as an option, primarily by trial-lawyer money and the opposition of the bar associations.

*   *   *

If the loss of no-fault was a major setback, the fight over creation of a Consumer Protection Agency turned into a death blow to the consumer revolution. In 1978, President Jimmy Carter made a determined effort to enact the legislation dearest to the hearts of consumer leaders: the bill creating the Consumer Protection Agency. According to some opponents, it would make Ralph Nader a permanent federal agency. The bill's opponents believed it would create a new layer of bureaucracy, cost businesses millions of dollars, and be ineffective at representing often-differing consumer positions on different issues

The idea of a Consumer Protection Agency was started by Nader. His dynamic entrance into the public debate over the functioning of the government as it related to the market system changed everything. He had real power in the 1960s and 1970s. The press loved him, and he took advantage of ready-made publicity with both his brilliance and his intensity. Capitol Hill staff usually sought his testimony on major bills—his appearance ensured good press coverage. Nader was a master of the "zinger," the blazing one-liner that captured the guts of an issue. Nader and his corps of "raiders" were always good for a newspaper story, sometimes for a headline.

Consumer leaders understood that nothing lasts forever. Washington has a short attention span. They wanted to institutionalize some permanent pressure for the effective performance of government agencies charged with consumer protection and regulation of activities such as offshore oil drilling and the securities markets. So Nader shopped the idea of a consumer protection watchdog to Congressman Ben Rosenthal, a New York City Democrat. Rosenthal liked the idea and sold it to allies in the Senate: Abraham Ribicoff, Charles Percy, and Jacob Javits.[19]

Starting in 1970 and for eight years thereafter, Rosenthal was the lead sponsor of a bill to get a consumer protection agency created by the Congress. Rosenthal believed that "organization makes policy."[20] Unless consumerism was given an organization in the form of a permanent federal agency, it would, in his view, fade away.

The idea was that the proposed agency would not actually regulate anything. It would, however, have the ability to intervene before other federal agencies and the courts to advocate the point of view of the consuming public. It is not a new concept in the law. The attorneys general of many states intervene in cases with broad impact, as a "friend of the public"—*parens patriae*, derived from the Latin for "father of his country."[21]

Rosenthal's bill—and Nader's idea—would have created a kind of federal attorney general with standing to go before federal agencies, such as the Department of Transportation, the Federal Communications Commission, the Federal Reserve Board, the Food and Drug Administration, or even the courts, to argue for better, stronger consumer programs and regulations. The idea at first frightened American business—and then terrified it.

Rosenthal was not particularly well known before he took up the cause of the Consumer Protection Agency, known as the CPA. But he became a leader on consumer issues in the House of Representatives. He did not have the seniority and committee jurisdiction to accomplish what Moss could, but he and Moss were friendly, if distant, allies. Rosenthal took the lead on the proposed CPA bill because it involved the creation of a new federal agency, something that fell under the purview of the Government Operations Committee on which he served. Moss was a co-sponsor of the bill.

Rosenthal did not look like he would be a leading consumer advocate when he began his congressional career in 1962. He was an unknown, thirty-nine-year-old New York lawyer when he was chosen by the "regular" Democratic organization in Queens to run in a complicated special election to fill a vacant House seat.

The New York Democratic Party was then split between "reform" Democrats—generally the more activist, progressive wing of the party—and "regular" Democrats who were often more moderate or conservative. The fierce political infighting went on for years. The battles extended from the lowly job of local district leader to the election of the city's congressional delegation and mayor.

Rosenthal was the choice of the regulars. The reformers, led by former First Lady Eleanor Roosevelt and Senator Herbert Lehman, had just helped elect Robert F. Wagner Jr. mayor. But Rosenthal bucked the odds and won a special election to fill the seat. Once in office, he proceeded to confound some of his supporters by becoming one of the most outspoken and liberal consumer leaders in the House of Representatives. He was never again challenged by the New York Democratic Party's reform wing.

Rosenthal was an early opponent of the Vietnam War. He said, "perhaps ten percent of my constituents agreed with me."[22] Rosenthal showed his independence by his opposition to the war and by his ability to win reelection to Congress—in combative New York districts—eleven times. Over his twenty-two years in Congress, his major legislative initiative was the Consumer Protection Agency. The bill—and Rosenthal—faced ferocious opposition from the business community.

At first, the CPA bill looked like a winner. In 1972, it passed the House of Representatives by an overwhelming vote of 344 to 4. However, a conservative-led filibuster killed it in the Senate. Then, in the next Congress, the bill again passed the House, although by a lesser margin of 293 to 94. Again, the bill stalled in the Senate.[23]

Then in 1975, the process was reversed. Senator Abraham Ribicoff took the bill to the Senate floor first where it passed narrowly. Things were looking better for the unborn consumer agency, until votes in the House began melting away. Intensive lobbying by the Chamber of Commerce and the newly formed Business Roundtable was trained on the legislation. Consumer organizations fought back. Labor unions assisted them. It was democracy—and dollars—in action.

"I have been around here for twenty-five years," said House Speaker Tip O'Neill in 1975. "I have never seen such extensive lobbying."[24] Both President Carter and his silver-haired consumer advisor, Esther Peterson, fought hard for the bill. Carter staked his prestige on passage. Peterson

walked the halls of Congress to drum up votes and led a White House-
sponsored national forum to generate public support.

* * *

If ever a person was a revered figure in progressive American politics,
Esther Peterson was. Like Nader, she has become an iconic leader in the
consumer movement. She was respected and soft-spoken, but a continuing force in the battle for consumer rights. Apart from the consumer
legislation she influenced, Peterson championed many significant pro-
consumer state and federal regulatory changes that benefit consumers
today. They include standardization of packaging, unit pricing on consumer goods, and open dating on foods.

Peterson served as an advisor on consumer issues to four American
presidents: John Kennedy, Lyndon Johnson, Jimmy Carter, and Bill
Clinton. Under Kennedy, she was the first person to hold the title of
Consumer Advisor to the president. Carter awarded her the Presidential
Medal of Freedom, the nation's highest civilian award. In 1993, when she
was eighty-seven years old, President Clinton named her as a delegate to
the United Nations General Assembly, where she continued to work for
international standards for safe products and for a United Nations code
of conduct for international corporations.

Peterson was born to a conservative Republican family in Provo, Utah,
in 1906. Her father was the city's superintendent of schools. The position
was not well paid, and the family took in boarders to make ends meet.
When she was twelve years old, the labor leader Eugene V. Debs organized a strike in Utah in an attempt to organize a railroad workers union.
The Union Pacific Railroad sent agents house-to-house in Provo seeking
to recruit strikebreakers. The roomers at her family's home were mostly
students at Brigham Young—farm kids who were short of money. Many
signed up to get a job. And that led to a defining moment in Peterson's
life:

> We were one of the few families to have a little car then. And I remember
> that we were to drive these students to the strike. . . . I shall never forget a
> woman—standing there with two little children. . . . It has haunted me to
> this day. And she looked at me and said, "Why do you do this to us?" And
> it hurts me. I can remember feeling that something was wrong. I wouldn't
> go back. I just wouldn't cross that line. I didn't know what was wrong, but I
> knew something was wrong.[25]

As members of the Mormon Church, Esther and her five brothers and
sisters were offered the choice of a college education or Mormon mission-
ary work. Esther chose a college education. She trained to be a physical

education teacher, graduating from Brigham Young University in 1927. Then Esther headed east where she graduated with a master's degree from Columbia University. After that, she took a job as a physical education teacher at the posh Winsor School in Boston. Along the way, she met her husband-to-be, Oliver Peterson, who introduced her to the work of the progressive Senator Robert La Follette of Wisconsin and labor leader Sidney Hillman—all of which led her into the labor movement.

Peterson also began teaching night school at the YWCA in Boston to a group of young women factory workers. Most of the girls in her class worked in the garment industry. One evening, Peterson went home with one of her students, a sixteen-year-old named Eileen. Inside the house, she met Eileen's brothers and sisters and her mother, all sitting at a table with a single light bulb hanging above them. Everyone was working. The youngest, a three-year-old, was sitting in a high chair counting out bobby pins into piles of ten. They made house dresses for $1.32 per dozen dresses. When company officials changed the pockets on the dresses from a square to heart shape, the workers could not sew them as quickly and their wages shrunk even lower.[26]

The following morning, Peterson walked beside her girls on a picket line in what became known as the "Heartbreakers Strike." As a result, Peterson became involved in the International Ladies Garment Workers Union.[27] Eventually, she ended up in Washington as a lobbyist where she worked for increased minimum wages and equal pay for women. In 1960, President Kennedy made her director of the women's bureau in the Department of Labor. Later, Peterson was named assistant secretary of labor to highlight the Kennedy administration's interest in women's status in the workplace.

Kennedy was killed soon after appointing her his presidential assistant for consumer affairs. She then became President Johnson's consumer advisor in the White House and, in 1976, consumer advisor to President Carter. It was in that role that she fought for enactment of the Consumer Protection Agency.

After she left the Carter administration, Peterson worked as vice president for consumer affairs at the big chain supermarket Giant Foods. Odonna Matthews, her successor at Giant, said, "Her friends in consumer activism asked, 'How can you work for business and represent the consumer?' She showed it could be done."[28]

When Peterson was named consumer advisor to Johnson, one trade group denounced her as "the most pernicious threat to advertising today." The advertising and food industries do not appear to have suffered at all from her efforts. Consumers have benefited.

\* \* \*

All of President Carter's and Peterson's efforts in support of the Consumer Protection Agency did not matter in 1978. The third time around in the House was the kiss of death. One consumer lobbyist was told by a member of the House, "I'm with you on the merits, but I cannot convince my constituents that this bill is not a move toward big government."[29]

Peter Barash was staff director of Rosenthal's Commerce, Consumer and Monetary Affairs Subcommittee in the House. The subcommittee was in the middle of the fight for enactment of the legislation for almost a decade. Barash said that when the bill narrowly passed the House in 1975, a veto threat by President Ford deterred the Democratic leadership from even sending the legislation to the president. They did not have the votes to override a veto.

While Nader was an important leader in fighting for the Consumer Protection Agency, he was also a lightning rod that generated a lot of opposition. Barash was on the House floor when the CPA came up for a third and final vote. As one Republican member voted—by pushing his card in a newly installed electronic voting machine—Barash heard him say, as he entered his "no" vote, "This one is for you Ralph."[30]

Richard Lester, president of the U.S. Chamber of Commerce, said the vote against the Consumer Protection Agency was not surprising. "The House was reacting to public opposition to a growing federal bureaucracy. The American people are weary of too much government in their lives—too much protection; too much of what other people think is good for them."[31]

Peterson blamed the defeat squarely on business lobbying. "We tried," she said. "We tried mighty hard. We were a little David against a tremendous Goliath, and I guess our little slingshot didn't matter."[32] Mary Jo Jacobi of the National Association of Manufacturers scoffed at the notion that members of Congress caved into pressure from big business. "Contrary to public opinion, we used no strong-arm tactics," she said. "We just did our homework."[33]

Rosenthal took the defeat hard.[34] He had put years into the fight. He soldiered on and compiled a record of financial and bank oversight in the years between 1978 and 1983. He was sworn in for his eleventh term in January of 1983 in a hospital bed in Washington, not far from his Capitol Hill office. He died of cancer a few days later, still representing his New York constituents.

Barash stayed on the committee staff as counsel to the subcommittee under its new chairman, Congressman Doug Barnard, a self-described "populist banker" from Georgia. Surprisingly, there was not much difference in bank oversight between the New Yorker and the Georgian. But there was no consumer protection agency to fight for anymore.

Rosenthal had been denied his crowning achievement. The consumer movement had suffered a grievous defeat. When Barash and Barnard, the new subcommittee chairman, visited the Federal Reserve Board for a breakfast meeting with Chairman Paul Volker, Barash was introduced to Volker for the first time. "Oh I know Peter Barash," said the financial eminence. "You were committee counsel to Ben Rosenthal. We've got a room down here named the Benjamin S. Rosenthal Memorial Subpoenaed Documents Room." It was a fitting memorial to a determined congressman—and to a defeat that signaled the end of the consumer decade.

"You can draw a straight line from that defeat in 1978 to the 2008 collapse of the stock market and the inadequate performance of the bank regulatory agencies," Barash said. "The consequences of not having a federal watchdog pressuring for vigorous enforcement of bank safety and soundness and mortgage regulation was a major reason for the 2008 market debacle." He added, "Rosenthal's CPA would have kept the bankers and bank regulators honest and saved a lot of people's money."[35]

\* \* \*

Two years after the defeat of no-fault, Bob Eckhardt's turn came. The big Texan had represented a safe Houston district with a large minority population for decades. Eckhardt fit the district. He was a defender of the little guy. Kinzler says Eckhardt was brilliant in negotiations, brilliant in committee, but a disaster when speaking on the House floor. Congressman Manuel Lujan Jr., a Republican from New Mexico, once told Kinzler that the reason Eckhardt was so bad at speaking before the full House was that he had this awful habit of continually referring to, even quoting from, the Constitution.

"I guess the members don't want to hear that much about the Constitution," said Lujan.[36]

Eckhardt was defeated for reelection in the Reagan landslide of 1980. As election day neared, he was trailing badly in the polls. Eckhardt mostly stayed in Washington and worked on price controls in natural gas pipeline legislation, which he thought would reduce gas prices to people in his Houston district. He favored price controls, on natural gas, to protect users who were tied to a single distribution system.

In 1980, Eckhardt was redistricted from his inner-city Houston district to a new district in the suburbs. When Eckhardt finally roused himself to go back to Houston and do some campaigning, his advertisements showed him sitting at his desk in Washington—talking about the Constitution.

Moss, who was then living in Sacramento, expressed deep regret at the defeat of his old ally. Moss thought Eckhardt compromised and negotiated with their opponents a bit too much. But he knew his friend had the interests of the average person at heart. He knew Bob Eckhardt would be very hard to replace.

Many consumer-oriented legislators—including Eckhardt and Warren Magnuson—were defeated in the Reagan landslide of 1980. Reagan's victory over Jimmy Carter and the emergence of a new group of congress-men changed the complexion of the House of Representatives and the Senate. The Reagan years, followed by the presidencies of George H. W. Bush, Bill Clinton, and George W. Bush, marked a long period of decline for consumer protection. The movement's supporters did not fold up their tents and go away. There were still strong consumer advocates in the Congress and in the country. They were just outspent and outvoted. The nation had turned its eyes in a different direction—toward faith in an unregulated, self-correcting marketplace.

It would be nearly thirty years before the pendulum began to swing back. In 2008, Congress—aroused by a growing number of reports of the deaths of children strangled in cribs, killed by small magnets in their toys, or brain-damaged by lead content—enacted the Consumer Product Safety Improvements Act. It was a modest step intended to rejuvenate the doz-ing, neglected Consumer Product Safety Commission created with such high hopes by Moss and Magnuson so long ago.

Later that year, the stock market crashed, yet again, and the country elected a new president—Barack Obama. Obama seemed to suggest a new role for government in the marketplace. Within six months of tak-ing office the Obama White House released a proposal which resulted in the creation in 2010 of a new Consumer Financial Protection Bureau, an independent branch of the Federal Reserve Board.

The agency was the brainchild of Elizabeth Warren, a Harvard Law School professor. At the time, she chaired a congressionally appointed panel overseeing the $700 billion federal bailout of America's failing banks. Warren, who had an eye for history, argued that a new consumer protection agency was needed to keep bank practices fair to their custom-ers—and to keep the banks solvent.

Seeming to take a cue from Moss, Magnuson, and Nader, she proposed the idea of a Consumer Financial Protection Agency in an essay entitled "Unsafe at Any Rate."[37] "Just as the Consumer Product Safety Commission protects buyers of goods and supports a competitive market," she wrote, "we need the same for consumers of financial products . . . a new regula-tory regime and even a new regulatory body to protect consumers who use credit cards, home mortgages, car loans, and a host of other products."[38]

The economic meltdown and the election of a new president in 2008 followed decades of neglect of consumer issues. For some thirty-odd years, the public had put its trust in deregulation and the self-correcting capability of markets. It had lost its faith in the ability of legislation and government agencies to police those markets. Years of well-funded business opposition to consumer protection regulation and the pull of "Reagonomics" had contributed to these trends. Whether the public's mistrust of government—in contrast to Moss's ideas—would ultimately prevail, remained unclear.

With his close friend and ally, Congressman John Dingell of Michigan (left), 1978. Moss holds up a Firestone tire, symbol of his oversight investigation of tire blowouts. Credit: courtesy, California State University at Sacramento Archives (by the Office of Photography, U.S. House of Representatives).

With wife Jean and Republican Congressman Jim Broyhill (left), 1978. Moss and Broyhill reached across party lines to push consumer and investor protection bills to enactment. Credit: courtesy, California State University at Sacramento Archives (by the Office of Photography, U.S. House of Representatives).

*Freshman Congressman Al Gore (left) with John and Jean in 1978. In his first term, Gore elected to join Moss's Oversight and Investigations Subcommittee. Credit: courtesy, California State University at Sacramento Archives (by the Office of Photography, U.S. House of Representatives).*

*Moss greets a young Senator Ted Kennedy. Kennedy played a significant role with Moss in strengthening the Freedom of Information Act after its initial passage in 1966. Credit: courtesy, California State University at Sacramento Archives (by the Office of Photography, U.S. House of Representatives).*

# 11

# Freedom of
# Information Today
## *The Torture Memos*

*Whenever a general knowledge and sensibility have prevailed among the people, arbitrary government and every kind of oppression have lessened and disappeared in proportion.*

—John Adams, *A Dissertation on the Canon and Feudal Law*

Baghdad Central Prison stands on barren, treeless land about twenty miles west of Baghdad. It is a low, sand-colored compound. Its walls surround dusty acres of arid land. Designed and built by American engineers in 1958 for the former Iraqi government, Baghdad Central Prison was, until recently, known as Abu Ghraib.

As many as fifteen thousand common criminals and political prisoners were housed in Abu Ghraib during the régime of Saddam Hussein. Mass graves nearby of hundreds of former prisoners are evidence that Abu Ghraib will be remembered as a brutal and inhumane place under the reign of Saddam.[1]

But Abu Ghraib's permanent place in American and world history was established after Saddam's régime had been driven from power. It was taken over by the United States Army and became a military prison after the defeat of Saddam in 2003. The prison complex was rebuilt and used by American forces to hold thousands of civilian and military prisoners who were thought to be dangerous.

The commander of Abu Ghraib in 2003 was reserve Brigadier General Janis Karpinski. She was an experienced operations and intelligence officer, a business consultant in civilian life. Karpinski had never run a prison before. Most of the thirty-four hundred Army reservists she commanded had not been trained in the handling and treatment of enemy prisoners.

As a result of a complaint filed by a member of the 320th Military Police battalion suggesting that prisoners were being mistreated, a military investigation of Abu Ghraib was authorized by General Ricardo Sanchez, the senior U.S. commander in Iraq. The investigation, conducted by Major General Antonio Taguba, was highly critical of the operation of Abu Ghraib. Taguba found numerous instances of "sadistic, blatant, and wanton criminal abuses" by U.S. troops and other government "interrogators" at the prison. Taguba's report was never meant to be made public.

The report was leaked to Seymour Hersh of the *New Yorker* magazine by persons who remain unknown. The magazine published a graphic description of the treatment of prisoners at the prison. The article by Hersh, "Torture at Abu Ghraib," was published in May 2004.[2]

While that part of the story was shocking enough, no one would have known the full story of Abu Ghraib without the Freedom of Information Act that John Moss pushed through Congress in 1966.

Soon after the *New Yorker* article appeared, pictures of Iraqi inmates were leaked to the press. The pictures will forever document the horror of American actions at Abu Ghraib. They include graphic scenes of naked Iraqi men piled one upon another by Army guards, American soldiers threatening Arab prisoners with unmuzzled attack dogs, and American military police beating Iraqi prison inmates. One picture, which circulated worldwide, shows a hooded Iraqi prisoner with electrical wires attached to his fingers, toes, and genitals standing on a box. According to Army documents, the prisoner was warned that if he fell or stepped off the box, he would be electrocuted. Another picture shows a female military police officer kneeling over the dead body of an Iraqi prisoner who was apparently beaten or suffocated to death. The female officer, Specialist Sabrina Harmon, is smiling broadly and giving a "thumbs-up" sign to the camera.[3]

Major General Taguba's report and the photographs of prisoner abuse caused great embarrassment to the United States government. Brigadier General Karpinski was suspended from command. Seven low-ranking American soldiers were court-marshaled and given short jail sentences or reprimanded for their conduct at Abu Ghraib.[4]

When the *New Yorker* published its article describing the Taguba report and the American media showed photographs of U.S. soldiers abusing prisoners, the immediate reaction of the Bush administration was to reassure the public that the abuse was isolated. President Bush discussed Abu Ghraib in May 2004, saying that the "cruel and disgraceful abuses" were the work of "a small number" of soldiers, and that those responsible had already been charged with crimes.[5]

Secretary of Defense Donald Rumsfeld offered similar comments in a visit to Abu Ghraib a few days later.[6] Rumsfeld did not discuss who might have authorized or been aware of the actions of U.S. soldiers. In congressional testimony a few days later, he said, "It breaks our hearts . . . I wish we had known more, sooner . . . but we didn't."[7]

Paul Wolfowitz, then deputy secretary of defense and a primary architect of the Iraq War, added that the abuses at Abu Ghraib were the actions of a few "bad apples."[8]

Thus, as of 2004, Brigadier General Karpinski and seven low-ranking American soldiers had been disciplined. But questions remained: How could the American soldiers and officers at Abu Ghraib have come to engage in such conduct? Who authorized and ordered torture?

* * *

Two lawyers at the American Civil Liberties Union had noticed the news reports about the abuse of prisoners in American custody. Jameel Jaffer and Amrit Singh, newcomers to the ACLU staff, wondered whether there was a broader pattern of abuse and whether a Freedom of Information Act (FOIA) request could uncover it. Most of their colleagues thought a FOIA request would be useless. One of them made a joking offer to give Jaffer and Singh one dollar for every page they turned up. The two decided to attempt to determine if Abu Ghraib was the tip of an iceberg.[9]

Five years later, after thousands of hours of legal work and numerous appearances before a federal judge in the United States District Court in Manhattan, the ACLU's FOIA request and subsequent lawsuit produced over one hundred thousand pages of previously secret documents detailing how Abu Ghraib happened.

The lawsuit and the tenacity of ACLU's lawyers forced disclosure of documents showing that senior officials at the Department of Justice, the Department of Defense, and the White House authorized and approved the torture of American-held prisoners.[10] Jaffer and Singh published a book in 2007 to publicize the materials they had obtained under FOIA from government files. In the forward to the book, ACLU President Anthony Romero referred to the words of Supreme Court Justice Louis Brandeis: "Sunlight is said to be the best disinfectant." He added, "The Freedom of Information Act embodies that principle and this book embodies that hope."[11]

The documents established that a Justice Department memorandum was the main justification for the orders that led to Abu Ghraib. It was written by John Yoo, then a deputy assistant attorney general in the department's office of legal counsel. The memorandum was based on an earlier Justice Department opinion by Assistant Attorney General Jay

Bybee, who was later appointed a federal judge, justifying the harshest interrogation techniques—short of serious physical injury or death.[12]

The Yoo memorandum was sent to the Department of Defense in March 2003, just as the Army was taking control of the Abu Ghraib prison. In what the ACLU called a "disgraceful legal analysis," Yoo asserted an extremely broad view of the president's powers as commander-in-chief. He concluded that the president can, in effect, suspend the Constitution in some situations.[13] The Department of Defense used the Justice Department memoranda to approve harsh and abusive treatment of prisoners of Abu Ghraib.[14]

There are some who argue that the suspension of the United States Constitution is justified—in the case of noncitizen suspects held abroad—to protect America from another terrorist attack like September 11, 2001, at the World Trade Center. Others assert that such conduct undermines national values and violates U.S. law. Some military officials have suggested that information obtained through torture is largely misleading and useless anyway. Whatever position one takes on this question, it never would have come to public attention, never would have been debated by Congress, in the media, and by the American people—without the Freedom of Information Act that John Moss pushed through Congress.

\* \* \*

The Freedom of Information Act was eight years old in 1974. A series of oversight hearings were held between 1972 and 1974 by the Government Information Subcommittee, once chaired by Moss, but by then under the direction of Representative William Moorhead of Pennsylvania (with Moss as the senior member). The hearings had shown that FOIA was facing major bureaucratic resistance. Some examples illustrate the barriers that federal agencies had placed in the path of information disclosure:

- The cost of copying documents was as high as one dollar a page. The cost of searching for documents to copy went up to seven dollars an hour.
- Many requestors were told that their requests were not specific enough, and also were not allowed to see agency indices of available documents since they were considered exempt from disclosure.
- Some agencies used the "contamination tactic" of mixing confidential, exempt materials with other materials in the same folder, then refusing to sort out what could be released.[15]

In addition, the Supreme Court decision in *EPA v. Mink* in 1973 had erected a major barrier to the disclosure of information. The court held that an agency's claim of withholding documents based on the national defense or foreign policy exemption to the law must be sustained on the basis of a simple sworn statement from the government that the withheld materials were, in fact, important to national security or foreign affairs and thus "classified."

The court found that the original 1966 law had not given judges the power to look behind executive claims of the national security or foreign policy classifications. The *Mink* ruling thus gave the executive branch virtual carte blanche to rubber-stamp a document "classified" and prevent disclosure. All a court could do was verify that the document had actually been so classified.

Congress, by large majorities, voted in 1974 to override the *Mink* decision and give the Freedom of Information Act new force. [16]

President Gerald Ford had just taken office following the resignation of Richard Nixon in August 1974. Ford's chief of staff, appointed in September 1974, was Donald Rumsfeld, who had co-sponsored the Freedom of Information Act in 1966 with John Moss. Rumsfeld's deputy chief of staff was Richard Cheney, who became vice president of the United States under George W. Bush. Ford had taken office pledging to open up government and restore public trust after the divisive Watergate scandal had forced Nixon to resign over the break-in at Democratic headquarters and its cover-up. The White House staff, led by Cheney—and actively assisted by Antonin Scalia, later a Supreme Court Justice, but then head of the Justice Department's office of legal counsel—was determined to persuade President Ford to veto the Freedom of Information Act amendments.[17]

What the 1974 amendments proposed regarding *Mink*—and what Cheney and Scalia decided to kill—was quite simple. Courts were to be authorized to hold a hearing to determine if the claim of national security was proper. Congress was moved to act after the White House withheld tape recordings from the public and the courts of President Nixon approving the Watergate break-in. Congress was reacting as well to eight years of resistance by the executive branch to the original Act.

Led by subcommittee chairman Moorhead, ranking Republican Frank Horton, Moss, and Senators Ted Kennedy, Phil Hart, and Ed Muskie, the House and Senate acted with surprising speed. The 1974 bill was written to allow any federal court to examine *in camera*—or in private—documents that were subject to executive claims asserting national security or foreign policy as necessary reasons for exemptions from the Act. Then, the courts would decide—after a hearing if necessary—if the executive branch was right.

Cheney and Scalia led the attack on the information amendments, according to the National Security Archive. [18] They did not believe that executive power should be subject to such court review or to limitation by the federal courts or Congress. Even before the amendments had arrived at the White House, Scalia began organizing pressure on the president for a veto. Ford was not quite convinced. As a congressman, Ford had been a co-sponsor of the original Act. He wrote on a legislative briefing document just after taking office: "a veto [of the FOIA bill] presents problems. How serious are our objections?"[19]

Donald Rumsfeld's role in the FOIA veto fight is intriguing. He had been a vigorous supporter of Moss in getting the law enacted in 1966. Would he reverse himself in 1974?

Rumsfeld told me in an interview in 2010 that he was serving as Ambassador to NATO in Belgium when Ford took office in August 1974. Ford named him White House chief of staff in September, after meeting with him when he returned to the U.S. for his father's funeral.

Then, Rumsfeld said, he returned to Belgium to conclude his work as U.S. ambassador to NATO and did not return until sometime in October. He said he did not recall having any role at all in the Ford veto of the FOIA amendments.[20] Ford vetoed the amendments on October 17, but the White House's opposition to the bill already had been clear in August. Even if Rumsfeld had been involved and argued in favor of signing the FOIA amendments, which would have put him at odds with his deputy, Cheney, he would probably have been severely outnumbered within the White House.

So, most of the credit for the indefensible and politically damaging Ford veto must go to Cheney and Scalia.

According to documents obtained by the National Security Archive, most federal agencies, including the Central Intelligence Agency (CIA), already opposed the bill. But Scalia told CIA officials, "If we want to have any impact, we should move quickly to make our views known directly to the president."[21] Expecting that "neither state nor defense would be recommending a veto," Scalia followed up his memorandum by telephoning the CIA on September 26, 1974, to urge direct contact with the White House in opposition to the amendments.[22] Scalia was determined to thwart any limitation of executive power.

"The idea that a judge could overrule a decision by the president was heresy to Scalia—and even bigger heresy to the intelligence community," said Tom Blanton, director of the National Security Archive at George Washington University.[23]

There is also a telling document that Senator Kennedy's counsel, Thomas Susman, obtained from FBI files under the Freedom of Information Act. The memorandum Susman obtained, directed to the administration's Senate negotiators, said in substance: "White House legislative counsel tells us to stop meeting with Kennedy staff to work out compromises on the Freedom of Information Act bill." So it seems the White House—meaning primarily Cheney and Scalia—"wanted the bill to be as bad as possible, in order to better justify a presidential veto," according to Blanton.[24]

Two weeks later, the Freedom of Information Act amendments were sent to President Ford. The Department of Justice and most federal agencies joined the CIA in recommending a veto. But one White House staff member, Ken Cole, advised Ford that there was "significant political disadvantage to vetoing a Freedom of Information Act bill—especially just before an election—when [his] administration's theme is one of openness and candor."[25] Ford, however, followed the Cheney-Scalia advice. He vetoed the amendments on October 17, 1974, sending the bill back to the House and Senate. Ford's veto statement said the bill was "unconstitutional and unworkable." Moss had heard the same arguments eight years earlier during the fight to get the bill signed by Lyndon Johnson.

Despite the efforts of Cheney, Scalia and the White House staff, the House of Representatives easily overrode the Ford veto on November 20, 1974. The margin was overwhelming: 371 to 31. The following day, the Senate overrode by a vote of 65 to 27. The Freedom of Information Act amendments were law, despite the presidential veto. They gave new teeth to John Moss's vision.

Twenty-seven years later, Cheney, then vice president, was interviewed about his refusal to furnish Congress with the names of oil industry executives he was meeting with on official business. Cheney was running the Bush administration's Energy Task Force in 2001. Representatives from Enron and major oil and coal companies were in the meetings helping to draft the administration policy. But Cheney would not tell Congress or the press who was on the task force writing the Bush administration's energy legislation.

When ABC's Cokie Roberts asked him on a Sunday news program why the administration was making such a big issue over names of a few people from the oil industry, Cheney told her, "This is where the lawyers said we should draw the line."[26] Then the vice president and former White House staff member added, "Well, Cokie, the power of the presidency has been eroded over the last thirty years by a series of unwise compromises, and we are determined to restore the power in the presidency."[27]

\* \* \*

The 1974 amendments were a shot in the arm for John Moss's information law. Using the Freedom of Information Act, newspapers all over the United States obtained documents that allowed them to write stories with dramatic impact on their readers:

- The *Los Angeles Times* reported in 2006 on documents obtained under the act exposing FBI efforts to gather information about antiwar and environmental protestors and other activists in Colorado and elsewhere.

- The *Minneapolis Star Tribune* used FOIA information to write a story showing that the rates of salmonella bacteria contamination were more than twice the national average in twenty-two plants in Minnesota that produced ground turkey.
- Based on newly declassified documents obtained under FOIA, the *Los Angeles Times* reported that a secret U.S. military program funded publication of favorable newspaper articles about the Iraq War.
- A study reported in the *New York Sun*, based on data disclosed following a lawsuit under the Act, showed that thousands of people had been wrongly identified as immigration law violators and concluded that 82 percent could not be confirmed as having violated any law.
- The *New York Times* reported that, according to a government memorandum, National Security Agency officers deliberately skewed information given to policymakers. The distorted information falsely suggested that North Vietnamese ships had attacked American destroyers in the Gulf of Tonkin, triggering the Vietnam War.[28]

\* \* \*

Even with the 1974 amendments, the Freedom of Information Act—John Moss's 1966 triumph—was not a complete victory. Moss said it was "a never-ending battle."[29] The lawsuit won by the American Civil Liberties Union to obtain the torture documents continued for more than six years. The difficulties involved suggest that, in the case of some FOIA requests, only skilled and determined advocacy—and major funding—can obtain the release of important government documents. There are, however, hundreds of thousands of FOIA requests each year that are granted without opposition by the government.

In 2001, government secrecy became more heavy-handed. During the administration of George W. Bush, Attorney General John Ashcroft issued a memorandum that attempted to reverse the Act's presumption in favor of public disclosure originally enacted in 1966.[30] The Ashcroft memorandum, issued immediately after the terrorist attack on the World Trade Center, encouraged federal agencies to resist information requests in order to assist in "safeguarding national security and enhancing the effectiveness of law enforcement agencies." For some reason, the attorney general added the seemingly unrelated direction to also protect "sensitive business information." Ashcroft went further in undermining open government and attempting to reverse the Freedom of Information Act. His memorandum advised federal agencies, "You can be assured that the Department of Justice will defend your decisions unless they lack a sound legal basis."[31] The memorandum offered a lot of room for denial of legitimate information requests by government lawyers.

Despite public fear of another terrorist attack, Ashcroft's memorandum was widely criticized.[32] It was reversed by President Barack Obama in 2009 on his first day in office.[33]

Toward the end of President George W. Bush's administration, there was some change of direction. Congress passed the Open Government Act in 2008,[34] which was jointly sponsored by Senators Patrick Leahy of Vermont, chairman of the Senate Judiciary Committee, and John Cornyn of Texas, the ranking Republican.

The Open Government Act addressed the problem of the executive branch's periodic reluctance to comply with the purposes of the Freedom of Information Act: it created an independent "ombudsman" within the National Archives and Records Adminstration to mediate citizen disputes with government agencies over information requests; it set up a system for public tracking of the status of information requests; and when a federal agency improperly denied a request, it allows a requester to recover legal costs from the government more easily.

President Bush signed the Open Government Act in January 2008. The Society of Professional Journalists called it an "open government victory," and thanked the president for signing the law. The Freedom of Information Act, said the journalists, is one of the strongest tools Americans have to hold elected officials accountable.[35]

Significant delays continue to plague members of the press and public who attempt to obtain information under the Freedom of Information Act. The tension between executive branch instincts against disclosure and greater disclosure of public information goes on. Yet the successes of the Act far outweigh its shortcomings.

The law has been a major factor in the passage of similar laws in more than sixty nations around the world. When it was enacted, the United States law was an oddity. A few nations, such as Sweden and Finland, had laws affirming a right to "official documents." The Freedom of Information Act gave the public potentially broader access by using the term government "records."

The Act has served as a model for antisecrecy advocates in many countries, yet many governments were at first slow to replicate the U.S. law. It was not until the late 1980s that more nations began to adopt freedom of information laws, but the pace became remarkable. Japan, the United Kingdom, and nations in Eastern Europe recently liberated from Soviet domination, were among the leaders.[36]

More recently, Mexico enacted a freedom-of-information law in 2002. Vicente Fox was the first opposition candidate to win the Mexican presidency after seventy years of one-party rule by the Revolutionary People's Party (PRP). The U.S. press had used FOIA to obtain documents from State Department files showing extensive corruption and other unprosecuted criminal activities in Mexico under the PRP. After his election, Fox pressed the Mexican legislature to pass a freedom-of-information law. It responded.

The Mexican statute may in fact go beyond American law. Mexico's Freedom of Information Act creates a government information commission with power to override objections to the release of information by a federal agency. The only appeal from the government information commission's decisions is to the president. The process appears to offer an easier path than filing a Freedom of Information Act lawsuit under the United States statute—depending on the makeup of the information commission and who fills the president's chair.

\* \* \*

Few could argue that there are no real national security secrets. Over the decades, the debate has centered on what is truly necessary to be kept secret in balancing the best interests of the nation. In times of national crisis, security classification of documents—and thus nonaccessibility—grows dramatically. By 2005, four years after the the World Trade Center attack, the number of government decisions to classify documents had grown by 14.2 million in a single year. The process of declassifying documents had been slowed, and those numbers started declining. The decade ending in 2005—which included the government's reaction to the 2001 terrorist attack—*added* 100 million classified documents to the total.[37]

Tom Blanton, director of the National Security Archive at George Washington University, concedes that there "is a real national security interest." But he notes that, "it has been stretched—in both the national security arena and the executive privilege arena. It should be the size of a bikini, and it's become the size of a burka."[38]

Some would assert that Blanton's interpretation is too narrow and that the executive branch should have broad, perhaps unreviewable, authority to withhold information. Scalia and Cheney might be in that number, but Rumsfeld might not be among them. In an interview in 2010, Rumsfeld said, "FOIA is a good law. The American people are required to participate in guiding the course of their country. . . . They do that better if they have information available to them about what is taking place in their government. It may at times be irritating to government agencies. There are some hard decisions about government secrecy in the interest of national security that have to be made under it. It is a balance."[39]

The conflict over the scope of the Freedom of Information Act is not likely to be resolved soon. Sometimes the trend appears to be toward a more open government; at other times, toward increased secrecy. It is a debate and a process that would never have started without John Moss's legislative achievement.

"Nothing inspires greater journalistic confidence than the words 'according to public records,' when attached to an important story," said Jay Smith, president of Cox Newspapers, Inc. "And I am hard-pressed to think of anything that has advanced the accessibility and usability of public records the way the Freedom of Information Act has."[40]

"Moss lit a spark . . . that secrecy had gone too far. It was not just bad for citizens. It was actually bad for the government as well," said Blanton.[41]

\* \* \*

Brigadier General Karpinski would probably agree. She was demoted, retired from the Army, and sent home. She maintains that she and her troops at Abu Ghrarb were following written interrogation guidelines approved by top administration and Defense Department officials. Karpinski says she was a scapegoat, that top officials knew all about what was going on at Abu Ghraib.[42]

General Taguba who investigated the abuses at Abu Ghraib would probably agree, too. He received a telephone call from General Richard Cody, the Army's vice chief of staff in early 2006. Cody fired Taguba, ordering him to resign within a year. He offered no reason. "They always shoot the messenger," Taguba said.[43]

Former Secretary of Defense Donald Rumsfeld said that the day the Abu Ghraib scandal broke was his worst day as secretary of defense.[44] Rumsfeld's responsibility for the events at Abu Ghraib became public because of the Freedom of Information Act he helped John Moss enact forty years earlier.

*Abu Ghraib prison near Baghdad, Iraq. The Freedom of Information Act was instrumental in obtaining the facts about who authorized the torture of Iraqi prisoners. Credit: Courtesy, United States Marine Corps/Wikipedia.*

*John and Jean, together as usual, in their Washington, D.C. townhouse toward the end of his congressional career. Credit: Courtesy, Moss family.*

# Epilogue

The consumer revolution that defined John Moss's career is with us today. The laws, the consumer protection agencies, the change in business attitudes toward consumer opinion remain its legacy. The gains of that era have at times been curtailed—but they have never been erased. Consumer programs from that time have been slashed and slowed—but they have never been repealed.

Americans can see the impact of the consumer revolution every day. It is visible in the stunning reduction of highway deaths and injuries since 1966; in the millions of consumer products—from foods, to automobiles, to toys—that are recalled every year for safety reasons under government direction; in the nutrutional and other labeling now required on food products; in the automobile crash and damageability information available from the Department of Transportation and U.S. car dealers. It can be measured in the hundreds of thousands of government responses each year—sometimes slow, sometimes incomplete—to Freedom of Information Act requests by American citizens.

The effects of the consumer revolution in the United States can also be seen in the more than sixty nations around the world that have adopted freedom of information laws based on ours, in the new worldwide awareness of the dangers of toxic substances in consumer products and the environment and in an apparent determination of Congress to fix the Toxic Substances Control Act, the flawed law that was enacted at the close of the consumer decade.

The consumer revolution of that era joins earlier waves of consumer progress, from Theodore Roosevelt's progressive movement to Franklin

Roosevelt's New Deal, to John F. Kennedy's Consumer Bill of Rights. But its story is far from complete. There is unfinished business.

An issue that John Moss was deeply concerned about years ago has only grown worse over time: the amount of money in politics—contributions to political campaigns and fees to an army of highly paid lobbyists. As Moss said after leaving Congress, too much money corrupts the political process.

Money can also drown out the consumer's voice. How can consumer interests be met when a narrow majority of the Supreme Court, among others, has equated corporate advertising and cash with the hallowed *individual* right of free speech under the First Amendment to the Constitution?

Beyond political money, there are other forces weakening the ability to make the case for consumers. Can consumers be heard when the press that gave them a powerful voice in the consumer decade seems to be slowly withering? When labor unions are weakened as a political balance to business interests?

In time, these questions will be answered. As in the consumer eras of the past, generations of Americans will devise new solutions to the everyday problems they face.

Consumers have great power at their disposal. Their consumption fuels the American economy. Their votes elect its leaders. Without consumer spending and consumer assent, our economy slows and our political system withers. Consumers have only to decide, once again, to use their power.

There were some signs at the start of the twenty-first-century's second decade that a modest consumer revival might be under way. Lack of government oversight of the stock market and a new wave of speculation brought on the "Great Recession" of 2008 that cost ordinary Americans billions of hard-earned dollars. It may have shocked some people out of their antigovernment, antiregulation myopia. The BP oil disaster in the Gulf of Mexico may have further demonstrated the need for government safety regulation, at least over oil well drilling companies. The excesses that these events demonstrated and the pain they caused in so many lives served to remind Americans that they need an effective government.

In 2008, Congress renewed Moss's Consumer Product Safety Act. The rewrite improved on the original law in several ways. Two unique concepts were added in the new statute, which was triggered by public outrage over deaths of children from unsafe toys and children's products, such as cribs. The press, smaller now and less able to grab the public's attention, nonetheless covered the issue to great effect. It energized politicians enough to get them to add new concepts to the consumer product safety law.

Congress wrote and President George W. Bush signed an amendment to the Consumer Product Safety Act that authorized state attorneys general to help the federal government enforce federal safety regulations. The law included more funding for the largely forgotten Consumer Product Safety Commission. And it added a new program to help consumers help themselves in the marketplace: a consumer databank of information on the safety of products available to the public. If implemented effectively and used wisely, the broadened authority of state attorneys general and the consumer databank will surely suggest other creative approaches to consumer protection in the future.

In 2010 President Obama looked back to John Moss's Consumer Product Safety Commission to propose a Consumer Financial Protection Bureau that would assist consumers by regulating credit card terms, loans, and mortgages. It may have taken a near depression to suggest to Americans that a system of competitive business and effective government oversight is good for them.

\* \* \*

John Moss died in California in 1997 of complications from asthma—the disease that first affected him in Utah so many years before and plagued him throughout his life. When he retired from Congress in 1978 and returned to California, Ward Sinclair wrote in the *Washington Post*, "By the time Moss left Washington, he had achieved something that others can only lay spurious claim to: an imprint on the way life is lived in the United States; an imprint on the way government governs"—words that could serve as his obituary.[1]

Donald Rumsfeld, looking back at Moss's role in the enactment of the Freedom of Information Act, said, "If you think about it, most members of Congress do not end up with legislation that they craft, sponsor and eventually achieve. Now, decades later, it still stands the test of time. Clearly, it is a mark of his success as a legislator."[2]

Californian Henry Waxman, who rose to become chairman of the House Commerce Committee thirty years after Moss left Washington, recalled when Moss died,

> I was privileged to begin my career in Congress as a member of the Subcommittee on Oversight and Investigations. . . . John Moss chaired that subcommittee. . . . He used his power to make government programs carry out the laws and serve the public. . . . I consider myself lucky to have had the opportunity to serve with him. He has been gone from this House for many years, but the public that he championed continues to benefit because of his work and accomplishments. We would all be proud to leave such a legacy.[3]

The history of Moss's consumer information revolution will remain a pathway for dealing with the unfinished business of the future. No other American leader of his generation so clearly epitomized a deep and continuing commitment to the common man. Perhaps Moss said it best himself: "Sometimes you have to embrace controversy, sometimes you have to take on a fight."[4]

# Notes

## 1. TROUBLED ROOTS

1. Jerry Wymore (Moss's District Representative), interview by Author, December 14, 1997, 10 (hereafter cited as *Wymore interview*).

2. *Wymore interview*, 10.

3. William W. Stiles, "How a Community Met a Disaster: Yuba City Flood, December 1955," *American Academy of Political and Social Science, Annals*, 1957, 160–69.

4. *Wymore interview*, 11.

5. "John E. Moss Papers, 1953–1978," Sacramento: Department of Special Collections and University Archives, The Library, California State University, box 776, folder 55 (hereafter cited as *Moss Papers*).

6. *Moss Papers*, box 776, folder 55.

7. John E. Moss, interview by Author, March 16–18, 1996, 14 (hereafter cited as *John Moss interview, 1996*).

8. "Joe Hill (1879–1915)," American Federation of Labor and Congress of Industrial Organizations, http://www.aflcio.org/aboutus/history/history/hill.cfm.

9. *John Moss interview, 1996*, 104.

10. Steven M. Avella, *Sacramento: Indomitable City* (Chicago: Arcadia Publishing, 2003).

11. Leo Rennert (former Washington Bureau Chief, *Sacramento Bee*), interview by Author, October 29, 2007, 3.

12. T. Severson, *Sacramento: An Illustrated History*. (San Francisco: California Historical Society, 1973), 76, 125–27.

13. Avella, *Indomitable City*, 90–94.

14. John F. Burns and Lori Parks, *Sacramento: Gold Rush Legacy, Metropolitan Destiny* (Dallas: Heritage Media, 1999), 98-113.

15. Avella, *Indomitable City*, 98.

16. Burns, *Gold Rush Legacy, Metropolitan Destiny*, 98–113.

17. Avella, *Indomitable City*, 100–101.

18. Burns, *Gold Rush Legacy, Metropolitan Destiny*, 101.

19. Avella, *Indomitable City*, 77.

20. *John Moss interview*, 1996, 16.

21. *John Moss interview*, 1996, 5.

22. *John Moss interview*, 1996, 16.

23. *John Moss interview*, 1996, 107–8.

24. "Letter from Lt. Governor-Elect Ellis E. Patterson, December 15, 1938 to John Moss," *Moss papers*, box 778, folder 65.

25. *John Moss interview*, 1996, 19.

26. Allison Moss, interview by Author, September 23, 2005, 18 (hereafter cited as *Allison Moss interview*).

27. *Allison Moss interview*, 34–35.

28. *Allison Moss interview*, 18.

29. *Allison Moss interview*, 9.

30. Albert S. Rodda, letter to Author, January 19, 1998.

31. Editorials. *The Sacramento Bee*, May 26, 1948, and October 20, 1948, *Moss Papers*, box 776, folder 3.

32. *Sacramento Union*, October 24, 1948, *Moss Papers*, box 776, folder 3.

33. State of California, Statement of Vote, General Election, State Assembly 1948, 12.

34. California State Archives, Oral History Program, "Interview with John E. Moss," October 3, 17, 24, and November 2, 1989, 149–50 (hereafter cited as *California Oral History*).

## 2. DANGEROUS GROUND

1. Rep. John D. Dingell, interview by Author, January 29, 2009, 2, (hereafter cited as *Dingell interview, 2009*).

2. *The Sacramento Bee*, March 25 1948, "John E. Moss Papers, 1953-1978"; Sacramento: Department of Special Collections and University Archives, The Library, California State University, box 776, folder 3 (hereafter cited as *Moss Papers*).

3. *The Sacramento Bee*, October 29, 1948, *Moss Papers*, box 776, folder 3.

4. California State Archives, Oral History Program, "Interview with John E. Moss," October 3, 1989, 105 (hereafter cited as *California Oral History*).

5. Arthur H. R. Samish and Bob Thomas, *The Secret Boss of California, the Life and High Times of Art Samish* (New York: Crown Publishers, 1971), 45–46.

6. *The Sacramento Bee*, August 15, 1949, 1; *Moss Papers*, box 776, folder 1.

7. California Oral History, 145.

8. Ibid., 140–45.

9. Ibid., 145.

10. Ibid., 105, 136.

11. Ibid., 134, 150.

12. Ibid., 112, 140.

13. Ibid., 151.

14. Ibid., 150.

15. Ibid., 150.

16. Ibid., 168.

17. "Election of Moss to Assembly is Urged by Ex Solon," *The Sacramento Bee*, October 25, 1948, *Moss Papers*.

18. *California Oral History*, 112, 140.

19. Ibid., 116–60.

20. *The Sacramento Bee*, October 5, 1951; *Moss Papers*, box 779, folder 7.

21. *California Oral History*, 139, 180.

22. Ibid., 114.

23. Ibid., 150.

24. Ibid., 135.

25. Ibid., 124.

## 3. I WENT TO BED A LOSER

1. John Moss, interview by Author, March 16–18, 1996, 22 (hereafter cited as *John Moss interview*, 1996).

2. *John Moss interview*, 1996, 22.

3. California State Archives, Oral History Program, "Interview with John E. Moss," October 3, 1989, 196 (hereafter cited as *California Oral History*).

4. *California Oral History*, 196.

5. *California Oral History*, 181, 182; *Moss Papers*, box 776, folder 22; *Woodland Democrat*, October 10, 1951. The population of Sacramento City and Sacramento County in 1952 was two hundred eighty thousand. By 2008 the population had grown to 1.3 million.

6. "Campaign Expenses, 1950," *Moss Papers*, box 776, folder 24.

7. *Colusa Sun Herald*, December 3, 1951; *Moss Papers*, box 776, folder 66; *Congressional General News Series*.

8. Burton R. Brazil, "The 1950 Elections in California," ed. Joseph P. Harris, *The Western Political Quarterly* 4, no. 1 (Mar. 1951): 67.

9. Jerry Wymore (Moss's District Representative), interview by Author, December 14, 1997, 8 (hereafter cited as *Wymore interview*).

10. *Moss Papers*, box 776, folder 1.

11. *John Moss interview*, 1996, 93.

12. *California Oral History*, 183.

13. Ibid., 95.

14. *Wymore interview*, 16

15. *Moss Papers*, box 779, folder 17.

16. Jean Moss, interview by Author, December 13–14, 1997, 1–3 (hereafter cited as *Jean Moss interview*).

17. Ibid., 3.

18. Ibid., 1.

19. Ibid., 1.

20. Ibid., 2.

21. Ibid., 3.

22. "Statement by John E. Moss, Jr. (Democratic Nominee for Congress, Third Congressional District), September 21, 1952," *Moss Papers*, box 276, folder 2.

23. "Speech by Assemblyman John E. Moss (Democratic Nominee for Congress) before the League of Women's Voters, Marysville, CA, October 14, 1952," *Moss Papers*, box 276, folder 1.

24. *Wymore interview*, 5.

25. Ibid., 6

26. Ibid., 6

27. *John Moss interview*, 1996, 31; *California Oral History*, 196.

28. Ivan Hinderaker, "The 1952 Elections in California," *The Western Political Quarterly* vol. 6, no. 1 (March, 1953): 102.

## 4. THE PEOPLE'S RIGHT TO KNOW

1. Carl Bernstein, *Loyalties* (New York: Simon & Schuster, 1989), 93.

2. Ibid., 93.

3. *Congressional Quarterly Almanac*, 1953 ( Washington, DC), 69.

4. Stewart McClure, Senate Oral History, U.S. Senate Library (December 16, 1982), 1, 41, 50.

5. Bernstein, *Loyalties*, 253.

6. John E. Moss, interview by Author, March 16–18, 1996, 14 (hereafter cited as *John Moss interview, 1996*); Jerry Wymore (Moss's District Representative), interview by Author, December 14, 1997, 9 (hereafter cited as *Wymore interview*).

7. "Tidelands Oil Controversy," http://www.encyclopedia.com/doc/1O184-TidelandsOilControversy.html (hereafter cited as *"Tidelands Oil Controversy"*); see also Ernest R. Bartley, *The Tidelands Oil Controversy* (Austin: University of Texas Press, 1953).

8. *"Tidelands Oil Controversy"*.

9. California State Archives, Oral History Program, "Interview with John E. Moss," October 1989 (hereafter cited as *California Oral History*).

10. *John Moss interview, 1996*, 87.

11. Ibid., 64.

12. Ibid., 60.

13. Ibid., 55–56.

14. Ibid., 149.

15. Ibid., 149.

16. Ibid., 60. Moss served as deputy whip from 1961 until 1971, when Carl Albert (D-Ok.) became the Speaker. He did not seek to continue as deputy whip after his confrontation with the White House and the House leadership over the Freedom of Information Act and the Vietnam War in the mid 1960s. He said he wanted to pursue his own agenda and that he was not asked to resign.

17. Bruce Ladd, *Crisis in Credibility* (New York: The New American Library, 1968), 188.

18. bid., 189.

19. *California Oral History*, 90.

20. Ladd, *Crisis in Credibility*, 190.

21. Kent Cooper, *The Right to Know: An Exposition of the Evils of News Suppression and Propaganda* (New York: Farrar, Strauss & Cudahy, 1956), xii–xiii; quoted in Herbert N. Foerstel, *Freedom of Information and the Right to Know* (Westport, Connecticut: Greenwood Press, 1999), 15.

22. Foerstel, *Right to Know*, 15.

23. Ibid., 16.

24. Harold L. Cross, *The People's Right to Know* (New York: Columbia University Press, 1953), xiii.

25. Ibid., 197.

26. Ibid., 132.

27. Foerstel, *Right to Know*, 20.

28. Ibid., 20.

29. Ibid.

30. Ibid., 21.

31. Ladd, *Crisis in Credibility*, 190.

32. Ibid.

33. Foerstel, *Right to Know*, 22.

34. John Moss interview, 1969, 7–9; Ladd, *Crisis in Credibility*, 190.

35. Ladd, *Crisis in Credibility*, 190.

36. Ibid., 191.

## 5. THE FREEDOM OF INFORMATION ACT

1. Ladd, *Crisis in Credibility*, 205; The John E. Moss Foundation, Freedom of Information Pages, George Kennedy, *How Americans Got Their Right to Know*, http://www.johnemossfoundation.org/foi/kennedy.htm; John E. Moss, interview by Author, March 16–18, 1996, 7-9 (hereafter cited as *John Moss Interview, 1996*).

2. Ladd, *Crisis in Credibility*, 206.

3. *John Moss interview*, 1996, 9.

4. John E. Moss Foundation, Freedom of Information Pages, George Berdes, "Interview with Congressman John E. Moss, April 13, 1965," http://www.johnemossfoundation.org/foi/fogis.htm (used with permission of the Marquette University Press), 7.

5. *Hearings on Federal Public Records Law, Before the House, Committee on Government Operations, Subcommittee on Foreign Operations and Government Information,* 89th Cong., 1st sess., 1 (March 30, 1965) (hereafter cited as *House Hearings*).

6. *House Hearings*, 2.

7. Grace-Ellen McCann (Professor, City College of New York), "An Examination of the Conditions Surrounding the Passage of the 1966 Freedom of Information Act," *Open Government, A Journal on Freedom of Information* (April 24, 2007): 9.

8. McCann, *Open Government*, 10.

9. *House Hearings*, 5.

10. Ibid., 16.

11. Ibid., 5.

12. Ibid., 6.

13. Ibid., 17.

14. Ladd, *Crisis in Credibility*, 208.

15. Cross, *The People's Right to Know*, viii.

16. Ibid., xiii.

17. Ibid.

18. "Congress and the Nation," Chapter 17, Investigations, *Congressional Quarterly Service*, 1956, 1738 (hereafter cited as *Congressional Quarterly Service, 1956*).

19. Ibid.

20. Ibid.

21. Availability of Information from Federal Departments and Agencies, H.R. Rep. No. 2947, at 93 (1956), 84th Cong, 2d Sess. (hereafter cited as *House Report 2947*).

22. *Congressional Quarterly Service*, 1956, 1738.

23. Ibid.

24. Ibid., 1739.

25. *House Report 2947*, 93.

26. *House Report 2947*, 93; the report was unanimous. However, ranking member Clare Hoffman (R-Michigan) filed additional views that were critical of possible legislation regarding public and congressional access to federal records. Hoffman stated "the right of the citizen, of the Congress, to be advised of the information possessed by the executive departments is subject to several limitations, as is the right to a free press, to free speech, to freedom of petition, and every other right guaranteed by the Constitution. There must be a reason for the exercise of the right. The right is limited by the fact that the Constitution grants to the President certain Authority, imposes upon him certain duties. Acting in performance of those duties, within the scope of the authority granted, he is under no obligation to explain or justify his acts, either to individuals or to the Congress."

27. Foerstel, *Freedom of Information and the Right to Know*, 35.

28. Clarifying and Protecting the Right of the Public to Information, H.R. Rep. No. 1497, at 2, 6 (1966).

29. *John Moss interview*, 1996, 8, 9.

30. "Letter from James S. Pope (Executive Editor, Louisville Courier Journal) to Rep. William L. Dawson," file 2 of 2, 84A–F.7.23, RG 233, National Archives.

31. Donald M. Rumsfeld, interview by Author, April 12, 2010 (cited as *Rumsfeld interview*), 2–3.

32. Ladd, *Crisis in Credibility*, 207.

33. Ibid.

34. Ibid., 208.

35. *Washington Post Times-Herald* (March 1, 1965), A-17, ProQuest Historical Newspapers, http://www.proquest.com/en-US/.

36. Benny L. Kass, former counsel, House Committee on Government Operations, interview by Author, September 18, 2007, 5 (hereafter cited as *Kass interview*).

37. Ibid., 6.

38. Ibid.

39. Ladd, *Crisis in Credibility*, 203.

40. Ibid., 201–2.

41. Ibid., 202.

42. Ibid., 203.

43. Ibid.

44. Biographical Directory of the United States Congress, http://biograde. congress.gov/scripts/biodisplay.pl?index=c000264.

45. Jewish Virtual Library, http://www.jewishvirtuallibrary.org/jsource/ biography/Celler.html.

46. Ibid.

47. Ibid.

48. Spaticus Educational, http://www.spartacus.schoolnet.co.uk/USAceller. htm.

49. Emanuel Celler, *You Never Leave Brooklyn: The Autobiography of Emanuel Celler* (New York: The John Day Company, 1953), 29.

50. *Kass interview*, 9–10, 15. House Speaker Tip O'Neill found Celler "difficult to deal with . . . arrogant and stubborn," which if true did not seem to apply to his relations with Moss. William Novak, *Man of the House, The Life and Political Memories of Speaker Tip O'Neill* (New York: Random House, 1987), 249.

51. Ibid., 10.

52. Ibid., 11.

53. Ibid., 12; see also Hearings, Before the Senate Subcommittee on Administrative Practice and Procedure, Committee on the Judiciary (June 7, 1973), 126 (testimony of Benny L. Kass). Kass testified, "I don't think it was a sellout, but in any event, it was really the price of getting the bill. It was my legal advice to both the chairman of this committee and the chairman, Congressman Moss, that the legislative history only interprets and does not vitiate in any way the legislation and that the legislation was strong and was there."

54. "Journalism Under Fire", speech to the Society of Journalism Professionals" (September 11, 2004), http://www.commondreams.org/views.

55. Statement of President Lyndon B. Johnson on signing the Freedom of Information Act (July 4, 1966), Lyndon B. Johnson Library, Special Files, 1927–73, Statements of Lyndon B. Johnson, box 195.

56. *Rumsfeld Interview*, 5, 13.

57. J. Edward Murray, article in the *Bulletin of the American Society of Newspaper Editors*, no. 500 (August 1, 1966), 3–6.

58. *John Moss interview, 1996*, 98, 100, 101; California State Archives, Oral History Program, "Interview with John E. Moss," October 3, 17, 24, and November 2, 1989, 204.

59. *John Moss interview, 1996*, 7; George Kennedy, "How Americans Got Their Right to Know," The John E. Moss Foundation, Freedom of Information Pages, 5, http://www.johnemossfoundation.org/kennedy.htm.

60. Ibid.

61. House of Representatives, *Congressional Record* (June 20, 1966), statement of the Honorable John E. Moss, http://www.thejohnemossfoundation.org/foi/ cr_JEM.htm.

## 6. THE CONSUMER PRODUCT SAFETY ACT

1. Benny L. Kass, former counsel, House Committee on Government Operations, interview by Author, September 18, 2007, 5 (hereafter cited as *Kass interview*).

2. Ibid.

3. Ibid.

4. Michael Pertschuk, *Revolt Against Regulation: The Rise and Pause of Consumerism* (Berkeley: University of California Press, 1982), 31 (hereafter cited as "consumerism").

5. Ibid.. 32.

6. Eric Pryne, "Maggie's Legacy is More than Money," *Seattle Times*, May 22, 1989 (qtd. in S. Doc. 101–13, 1990).

7. "Ex-Senator Warren Magnuson Dies at 84," *Washington Post*, May 21, 1989, D6 (qtd. in S. Doc. 101–13, 1990).

8. Shelby Scates, *Warren G. Magnuson and the Shaping of Twentieth-Century America* (Seattle: University of Washington Press: 1998), 80, 339–141.

9 Ibid., 205.

10. Ibid., 207–8.

11. "Congressional Elections 1946–1996," *Congressional Quarterly* (Washington, DC, 1966), 99. The 1962 totals were: Magnuson 491,365 (52.1 percent), Christensen 446,204 (47.3 percent). Magnuson had won by 685,565 (61.1 percent) to 436,652 (38.9 percent) over his Republican opponent in the prior, 1958 election. His margin increased sharply again in 1968, after he began pushing consumer protection legislation.

12. Ralph Nader, qtd. in Scates, *Warren G. Magnuson*, 209.

13. Eric Pryne, *Seattle Times*, May 22, 1989 (qtd. in S. Doc. 101–13, 19).

14. "Honor and Lunch," *New Yorker*, July 11, 1959, 20–21.

15. Scates, *Warren G. Magnuson*, 213.

16. "Warren G. Magnuson," *American National Biography*, American Council of Learned Societies, vol. 14 (New York: Oxford University Press, 1999), 325–26.

17. Scates, *Warren G. Magnuson*, 225, Edward Merlis (former Staff Director, Senate Commerce Committee), interview by Author, September 16, 2009, 10.

18. Qtd. in Scates, *Warren G. Magnuson*, 216.

19. Scates, *Warren G. Magnuson*, 220, and Pertschuk, *Consumerism*, 13–36.

20. Pertschuk, *Consumerism*, 6, 22.

21. *Kass interview*, 18.

22. Drew Pearson, "House Group Listens to Auto Lobby," *Washington Post Times-Herald*, June 24, 1966, B15, ProQuest Historical Newspapers, http://www.proquest.com/en-US/.

23. *Congress and the Nation*, vol. 2, 1965-68 (Congressional Quarterly Service, Washington, DC), 803.

24. Pertschuk, *Consumerism*, 41–43.

25. J. O'Reilly, Food and Drug Administration (Colorado Springs: Shephard's McGrawHill, 1979). See sections 3.01–5 for an overview history of federal food and drug regulation.

26. Michael R. Lemov, *Consumer Product Safety Commission Regulatory Manual Series* (Colorado Springs: Shephard's McGraw Hill, 1981), sections 1.03-7.

27. Final Report of the National Commission on Product Safety (June 1970, Library of Congress No.76606753), 20, (hereafter cited as *NCPS Report*).

28. Ibid., 21.

29. Ibid., 17.

30. Ibid., 12.

31. Letter from John E. Moss to Harley O. Staggers, February 28, 1969, "John E. Moss Papers, 1953–1978," Sacramento: Department of Special Collections and University Archives, The Library, California State University, box 779, folder 27 (hereafter cited as *Moss Papers*).

32. Letter from John E. Moss, John D. Dingell, Paul G. Rogers to Harley O. Staggers, March 4, 1969, *Moss Papers*, box 779, folder 27.

33. Letter from Harley O. Staggers to Reps. Moss, Dingell, Rogers, March 5, 1969, *Moss Papers*, box 779, folder 27.

34. *NCPS Report*, 12–36.

35. *New York Times*, January 31, 1972, 40. ProQuest Historical Newspapers, http://www.proquest.com/en-US/.

36. "Consumer Product Safety Agency Created," *CQ Almanac*, 1972, 141.

37. *Hearings, Before the House Subcommittee on Commerce and Finance on Bills to Protect Consumers Against Unreasonable Risk of Injury from Hazardous Products*, (testimony of the National Association of Manufacturers 944, American Gas Association 763, Electronic Industries Association 858, Chamber of Commerce of the United States 1316), H.R. Doc. 92–59 at 944, 763, 858, 1316 (1972).

38. James Thomas Broyhill, Biographical Directory of the United States Congress, September 2008, http://bioguide.congress.gov/.

39. James Thomas Broyhill, "Candidate Biographies, 1986," *Associated Press*, Associated Press Political Service.

40. "Senator Jim Broyhill, Personal Biography," May 1, 2008, furnished to the Author by former Senator Broyhill.

41. Rep. John D. Dingell (Chairman Emeritus House Commerce Committee), interview by Author, January 29, 2009, 9.

42. Alan Ehrenhalt, ed., *Politics in America: Members of Congress in Washington and at Home* (Washington, DC: Congressional Quarterly Books, 1984), 1142.

43. Alan Ehrenhalt, ed., *Politics in America, Members of Congress in Washington and at Home*, 3d ed. (Washington, DC: Congressional Quarterly Books, 1986), 1156.

44. "Truer Blue," Time/CNN, Prime Archive/Partnership, May 5, 1986, http://www.time.com/.

45. *New York Times*, October 6, 1962, 89, ProQuest Historical Newspapers, http://www.proquest.com/en-US/.

46. Ibid.

47. *Washington Post Times-Herald*, October 5, 1972, H7, ProQuest Historical Newspapers, http://www.proquest.com/en-US/.

48. *Washington Post Times-Herald*, October 14, 1972, A1, ProQuest Historical Newspapers, http://www.proquest.com/en-US/.

49. *Public Papers of the Presidents of the United States*, "Richard Nixon, 1968–72," 379, Statement About Decision to Sign 37 Bills; "The Consumer Product Safety Act," http://www.presidency.ucsb.edu/ws/index.php ?pid=3662&st=&st1= (accessed April 13, 2010); see also *Washington Post Times-Herald*, October 29, 1972, A1, ProQuest Historical Newspapers, http://www.proquest.com/en-US/.

50. Morton Mintz, ". . . milestone for product safety," *Washington Post*, December 9, 1972, A23; John D. Morris, ". . . regarded as a landmark in consumer protection . . . ," *New York Times*, October 29, 1972, 1.


## 7. REVIVING THE FEDERAL TRADE COMMISSION

1. House Committee on Interstate and Foreign Commerce, Subcommittee on Commerce and Finance, September 28, 1971, 98 (testimony of Rep. John Dingell).

2. 120 Cong. Rec. H31316–23, (September 17, 1974) (statement of Rep. John E. Moss) (hereafter cited as *John Moss statement*).

3. See *Dr. Miles Medical Co. v. J. D. Parkinsons Creative Products, Inc.* 220 U.S. 373(1911); *but see Leegan v. PSKS* 123 Sup. Ct. 2705 (2007) where the Supreme Court reversed itself, holding that resale price maintenance is unlawful only under *some* circumstances. State attorney generals continue to prosecute retail price maintenance under state antitrust laws.

4. Michael Pertschuk, *Revolt Against Regulation: The Rise and Pause of Consumerism* (Berkeley: University of California Press, 1982), 9.

5. It is not clear who first coined the term "sleepy old lady" to describe the FTC, but as demonstrated by the Nader and American Bar Association reports of 1969, it was well deserved.

6. Pertschuk, *Consumerism*, 8–9.

7. Cong. Rec. H31316 (September 17, 1974), (statement of John Moss), John Moss's floor statement used the current Consumer Price Index of 11.9 percent to support the need for the legislation (hereafter cited as *John Moss floor statement*).

8. Nord was acting chair of the Consumer Product Safety Commission from 2006 to 2009, during the presidency of George W. Bush. She continued to serve as a commissioner after the Bush administration ended. Her actions as acting chair, in opposing new legislative authority for the CPSC, caused the chairs of the House and Senate Commerce committees, as well as the primary sponsors of the 2008 amendments that gave new powers to the CPSC to accuse her of "grossly mishandling" the law's implementation and to calling for her replacement by President Obama. See Letter from Chairmen Jay Rockefeller, Henry Waxman, et al. to President Barack Obama, February 3, 2009.

9. David Schmeltzer (former Attorney, National Highway Traffic Safety Administration, 1966; Director of Compliance, Consumer Product Safety Commission 1972–98), interview by Author, January 16, 2009.

10. Edward Finch Cox, Robert C. Fellmeth, and John E. Schulz, preface by Ralph Nader, *The Nader Report on the Federal Trade Commission* (New York: Richard W. Barron, 1969).

11. Ibid., 1.

12. Ibid., 26.

13. Ibid., 22.

14. Ibid., VII.

15. Ibid., 221.

16. American Bar Association, *Report of the Commission to Study the Federal Trade Commission* (Chicago: American Bar Association, 1969), 119 .

17. See *The President's Task Force Report on Appliance Warranties and Service* (1969) (qtd. in 120 Cong. Rec. H3317-22 (September 17, 1994)), "Interstate and Foreign Commerce Committee, Subcommittee on Commerce and Finance, Staff Report" (hereafter cited as *Task Force Report Appliance Warranties and Service*).

18. Staggers and his approach to chairing the House Interstate and Foreign Committee are described in chapter 6.

19. *Hearings on Consumer Warranty Protection, Before the Committee on Interstate and Foreign Commerce, Subcommittee on Commerce and Finance*, H.R. Doc. 92–50, 1 (September 28, 1971) (hereafter cited as *Warranty Hearings*).

20. Ibid., 2.

21. Ibid., 146–79.

22. Ibid., 150.

23. Ralph Nader, interview by Author, October 14, 2009, 14.

24. *Warranty Hearings*, 154.

25. Ibid., 176.

26. Ibid.

27. Ibid., 177.

28. Ibid., 178.

29. Thomas Greene (Special Assistant Attorney General, State of California; former legislative counsel to Congressman Moss), interview by Author, December 12, 2008.

30. Clarence Ditlow (Director, Center for Auto Safety), interview by Author, September 2, 2009 (hereafter cited as *Ditlow Interview*).

31. *John Moss floor statement*, 31317–22.

32. *Congressional Quarterly Almanac* (Washington, DC: 1974), 328.

33. Carole Shifrin, "Warranty-FTC Bill Voted by House Unit," *Washington Post*, May 23, 1974, A-5, Proquest Historical Newspapers, http://www.proquest.com/en-US/.

34. 120 Cong. Rec. (December 18, 1974), S40712.

35. Curtis Reitz, *Consumer Product Warranties Under Federal and State Laws*, 2d ed. (Philadelphia: American Law Institute, 1987), 3, 10, 133, 235–41.

36. *Ditlow interview*, 1–6.

37. Moss tried hard to avoid this result. He directed that the committee reports and the bill only Authorize the extensive and costly cross-examination process regarding "material facts" at issue, not policy issues, or issues of lesser importance. But the undermanned FTC largely gave up on the Magnuson-Moss rule-making procedures, without attempting to limit the procedures by rule or order. Only where Congress has in later legislation specifically Authorized informal rule-making, without trial-type procedures, has the FTC issued national rules against deceptive practices.

38. "FTC to Toughen Tactics Against Firms Practicing Deception Under New Statute," *Wall Street Journal*, January 20, 1975, 24.

39. Jodi Bernstein (former director, Bureau of Consumer Protection, Federal Trade Commission, 1995–2001), interview by Author, January 21, 2009 (hereafter cited as *Bernstein interview*).

40. Bruce K. Mulock, *Congressional Research Service*, Economics Division, Federal Trade Commission, "Background and Selected Consumer Protection Issues," January 23, 1981.

41. Michael Pertschuk, interview by Author, January 26, 2009, 13. The title of the Consumer Product Warranty-FTC Improvements Act was changed by a Senate floor amendment to the Magnuson-Moss Act. Mike Pertschuk, by then general counsel of the Senate Commerce Committee, decided on the new name for the law to honor its chief Senate and House sponsors. Pertschuk tells of how he described the renaming amendment to Magnuson. For some reason, the Senator did not hold Utah's Frank Moss in particularly high regard. Frank Moss was then chairman of the Consumer subcommittee of the Senate Commerce Committee. He had played an important role in supporting enactment of the law. But Magnuson, whether because of his feelings toward Frank Moss, or his inclination not to share the spotlight, would not have approved calling it the Magnuson-Moss Act, if the Moss was Frank Moss. So, Pertschuk says, he assured Magnuson that the Moss was John Moss who had rammed the bill through the House of Representatives. Magnuson beamed. Pertschuk later ensured that the legislative history established that "the Moss" in Magnuson-Moss forever enshrined the names of both Mosses.

42. *Bernstein interview.*

43. Christian White (Deputy General Counsel, Federal Trade Commission), interview by Author, January 22, 2009.

## 8. INVESTOR PROTECTION

1. Joel Seligman, *The Transformation of Wall Street: A History of the Securities and Exchange Commission and Modern Corporate Finance*, rev. ed. (Boston: Northeastern University Press, 1992), 450–52.

2. Hurd Baruch, *Wall Street: Security Risk* (Washington, DC: Acropolis Books, 1971) 72, 171, 219, 228; Seligman, *Transformation of Wall Street*, 455, 457.

3. John E. Moss, interview by Author, March 16–18, 1996 (hereafter cited as *Moss interview*).

4. Seligman, *Transformation of Wall Street*, 454–55.

5. *The Hartford Courant*, November 27, 1970, 38, ProQuest Historical Newspapers, http://www.proquest.com/en-US/.

6. Ibid.

7. Baruch, *Wall Street: Security Risk*, preface, ix.

8. *New York Times*, March 18, 1970, 85; ProQuest Historical Newspapers, http://www.proquest.com/en-US/.

9. Robert Metz, "Marketplace," *New York Times*, November 17, 1970, 64, ProQuest Historical Newspapers, http://www.proquest.com/en-US/.

10. Mike Dash, *Tulipmania: The Story of the World's Most Coveted Flower & the Extraordinary Passions it Aroused* (New York: Three Rivers Press, 1999); Charles MacKay, *Extraordinary Popular Delusions and the Madness of Crowds*, with a foreword by Andrew Tobias (1841; New York: Harmony Books, 1980); Ann Goldgar, *Tulipmania* (Chicago: University of Chicago, 2007), 32.

11. *Wall Street Journal*, September 3, 1968, 14, ProQuest Historical Newspapers, http://www.proquest.com/en-US/.

12. *Wall Street Journal*, April 28, 1970, 1, ProQuest Historical Newspapers, http://www.proquest.com/en-US/.

13. Charles Moritz, ed., *Current Biography Yearbook 1968* (New York: H. W. Wilson, 1968), 278, also available at http://www.hwwilson.com; R. W. Apple Jr., "Edmund S. Muskie, 81, Dies; Maine Senator and a Power on the National Scene," *New York Times*, March 27, 1996, 21.

14. Baruch, *Wall Street: Security Risk*, 71, 298.

15. Eileen Shanahan, "The securities industry wants to run its own broker-dealer insurance program . . . ," *New York Times*, April 17, 1970, 66.

16. Baruch, *Wall Street: Security Risk*, 72.

17. Ibid., 76.

18. Ibid., 74.

19. Ibid., 76

20. Securities Investor Protection Act of 1970, H.R. Doc. No. 91–1613 at 3 (October 21, 1970).

21. Baruch, *Wall Street: Security Risk*, 80.

22. Ibid., 78.

23. Ibid., 70.

24. *New York Times*, March 18, 1970, 85, ProQuest Historical Newspapers, http://www.proquest.com/en-US/.

25. *New York Times*, June 21, 1970, 123, ProQuest Historical Newspapers, http://www.proquest.com/en-US/.

26. *New York Times*, November 17, 1970, 63, ProQuest Historical Newspapers, http://www.proquest.com/en-US/.

27. "Congress Clears Securities Investor Protection Bill," *Congressional Quarterly Almanac*, 1970, 865, 870.

28. Harvey Rowen, interview by Author, February 9, 2009, 3 (hereafter cited as *Rowen interview*).

29. Ibid., 19.

30. Harvey Rowen, supplemental e-mail interview by Author, August 9, 2009.

31. *Rowen interview*, 6.

32. Ibid., 5.

33. James Broyhill, interview by Author, February 22, 2009, 14; *Rowen interview*, 21.

34. *Broyhill interview*, 14; *Rowen interview*, 21.

35. "John E. Moss Papers, 1953-1978," Sacramento: Department of Special Collections and University Archives, The Library, California State University, box 779, folder 7, *Ralph Nader Congress Project*, October 1972, "Congressional Profile on John E. Moss," 2.

36. *Washington Post*, January 8, 1975, D–8, Proquest Historical Newspapers, http://www.proquest.com/en-US/. Moss had used blunt words to challenge the securities industry before. In 1970, when the industry defeated a Moss backed provision to limit customer fees charged by mutual funds in legislation before his subcommittee, Moss announced that he opposed his own bill and would kill it. The Republican sponsor of the mutual fund amendments that were voted into in the Moss legislation was asked who had written them. He said, "Carl Shipley [a Washington lawyer who represented a number of the funds] had done the drafting." Moss said that the way they had gone about opposing the mutual fund bill had turned members "against the securities industry," and that the industry

"might face reprisals" when his broader securities bill was considered in the next Congress (see *New York Times*, May 15, 1970, 51, ProQuest Historical Newspapers, http://www.proquest.com/en-US/).

37. "Big Board Likes Securities Bill," *New York Times*, May 27, 1975, 39; Proquest Historical Newspapers, http://www.proquest.com/en-US/; "Moss and Williams in Different Ways Act to Goad SEC to Modernize Securities Industry," *Wall Street Journal*, August 17, 1972, 28, ProQuest Historical Newspapers, http://www.proquest.com/en-US/.

38. *Rowen interview*, 4.

39. Ibid., 27–28.

40. Harvey L. Pitt (former Chairman and General Counsel of the Securities Exchange Commission), interview by Author, June 27, 2010, 4–6.

## 9. CARS, CHEMICALS, AND ARAB OIL

1. OPEC consisted of the twelve major oil producing nations, including seven Arab countries (the primary producers being Saudi Arabia and Iraq), as well as Iran, Venezuela, Indonesia, Nigeria, and Ecuador.

2. David Frum, *How We Got Here: The '70s* (New York: Basic Books, NY, 2000), 318.

3. "Chart, January 1974-December 1981," http://inflationdata.com/inflation/; "Historical CPI Data," U.S. Bureau of Labor Standards, www.bls.gov.

4. Philip E. Davis, "Comparing Bear Markets—1973 and 2000," *National Institute Economic Review* 183.1 (January 2003): 78–89.

5. *Weekly Compilation of Presidential Documents*, President Richard M. Nixon, March 1, 1971, "Consumer Protection;" "John E. Moss Papers, 1953-1978," Sacramento: Department of Special Collections and University Archives, The Library, California State University, box 65 folder 3.

6. "Estimated Repair Costs for Slow Speed Car Crashes" (citing Insurance Institute for Highway Safety testimony), *Congressional Quarterly Almanac*, 1972, 379.

7. *New York Times*, September 10, 1966, 12. Text of remarks by President Lyndon B. Johnson on signing of the National Traffic and Motor Vehicle Safety Act of 1966, Proquest Historical Newspapers, http://www.proquest.com/en-US/.

8. Ibid.

9. Ibid.

10. *House Hearings on Automobile Property Damage and Consumer Information Program*, 92d Cong., 1st sess. (November 9, 1971), Serial No. 92–55, 2.

11. "Table 2, Persons Killed or Injured and Fatality and Injury Rates Per Population, Licensed Drivers, Registered Vehicles, and Vehicle Miles Traveled, 1966–2008," *Traffic Safety Facts 2008: Early Edition* (U.S. Department of Transportation, National Highway Traffic Safety Administration), 15.

12. Don Randall, interview by Author, October 12, 2009.

13. Ibid.

14. Ibid.

15. "House Committee Kills Proposal to Reduce Cost of Auto Repairs," *Washington Post Times-Herald*, March 1, 1972, A6; Proquest Historical Newspapers,

http://www.proquest.com/en-US/; "House Panel Rejects Senate Bill to Reduce Cost of Auto Repairs," *Wall Street Journal*, March 1, 1972, 32, Proquest Historical Newspapers, http://www.proquest.com/en-US/.

16. "A Bill to Cut Auto Repairs is Shelved by House Panel," *New York Times*, March 22, 1972, 93, ProQuest Historical Newspapers, http://www.proquest.com/en-US/.

17. California State Archives, Oral History Program, "Interview with John E. Moss," October 3, 17, 24 and November 2, 1989, 204.

18. Herman Brandeau (former Associate General Counsel, State Farm Insurance Company, 1984–2006), interview by Author, February 5, 2010, (hereafter cited as *Brandeau interview*).

19. State Farm remains a major financial supporter of the consumer-industry safety organization, Advocates for Highway and Automobile Safety, which was established in 1989.

20. *Relative Collision Insurance Cost Information Booklet*, 2009, www.nhtsa.dot .gov; for safety ratings see www.autosafety.org.

21. Report on the Motor Vehicle Defect Remedy Act, S. Rep. 93–150, 6, 93d Cong., 1st sess. (May 14, 1973).

22. Report on the Motor Vehicle and School Bus Safety Amendment of 1974, H.R. Rep. 93–1191, 14, 93d Cong., 2d Sess. (July 11, 1974).

23. Ibid., S. Rep. 93–150, 7.

24. "Auto Industry Fines," The Center for Auto Safety, www.autosafety.org. General Motors paid a fine of one million dollars in 2004 because it had failed to give owners timely notification of defective windshield wipers on Chevrolet Trailblazers and other models.

25. Joan Claybrook (former President of Public Citizen and Administrator of the National Highway Traffic Safety Administration), interview by Author, February 17, 2009, 2–3.

26. Ibid., 10.

27. General Motors Corporation v. Adams 565 F.2d 754, 760 (Court of Appeals DC, 1977), Skelly Wright, Judge.

28. General Counsel's Office (National Highway Traffic Safety Administration), interview by the Author, December 4, 2009. The total number of vehicles recalled for safety defects since 1966 exceeds 330 million.

29. David Shepardson and Christine Tierney, "NHTSA Fell Short Investigating Acceleration Complaints," *Detroit News*, February 23, 2010.

30. *Congressional Quarterly Almanac*, 1974, 687.

31. Ibid.

32. Ibid.

33. "Train Asks Stiff Toxic Chemical Law," *New York Times*, February 27, 1976, 64, ProQuest Historical Newspapers, http://www.proquest.com/en-US/.

34. "Showdown on Toxics," *New York Times*, August 25, 1976, 28, ProQuest Historical Newspapers, http://www.proquest.com/en-US/.

35. *Hearing on Toxic Substances Control Act, Before the House Committee and State and Foreign Commerce, Subcommittee on Commerce and Finance*, 92d Cong., 2d sess., May 18 and 23, 1972, Serial No. 92-73, 1.

36. Ibid.

37. Biographical Directory of the United States Congress, Samuel Hollingsworth Young, http://bioguide.congress.gov/scripts/biodisplay.pl?index=y000052.

38. *Committee Minutes of the House Committee on Interstate and Foreign Commerce, Subcommittee on Commerce and Finance*, 23, 26, 30, 32, 93d Cong. 1st sess. (April 3, 4, 9, 1973).

39. "Ecology group blasts Young and donates funds to Mikva," *Chicago Sun-Times*, Oct. 14, 1971, 15; "Money fires Young-Mikva debate, *Chicago Sun-Times*, October 28, 1974, 46; "Mikva for Congress in 10th"; *Chicago Sun-Times*, October 15, 1974, editorial page.

40. Abner Mikva, *Conversations with History*, interview by Harry Kreisler Institute of International Studies, University of California Berkeley, 1999, http://globetrotter.berkeley.edu/people/Mikva/mikva-con0.html, accessed April 15, 2010.

41. "Chemicals That Can Kill," *Washington Post*, August 29, 1976, 26, Proquest Historical Newspapers, http://www.proquest.com/en-US/.

42. *Congressional Quarterly Almanac*, 1976, 123.

43. Ibid. 124

44. Ibid.

45. *Hearing on Chemical Regulation Options for Enhancing the Effectiveness of the Toxic Substance Control Act, Before the House Committee on Energy and Commerce, Subcommittee on Commerce, Trade and Consumer Protection* (testimony of Richard A. Dennison, Sr. Scientist, Environmental Defense Fund, p.2, the United States Government Accountability Office, p.3, Jay Clarence Davies, p. 4-5), 111th Cong., 1st sess. (February 26, 2009).

46. "Toxic Substances Control Act Reform Gets Hearing in House," *Product Safety Letter*, November 21, 2009, http://www.productsafetyletter.com/news/5916-1.html.

47. James Nelligan (former member of Congress and member of the Moss subcommittee staff) interview by the Author, December 14, 1997, 2; Jean Moss, interview by Author, December 13–14, 1997, 127.

48. Frank Silbey (former Moss staff member) interview by Author, January 11, 1997, 7 (hereinafter cited as *Silbey interview*).

49. Rep. John D. Dingell, interview by Author, January 29, 2009, 1, 7, 9 (hereafter cited as *Dingell interview*). Dingell on Moss: "He was an extraordinary man. He cared about people. He had the courage of a lion and we were in very strong agreement on most matters," 1; "He just did it instinctively. He had a wonderful sense of concern for the little guy, and he always put himself in the little guy's shoes. He tried to do the things that had to be done for the little guy to protect him and to help him and to see to it that he got a fair chance in a society which has a lot of respect for the big fellow," 7; "They had a very large staff up there, and they didn't do oversight. And we saw all these bad things happening," 9.

50. Elliot Segal (former Moss subcommittee staff member) interview with Author, October 9, 2007, 7. Moss's hearings on "Cost and Quality of Health Care: Unnecessary Surgery," commenced in 1975 when he was the newly elected chairman of the Oversight and Investigations subcommittee in the House. They were recommended to him by his health policy adviser (Segal), the former assistant dean at Yale Medical School, who Moss hired on the recommendation of Senator Magnuson's staff. Moss wanted to address the cost of health care as a way of pushing

national health insurance legislation. Segal says they focused on unnecessary surgery because there had been some recent studies in the *New England Journal of Medicine* and elsewhere suggesting deaths had resulted from unnecessary surgery and that a second opinion was important before most operations. Moss gave Segal the go-ahead and mostly a free hand. The succeeding series of hearings drew national headlines as well as a five-part series in the *New York Times*. The American Medical Association opposed the idea of second opinions. Medicare and most private insurance companies ultimately agreed to pay for second consultations.

51. *Report of the House Commerce Committee, Subcommittee on Oversight and Investigations on Federal Regulation and Regulatory Reform*, U.S. Gov. Printing Office, 1976, http://openlibrary.org. This site also lists ten other major reports by Moss's Oversight and Investigations subcommittee. Moss's commitment to congressional oversight was clear. He told his staff, "No federal program should go unaudited and unscrutinized for any serious length of time"; *Silbey interview*, 28.

52. Ralph Nader, interview by Author, October 14, 2009, 12.

53. *Dingell interview*, 11.


## 10. CONSUMER PROTECTION IN RETREAT

1. *Wall Street Journal*, July 19, 1972, 10, ProQuest Historical Newspapers, http://www.proquest.com/en-us/.

2. bid.

3. Peter Kinzler, interview by Author, June 12, 2009, 1 (hereafter cited as *Kinzler interview*).

4. Ibid., 17.

5. Dennis Hevesi, *New York Times*, August 4, 2007; Megan Tench, *Boston Globe*, July 3, 2007.

6. *Hearings, Before the House, Committee on Interstate and Foreign Commerce, Subcommittee on Commerce and Finance*, 92d Cong., 1st sess. (April 20, 1971), H.R. Doc. 92–25, 1.

7. Ibid.

8. Morton Mintz, "No-Fault bill Approved by Senate Unit," *Washington Post*, May 25, 1972, ProQuest Historical Newspapers, http://www.proquest.com/enus/.

9. *Kinzler interview*, 16. As of 2010, only sixteen states had no-fault insurance laws. They are of widely varying effectiveness.; Kinzler telephone interview by Author, April 16, 2010.

10. *Kinzler interview*, 16.

11. Ibid., 19.

12. Ibid., 25.

13. Ibid., 28.

14. Peter Kinzler, telephone interview by Author, April 16, 2010.

15. *Congressional Quarterly Almanac*, 1974, 315.

16. Rep. John E. Moss, *Press Release and Letter to President Gerald Ford*, September 9, 1974, California State University Archives, 1971–74 Press Book; see also "John

E. Moss Papers, 1953–1978," Sacramento: Department of Special Collections and University Archives, The Library, California State University, box 776, folder 55.

17. *Kinzler interview*, 12–13.

18. Ibid., 30; John E. Moss, interview by Author, March 16–18, 1996, 10, "I didn't back away from many things."; Christopher White (Deputy General Counsel, Federal Trade Commission), interview by Author, January 22, 2009, "I can't imagine anyone like him today."

19. Peter Barash (Congressman Rosenthal's Government Operations Committee Counsel), interview with Author, July 1, 2009 (hereafter cited as *Barash interview*), 10.

20. Ibid., 2.

21. For a discussion of the role of state attorney generals as "parens patriae," see http//legal-dictionary.thefreedictionary.com, "The parens patriae doctrine has its roots in English common law. In the United States the doctrine has its greatest application to the treatment of children, mentally ill persons, and other individuals who are legally incompetent to manage their affairs . . . the doctrine of parens patriae has been expanded in the United States to permit the attorney general of a state to commence litigation for the benefit of state residents for federal anti-trust violations (15 U.S.C.A. Section 15(c)) . . . states may also invoke parens patriae to protect interests such as the health, comfort and welfare of the people, interstate water rights, and the general economy of the state. For a state to have standing to sue under the doctrine, it must be more than a nominal party without a real interest of its own and must articulate an interest apart from the interests of particular private parties."

22. Quoted in Maurice Carroll, *New York Times*, January 5, 1983.

23. *Congressional Quarterly Almanac*, 1972, 703.

24. *Congressional Quarterly Almanac*, 1978, 473.

25. Esther Peterson, *New York Times Oral History Program*, The University of Michigan, Ann Arbor, Michigan, 1978, 2 (hereafter cited as *Peterson Oral History*); see also, Esther Peterson with Winfred Conkling, *Restless: The Memoirs of a Labor and Consumer Activist* (Washington, DC: Caring Publishing Company, 1997).

26. *Peterson Oral History,*7.

27. Esther Eggertsen Peterson, http://www.aflcio.org; Peterson, *Restless*, 33.

28. Irvin Molotsky, *New York Times*, December 22, 1997.

29. *Congressional Quarterly Almanac*, 1978, 473.

30. *Barash interview*, 11.

31. *Congressional Quarterly Almanac*, 1978, 473.

32. Ibid.

33. Ibid.

34. *Barash interview*, 12–13.

35. Ibid., 3–4.

36. *Kinzler interview*, 32

37. Catherine Rampell, "Elizabeth Warren on Consumer Financial Protection," *New York Times*, June 17, 2009, http://economix.blogs.nytimes.com/2009/06/17/elizabeth-warren-on-consumer-financial-protection/, accessed April 16, 2010.

38. Ibid.

## 11. FREEDOM OF INFORMATION TODAY

1. "Abu Ghurayb Prison," GlobalSecurity.org, http://www.globalsecurity. org/intell/world/iraq/abu-ghurayb-prison.htm; William Saletan, "Rape Rooms: A Chronology, What Bush Said as the Iraq Prison Scandal Unfolded," May 5, 2004, http://www.slate.com/id/2100014/, accessed April 16, 2010.

2. Seymour M. Hersh, "Annals of National Security: Torture at Abu Ghraib," *New Yorker*, May 10, 2004, http://www.newyorker.com/archive.

3. Jameel Jaffer and Amrit Singh, *Administration of Torture: A Documentary Record from Washington to Abu Ghraib and Beyond* (New York: Columbia University Press, 2007), 18, 19, 23.

4. Samira Simone, "Abu Ghraib Head Finds Vindication in Newly-Released Memos," CNN.com, April 22, 2009, http://www.cnn.com/2009/US/04/22/ us.torture.karpinski/index.html, accessed April 22, 2009 (hereafter cited as *Karpinski*).

5. Statement of President George W. Bush, "President Bush Reaffirms Commitments in Iraq," May 10, 2004, http://www.whitehouse.gov/news/releases/2004/05/20040510-3.html (also cited in Jaffer and Singh, *Administration of Torture*).

6. Remarks of Donald H. Rumsfeld at Abu Ghraib Prison, May 13, 2004, http://www.defenselink.mil/speeches/speech.aspx?speechid=121.

7. Testimony of Defense Secretary Donald M. Rumsfeld before the Senate and House Armed Services Committees, May 7, 2004, cited by Seymour M. Hersh, "Annals of National Security, The General's Report," *New Yorker*, June 25, 2007, 60 (hereafter cited as *General's Report*).

8. Paul Wolfowitz (Dept. of Defense, Deputy Secretary of Defense), interview May 4, 2004, U.S. Dept. of Defense News Transcript, www.defense.gov/transcripts/transcript; *Karpinksi*.

9. Scott Shane, "ACLU Lawyers Mine Documents for Truth," *New York Times*, August 30, 2009, http://www.nytimes.com/2009/08/30/world/30intel. html?scp=1&sq=august%2030,%202009%20&%20aclu&st=cse.

10. "Memo Contends that President Can Authorize Torture," ACLU, http:// www.aclu.org/national-security/secret-bush-administration-torture-memo-released-today-response-aclu-lawsuit, accessed April 16, 2010; Jaffer and Singh, *Administration of Torture*, 24, 28.

11. Jaffer and Singh, *Administration of Torture*, x.

12. Ibid., 14.

13. Ibid., 14, 28. The ACLU Authors state "abuse of prisoners was the result of decisions made at the very highest levels of the U.S. government."

14. "Veto Battle 30 Years Ago Set Freedom of Information Norms," *NSA Archive*, November 23, 2004, 3. http://www.gwu.edu/~nsarchiv/NSAEBB/ NSAEBB142/index.htm (hereafter cited as *NSA Archive*).

15. Ibid., 3.

16. Ibid., 6.

17. Ibid., 1, 13–15.

18. See http://www.gwu.edu/~nsarchiv/; *NSA Archive*, 1.

19. *NSA Archive*, 2.

20. Donald M. Rumsfeld, interview by Author, April 12, 2010 (hereafter cited as *Rumsfeld interview*); Donald M. Rumsfeld, supplemental memorandum to Author, April 15, 2010.

21. *NSA Archive*, 13.

22. Ibid.; see "Supreme Court Justice Scalia Fought Against Freedom of Information Act." http://www.thememoryhole.org/foia/scalia _foia.htm. Scalia's role in promoting a Ford veto of the 1974 FOIA amendments is detailed in memoranda from the Associate General Counsel of the Central Intelligence Agency to the General Counsel John Warner, September 23, 1974, and from Warner on September 26, 1974, which states, "Mr. Scalia stated that if we wanted to have any impact, we should move quickly to make our views known to the president. . . . Later in the day Mr. Scalia telephoned urging us to contact the White House. . . . I contacted Mr. Sheppard and stated our position."

23. Thomas Blanton (Executive Director, National Security Archive), interview by Author, October 14, 2009, 4 (hereafter cited as *Blanton interview*).

24. Ibid., 6.

25. *NSA Archive*, 2.

26 *Blanton interview*, 14.

27. Ibid., 15.

28. "Freedom of Information Act in the News," 3, *NSA Archive*, 2004–6, http://www.gwu.edu/~nsarchiv/nsa/foia/stories.htm.

29. John E. Moss, interview by Author, March 16–18, 1996, 7.

30. John Ashcroft, Attorney General, "Memorandum for Heads of All Federal Departments and Agencies, Re: The Freedom of Information Act," October 12, 2001, http://www.justice.gov/archive/oip/011012.htm.

31. Ibid.

32. "SPJ Asks Ashcroft Not to Stonewall Requests for Public Information," *Society of Professional Journalists*, News Release, October 19, 2001, http://www.spj.org/news.asp?ref=41.

33. President Barack Obama, "Memorandum for the Heads of Executive Departments and Agencies: Transparency and Open Government," January 21, 2009, http://www.whitehouse.gov/the_press_office/Transparency_and_Open_Government/.

34. Open Government Act of 2007, P.L. 110-81, passed the Senate on December 14, 2007, signed by President Bush December 31, 2007.

35. "Society of Professional Journalists Leaders Pleased Over Freedom of Information Act Bill Signing," January 2, 2008, http://www.spj.org/news.asp?ref=755.

36. Alasdair Roberts, *Blacked Out: Government Secrecy in the Information Age* (New York: Cambridge University Press, 2006), 14.

37. Ted Gup, *Nation of Secrets* (New York: Doubleday, 2007), 16.

38. *Blanton interview*, 29.

39. *Rumsfeld interview*, 10; e-mail from Mr. Rumsfeld to Author April 14, 2010.

40. *House Committee on Government Reform, Before the Subcommittee on Government Management, Finance and Accountability on the implementation of the Freedom of Information Act* (written statement of Jay Smith, President, Cox Newspapers, Inc.) 109th Cong, 1st sess., May 11, 2005, Service No. 109–46, 129, http://frwebgate.ac-

cess.gpo.gov/cgi-bin/getdoc.cgi?dbname=109_house_hearings&docid=f:22705. wais.

41. *Blanton interview*, 31.
42. *Karpinski*.
43. *General's Report*, 69.
44. Rumsfeld's statement quoted in *Karpinski*; see also, Report of the Senate Armed Services Committee, Inquiry into the Treatment of Detainees in U.S. Custody (November 20, 2008, Comm. Print 110th Cong., 2d sess.) which concluded, "President Bush made a determination in 2002 that the Geneva Convention did not apply to al Queda or Taliban detainees; members of the Bush cabinet discussed specific interrogation techniques; the General Counsel of the Department of Defense, William J. Hayes, cut short a legal and policy review of severe interrogation techniques; Secretary of Defense Rumsfeld's Authorization of aggressive interrogation techniques at GTMO was a direct cause of detainee abuse there and contributed to detainee abuse in Iraq; the abuse of detainees at Abu Ghraib in 2003 was not simply the result of a few soldiers acting on their own" (conclusions 1, 12, 13, 14, 19, pp. xxvi–xxviii;).

## EPILOGUE

1. Ward Sinclair, "The Man Who Perfected Oversight," *Washington Post*, January 14, 1979.
2. Donald M. Rumsfeld, interview by Author, April 12, 2010.
3. Henry A. Waxman (D-California), Tribute to John E. Moss, 144th Cong. Rec., Part I, 165 (January 27, 1998), 105th Congress, 2d Sess.
4. John E. Moss, interview by Author, March 16–18, 1996.

# Bibliography

## BOOKS

Avella, Steven M. *Sacramento: Indomitable City*. Chicago: Arcadia Publishing, 2003.

Bartley, Ernest R. *The Tidelands Oil Controversy*. Austin: University of Texas Press, 1953.

Baruch, Hurd. *Wall Street: Security Risk*. Washington D.C.: Acropolis Books Ltd., 1971.

Bernstein, Carl. *Loyalties*. New York: Simon and Schuster, 1989.

Burns, John F., and Lori Parks. *Sacramento: Gold Rush Legacy, Metropolitan Destiny*. Dallas: Heritage Media, 1999.

Caro, Robert A. *The Years of Lyndon Johnson: Master Of The Senate*. New York: Vintage Books, 2003.

Celler, Emanuel. *You Never Leave Brooklyn: the Autobiography of Emanuel Celler*. New York: The John Day Company, 1953.

Chambers, II, John Whiteclay. *The Tyranny of Change: America in the Progressive Era, 1900-1917*. New York: St. Martin's Press, 1980.

Claybrook, Joan, and The Staff of Public Citizen. *Retreat From Safety: Reagan's Attack On America's Health*. New York: Pantheon Books, 1984.

Cohen, Lizabeth. *A Consumers' Republic: The Politics of Mass Consumption in Postwar America*. New York: Alfred A. Knopf, 2003.

*Consumer Product Safety Act-Legislative History*. Washington, DC: The Bureau of National Affairs, Inc., 1973.

*Conversations with History*. University of California Berkeley, 1999. http://globetrotter.berkeley.edu/people/Mikva/mikva-con0.html (accessed April 15, 2010).

Cooper, Kent. *The Right to Know: An Exposition of the Evils of News Suppression and Propaganda*. New York: Farrar, Strauss & Cudahy, 1956.

Cox, Edward Finch, Robert C. Fellmeth, and John E. Schulz. Preface by Ralph Nader. *The Nader Report on the Federal Trade Commission.* New York: Richard W. Barron, New York, 1969.

Cross, Harold L. *The People's Right To Know.* Morningside Heights: Columbia University Press, 1953.

Dallek, Robert. *Nixon and Kissinger: Partners In Power.* New York: HarperCollins Publishers, 2007.

Dash, Mike. *Tulipmania: The Story of the World's Most Coveted Flower and the Extraordinary Passions it Aroused.* London: 1999.

Ehrenhalt, Alan, ed. *Politics in America: Members of Congress in Washington and at Home.* 3d ed. Congressional Quarterly Books, May 1986.

Foerstel, Herbert N. *Freedom of Information and The Right To Know: The Origins and Applications of the Freedom of Information Act.* Westport, Connecticut: Greenwood Press, 1999.

Frum, David. *How We Got Here: The '70s.* New York: Basic Books, 2000.

Goldgar, Anne. *Tulipmania.* University of Chicago Press, 2007.

Gup, Ted. *Nation of Secrets.* New York: Doubleday, 2007.

Jaffer, Jameel and Amrit Singh. *Administration of Torture: A Documentary Record from Washington to Abu Ghraib and Beyond.* New York: Columbia University Press, 2007.

Keith, Gary A. Forward by Al Gore. *Eckhardt: There Once Was A Congressman From Texas.* Austin: University of Texas Press, 2007.

Ladd, Bruce. *Crisis in Credibility.* New York: The New American Library, 1968.

Lemov, Michael R. *Consumer Product Safety Commission: Regulatory Manual Series.* Colorado Springs: Shepard's-McGraw-Hill, 1983.

Library of Congress. "Final Report of the National Commission on Product Safety." No.76606753, June 1970. 20.

MacKay, Charles. *Memoirs of Extraordinary Popular Delusions and the Madness of Crowds.* London, 1841.

Martin, Justin. *Nader: Crusader, Spoiler, Icon.* New York: Basic Books, 2002.

Miller, Clem, and Edited With Additional Text by John W. Baker. *Member of the House: Letters of a Congressman.* New York: Charles Scribner's Sons, 1962.

Mintz, Morton, and Jerry S. Cohen. *America, Inc.: Who Owns and Operates the United States.* New York: Dell Publishing Co., Inc., 1972.

Moritz, Charles., ed. *Current Biography Yearbook 1968.* New York: H.W. Wilson, 1968. Also available at http://www.hwwilson.com.

Nash, Gerald D. *The Crucial Era: The Great Depression and World War II, 1929-1945.* IL: Waveland Press, 2d ed. 1998.

O'Neill, William L. *Coming Apart: An Informal History of American in the 1960's.* New York: Times Books, 1971.

O'Reilly, J. *Food and Drug Administration.* Colorado Springs: Shephard's McGraw-Hill, 1979.

Pertschuk, Michael. *Revolt Against Regulation: The Rise and Pause of the Consumer Movement.* Berkeley: University of California Press, 1982.

Peterson, Esther, with Winfred Conkling. *Restless: The Memoirs of a Labor and Consumer Activist.* Washington, DC: Caring Publishing Company, 1997.

Randall, Donald A., and Arthur P. Glockman. *The Great American Auto Repair Robbery: A Report on a Ten-Billion Dollar National Swindle—And What You Can Do About It*. New York: Charterhouse, 1972.

Reitz, Curtis. *Consumer Product Warranties Under Federal and State Laws*. 2d ed. Philadelphia: American Law Institute, 1987.

Roberts, Alasdair. *Blacked Out, Government Secrecy in the Information Age*. New York: Cambridge University Press, 2006.

Rozell, Mark J., and Clyde Wilcox. *Interest Groups in American Campaigns: The New Face of Electioneering*. Washington, DC: CQ Press. 1999.

Samish, Arthur H., and Bob Thomas. *The Secret Boss of California, the Life and High Times of Art Samish*. New York: Crown Publishers, 1971.

Sandford, David, Ralph Nader, James Ridgeway, and Robert Coles. *Hot War On The Consumer*. New York: Pitman Publishing Corporation, 1969.

Scates, Shelby. *Warren G. Magnuson And the Shaping of Twentieth-Century America*. Seattle: University of Washington Press, 1997.

Seligman, Joel. *The Transformation of Wall Street: A History of the Securities and Exchange Commission and Modern Corporate Finance*. rev. ed. Boston: Northeastern University Press, 1992.

Severson, Thor. *Sacramento: An Illustrated History*. San Fransisco: California Historical Society, 1973.

Taylor, Robert J. et al., ed. *Papers of John Adams*,Vol. I. Cambridge, Massachusetts: Belknap Press of Harvard University, 1977.

Tolchin, Susan J., and Martin Tolchin. *Dismantling America*. Boston: Houghton Mifflin Company, 1983.

"Warren G. Magnuson." *American National Biography: American Council of Learned Societies*. New York: Oxford University Press, 1999.

Woods, Randall Bennett. *Quest For Identity: America Since 1945*. Fort Worth: Harcourt College Publishers, 2001.

## INTERVIEWS

Blanton, Thomas, (Executive Director, National Security Archives). Interview by Author. October 14, 2009. Transcript, Bethesda, MD.

Barash, Peter (former counsel, House Government Operations Committee). Interview by Author. July 1, 2009. Transcript, Bethesda, MD.

Bernstein, Jodi (former director, Bureau of Consumer Protection, Federal Trade Commission, 1995-2001). Interview by Author. January 21, 2009. Transcript, Bethesda, MD.

Brandeau, Herman (former associate general counsel, State Farm Insurance Company, 1984-2006). Interview by Author. February 5, 2010. Transcript, Bethesda, MD.

Brown, Michelle Lyon (Moss family member). Interview by Author. August 27, 2007, Transcript, Bethesda, MD.

Broyhill, James (former member, U.S. House of Representatives and former U.S. Senator). Interview by Author. February 22, 2009. Transcript, Bethesda, MD.

Claybrook, Joan (former administrator, National Highway Traffic Safety Administration and former President, Public Citizen). Interview by Author. February 17, 2009. Transcript, Bethesda, MD.

Dingell, John D. (member, U.S. House of Representatives and Chairman Emeritus, House Commerce Committee). Interview by Author. January 29, 2009. Transcript, Bethesda, MD.

Dodge, Lowell (former staff member Oversight and Investigations Subcommittee, House Commerce Committee). Interview by the Author, June 28, 2007. Transcript, Bethesda, MD.

Ditlow, Clarence (director, Center for Auto Safety). Interview by Author. September 2, 2009. Transcript, Bethesda, MD.

Greene, Thomas (special assistant attorney general, State of California; former legislative counsel to Congressman Moss). Interview by Author. December 12, 2008. Transcript, Bethesda, MD.

Kass, Benny L. (former counsel, House Committee on Government Operations). Interview by Author. September 18, 2007. Transcript, Bethesda, MD.

Kinzler, Peter (former counsel, House Commerce Committee). Interview by Author. June 12, 2009. Transcript, Bethesda, MD.

Merlis, Edward (former staff director, Senate Commerce Committee). Interview by Author. September 16, 2009. Transcript, Bethesda, MD.

Moss, Allison. Interview by Author. September 23, 2005. Transcript, Bethesda, MD.

Moss, Jean. Interview by Author. December 13–14, 1997. Transcript, Bethesda, MD.

Moss, Jennifer. Interview by the Author, September 23, 2005. Transcript, Bethesda, MD.

Moss, John E. Interview by Author. March 16–18, 1996. Transcript, Bethesda, MD.

Nader, Ralph. Interview by Author. October 14, 2009. Transcript, Bethesda, MD.

Nelligan, James (former staff member, Foreign Operations and Government Information Subcommittee, House Government Operations Committee; Subcommittee on Oversight and Investigations, House Commerce Committee; and former U.S. Representative. Interview by Author. December 14, 1997. Transcript, Bethesda, MD.

Pertschuk, Michael (former chief counsel, Senate Commerce Committee and former chairman, Federal Trade Commission). Interview by Author. January 26, 2009. Transcript, Bethesda, MD.

Pitt Harvey L. (former Chairman and General Counsel, Securities and Exchange Commission). Interview by Author. June 27, 2010. Transcript, Bethesda, MD.

Randall, Donald (former counsel, Senate Antitrust and Monopoly subcommittee). Interview by Author, October 12, 2009. Transcript, Bethesda, MD.

Ratcliff, Moina (former Moss staff member). Interview by Author. December 13, Transcript, Bethesda, MD.

Rennert, Leo (former Washington bureau chief, The Sacramento Bee). Interview by Author. October 29, 2007. Transcript, Bethesda, MD.

Rowen, Harvey (former securities counsel, Subcommittee on Commerce and Finance, House Commerce Committee). Interview by Author. February 9, 2009. Transcript, Bethesda, MD.

Rowen, Harvey. Supplemental interview by Author. August 9, 2009. E-mail.

Rumsfeld, Donald M. (former secretary of defense, White House Chief of Staff and U.S. Representative. Interview by Author. April 12, 2010. Transcript, Bethesda, MD.

Schmeltzer, David (former attorney, National Highway Traffic Safety Administration, 1966; director of compliance, Consumer Product Safety Commission 1972–98). Interview by Author. January 16, 2009. Transcript, Bethesda, MD.

Segal, Elliot (former staff member, Oversight and Investigations Subcommittee, House Commerce Committee). Interview by Author. October 9, 2007. Transcript, Bethesda, MD.

Silbey, Frank (former Moss staff member). Interview by Author. January 11, 1997. Transcript, Bethesda, MD.

White, Christian (deputy general counsel, Federal Trade Commission). Interview by Author. January 22, 2009. Transcript, Bethesda, MD.

Wymore, Jerry (Moss's district representative and adviser). Interview by Author. December 14, 1997. Transcript, Bethesda, MD.

## SELECTED LEGISLATIVE MATERIALS

U.S. Congress. House. *Availability of Information from Federal Departments and Agencies.* 84th Cong., 2d sess., 1956. H.R. Rep. 2947.

———. *Clarifying and Protecting the Right of the Public to Information.* 89th Cong., 2d sess., 1966.

———. Commerce Committee, Subcommittee on Oversight and Investigations. *Federal Regulation and Regulatory Reform,* U.S. Gov. Printing Office, 1976. http://openlibrary.org.

———. Committee on Energy and Commerce. *Testimony of Richard A. Dennison, Sr. Scientist, Environmental Defense Fund, Before the Subcommittee on Commerce, Trade and Consumer Protection.* 111th Cong., 1st sess., February 26, 2009.

———. Committee on Energy and Commerce. *Testimony of the United States Government Accountability Office on Chemical Regulation Options for Enhancing the Effectiveness of the Toxic Substance Control Act, Before the Subcommittee on Commerce, Trade and Consumer Protection.* 111th Cong. 1st sess., February 26, 2009.

———. Committee on Government Operations. *Hearings on Availability of Information from Federal Departments and Agencies. Special Subcommittee on Government Information.* 84th Cong., 2d sess., 1956.

———. Committee on Government Operations. Subcommittee on Foreign Operations and Government Information. *Hearings on Federal Public Records Law.* 89th Cong., 1st sess., March 30, 1965 to April 5, 1965.

———. Committee on Government Reform. *Written statement by Smith, Jay. President, Cox Newspapers, Inc., on the Implementation of the Freedom of Information Act, Before the Subcommittee on Government Management, Finance and Accountability.* 109th Cong. 1st sess., May 11, 2005. Serial No. 109–46.129. See also http://frwebgate.access.gpo.gov/cgi-bin/getdoc.cgi?dbname=109_househearings&docid=f:22705.wais.

———. Committee on Interstate and Foreign Commerce. *Hearings on Toxic Substances Control Act, Before the Subcommittee on Commerce and Finance*. 92d Cong., 2d sess., May 18 and 23, 1972. Serial No. 92–73.

———. Committee on Interstate and Foreign Commerce. *Hearings, Before the Subcommittee on Commerce and Finance on Automobile Property Damage and Consumer Information Program*. 92d Cong., 1st sess., November 9, 1971. Serial No. 92–55.

———. Committee on Interstate and Foreign Commerce. *Hearings, Before the Subcommittee on Commerce and Finance on Bills to Protect Consumers Against Unreasonable Risk of Injury from Hazardous Products*. 92d Cong., 1st sess., 1972. Serial No. 92-59.

———. Committee on Interstate and Foreign Commerce. *Testimony of Representative John Dingell, Before the Subcommittee on Commerce and Finance*. September 28, 1971.

———. Committee on Interstate and Foreign Commerce, *Hearings, Before the Subcommittee on Commerce and Finance on No Fault Motor Vehicle Insurance*, April 20, 1971. 92d Cong., 1st sess. 1972. Serial No. 92-25.

———. Committee on Interstate and Foreign Commerce, *Hearings, Before the Subcommittee on Commerce and Finance on Consumer Warranty Protection*. 92d Cong., 1st sess., September 28, 1971. Serial No. 92–50.

———. *Congressional Record*. 89th Cong., 2d sess. "Statement of the Honorable John E. Moss." June 20, 1966. Washington, DC. See also http://www.thejohnemoss-foundation.org/foi/cr_JEM.htm.

———. *Congressional Record*. 93d cong., 2d sess. "Statement of Representative John E. Moss." September 17, 1974. 31316–23.

———. *Congressional Record*. "Tribute to John E. Moss by Rep. Waxman, Henry A. (D-CA)." 105th Cong., 2d sess., January 27, 1998. Pt. I, p. 165.

———. *The Motor Vehicle and School Bus Safety Amendment of 1974*. 93d Cong. 2d sess., July 11, 1974. H.R. Rep. 93–1191.

———. *Securities Investor Protection Act of 1970*. 91st Cong., 2d sess., October 21, H.R. Rep. 91–1613. U.S.

———. *The Motor Vehicle Defect Remedy Act*. 93d Cong., 1st sess., May 14, 1973. S. Rep. 93-150.

———. Senate Armed Services Committee. *Inquiry into the Treatment of Detainees in U.S. Custody*. 110th Cong., 2d sess., November 20, 2008. Comm. Print. See also http://www.cfr.org/publication/19166/.

———. *Congressional Record*. 120. S40712. "Statement of Senator Warren G. Magnusen." 93d Cong., 2d sess. December 18, 1974.

## OTHER SELECTED CITATIONS
## (ALPHABETICAL BY ORIGIN OR AUTHOR)

"Abu Ghurayb Prison." http://www.globalsecurity.org/intell/world/iraq/abu-ghurayb-prison.htm (accessed April 16, 2010).

American Bar Association. "Report of the Commission to Study the Federal Trade Commission." 1969.

American Civil Liberties Union. "Memo Contends that President Can Authorize Torture." http://www.aclu.org/national-security/secret-bush-administrationtorture-memo-released-today-response-aclu-lawsuit (accessed April 16, 2010).

Ashcroft, John, Attorney General. "Memorandum for Heads of All Federal Departments and Agencies regarding The Freedom of Information Act." October 12, 2001. http://www.justice.gov/archive/oip/011012.htm.

Brazil, Burton R. "The 1950 Elections in California." Stanford University. *Political Research Quarterly*, 1951. 4, no. 1. 67-71.

Broyhill, James Thomas. *Biographical Directory of The United States Congress.* September 2008. http://bioguide.congress.gov/.

———. "Candidate Biographies, 1986." Associated Press. Associated Press Political Service.

California State Archives. "Interview with John E. Moss." *Oral History Program.* October 3, 17, 24 and November 2, 1989.

California State University Archives. "John E. Moss Papers, 1953-1978." Sacramento: Department of Special Collections and University Archives. The Library, California State University. certain materials relating to Moss's career have been transferred to the National Archives; Group 233; Records of the U.S. House of Representatives; "John E. Moss papers."

———. Moss, John E. "Press Release and Letter to President Gerald Ford." September 9, California State University Archives, 1971-1974 Press Book.

———. "Letter from John E. Moss to Harley O. Staggers." February 28, 1969. *Moss Papers.* Box 779, Folder 27.

———. "Letter from John E. Moss, John D. Dingell, Paul G. Rogers to Harley O. Staggers." *Moss Papers.* March 4, 1969. Box 779, Folder 27.

———. "Letter from Harley O. Staggers to Moss, Dingell Rogers." March 5, 1969. *Moss Papers.* Box 779, Folder 27.

Center for Auto Safety. "Auto Industry Fines." www.autosafety.org/.

*Detroit News.* Shepardson, David and Christine Tierney. "NHTSA Fell Short Investigating Acceleration Complaints." *Detroit News*, February 23, 2010.

*Congressional Quarterly*

———. "Congress Clears Securities Investor Protection Bill." *Almanac.* Washington, DC, 1970. 865, 870.

———. "Consumer Product Safety Agency Created." *Almanac.* Washington, DC , 1972, 141.

———. "Congress and the Nation." *Congressional Quarterly Service.* 1956. Chap. 17. Investigations.

———. "Estimated Repair Costs for Slow Speed Car Crashes." *Almanac.* 1972. 379.

CNN. Simone, Sahara. "Abu Ghraib Head Finds Vindication in Newly-Released Memos" April 22, 2009. http://www.cnn.com/2009/US/04/22/us.torture.karpinski/index.html.

Hall, Kermit L. "Tidelands Oil Controversy." The Oxford Companion to the Supreme Court of the United States. 2005. Encyclopedia.com. http://www.encyclopedia.com/doc/1O184-TidelandsOilControversy.html (accessed April 12, 2010).

Harris, Joseph P., ed. *The 1950 Elections in the West*. Berkeley: University of California.

Hartford Courant, November 27, 1970. 38. Proquest Historical Newspapers. http://www.proquest.com/en-US/.

Hinderaker, Ivan. "The 1952 Elections in California." The Western Political Quarterly, March 1953. 6. no. 1. 102.

Inflation Data. "Chart, January 1974-December 1981." http://inflationdata.com/inflation/.

McCann, Grace-Ellen (Professor, City College of New York). "An Examination of the Conditions Surrounding the Passage of the 1966 Freedom of Information Act." Open Government, *A Journal on Freedom of Information* 3, no. 1 (April 24, 2007).

Mikva, Abner. Conversations with History. Interview by Harry Kreisler (Institute of International Studies). University of California Berkeley, 1999. http://globetrotter.berkeley.edu/people/Mikva/mikva-con0.html (accessed April 15, 2010).

Moss, John E. (See California State Archives and California State University at Sacramento Archives)

Moyers, Bill. "Journalism Under Fire." (speech). Address to the Society of Journalism Professionals. September 11, 2004. 6. http://www.commondreams.org/views04/0917-02.htm.

Mulock, Bruce K. "Background and Selected Consumer Protection Issues, Federal Trade Commission." January 23, 1981. Economics Division, *Congressional Research Service*.

National Archives, Group 233, Records of the U.S. House of Representatives; "John E. Moss papers."

*National Institute Economic Review*. Davis, Philip E. "Comparing Bear Markets – 1973 and 2000." January 2003. 183 (1): 78-29.

National Security Archive. *Freedom of Information Act in the News*, 2004-2006. http://www.gwu.edu.

———. "Veto Battle 30 Years Ago Set Freedom of Information Norms." The National Security Archive. National Security Archive Electronic Briefing Book No. 142, November 23, 2004. 3-7. http://www.gwu.edu/~nsarchiv/NSAEBB/NSAEBB142/index.htm.

*The New Yorker*

———. Hersh, Seymour M. "Annals of National Security: Torture at Abu Ghraib." May 10, 2004. http://www.newyorker.com/archive.

———. Hersh, Seymour M. "Annals of National Security-The Generals Report." June 25, 2007. 69.

*New York Times*

———. "A Bill to Cut Auto Repairs is Shelved by House Panel." New York Times, March 22, 1972. 93. Proquest Historical Newspapers. http://www.proquest.com/en-US/.

———. "Big Board Likes Securities Bill." New York Times, May 27, 1975. 39. Proquest Historical Newspapers. http://www.proquest.com/en-US/.

———. Carroll, Maurice. New York Times, January 5, 1983.

——— Rampell, Catherine. "Elizabeth Warren on Consumer Financial Protection." June 17, 2009, http://economix.blogs.nytimes.com/2009/06/17/elizabeth-warren-on-consumer-financial-protection/ (accessed April 16, 2010).

────── Shane, Scott. "ACLU Lawyers Mine Documents for Truth." August 30, 2009. http://www.nytimes.com/2009/08/30/world/30intel.html?scp=1&sq=august%2030,%202009%20&%20aclu&st=cse.

──────. Metz, Robert. "Marketplace." New York Times, November 17, 1970. 64. *Proquest Historical Newspapers.* http://www.proquest.com/en-US/.

──────. Molotsky, Irvin. New York Times, December 22, 1997.

──────. October 6, 1962. 89. Proquest Historical Newspapers. http://www.proquest.com/en-US/.

──────. March 18, 1970. 85. Proquest Historical Newspapers. http://www.proquest.com/en-US/.

──────. April 17, 1970. 66. Proquest Historical Newspapers. http://www.proquest.com/en-US/.

──────. May 15, 1970. 51. Proquest Historical Newspapers. http://www.proquest.com/en-US/.

──────. June 21, 1970. 123. Proquest Historical Newspapers. http://www.proquest.com/en-US/.

──────. November 17, 1970. 63. Proquest Historical Newspapers. http://www.proquest.com/en-US/.

──────. January 31, 1972. 40. ProQuest Historical Newspapers. http://www.proquest.com/en-US/.

──────. "Showdown on Toxics." August 25, 1976. 28. Proquest Historical Newspapers. http://www.proquest.com/en-US/.

──────. "Text of remarks by President Lyndon B. Johnson on Signing of the National Traffic and Motor Vehicle Safety Act of 1966." September 10, 1966. 12. Proquest Historical Newspapers. http://www.proquest.com/en-US/.

──────. "Train Asks Stiff Toxic Chemical Law." February 27, 1976. 64. Proquest Historical Newspapers. http://www.proquest.com/en-US/.

Nixon, Richard (President). Public Papers of the Presidents of the United States: Richard Nixon, 1968-72. "379: Statement About Decision to Sign 37 Bills." http://www.presidency.ucsb.edu/ws/index.php?pid=3662&st=&st1 (accessed April 13, 2010).

Obama, Barack. (President). "Memorandum for The Heads Of Executive Departments and Agencies: Transparency and Open Government, January 21, 2009. http://www.whitehouse.gov/the_press_office/Transparency_and_Open_Government/.

Peterson, Esther Eggertsen. "New York Times Oral History Program." The University of Michigan. Ann Arbor, Michigan, 1978, 2. See also http://www.aflcio.org.

Product Safety Letter. "Toxic Substances Control Act Reform Gets Hearing in House."November 21, 2009. http://www.productsafetyletter.com/news/5916-1.html.

Pryne, Eric. "Maggie's Legacy is More than Money." *Seattle Times*, May 22, 1989.

Rumsfeld, Donald H. "Remarks of Donald H. Rumsfeld at Abu Ghraib Prison." May 13, 2004. Available at http://www.defenselink.mil/speeches/speech.aspx?speechid=121.

──────. "Rumsfeld's statement - Senate Committee on Armed Services, November 20, 2008." 110th Cong., second sess. (quoted in www.cnn.com/2009/us.04/22/us.torture.karpinski/, April 22, 2009).

Society of Professional Journalists. "Society of Professional Journalists Leaders Pleased Over Freedom of Information Act Bill Signing." January 2, 2008. http://www.spj.org/news.asp?ref=755.

———. "SPJ Asks Ashcroft Not to Stonewall Requests for Public Information." News Release, October 19, 2001. http://www.spj.org?news.asp?ref=41.

*Slate.* Saletan. William. "Rape Rooms: A Chronology, What Bush Said as the Iraq Prison Scandal Unfolded." Updated May 5, 2004. http://www.slate.com/id/2100014/ (accessed April 16, 2010).

*Supreme Court Justice Scalia Fought Against Freedom of Information Act.* http://www.thememoryhole.org/foi/scalia_foia.htm (accessed April 16, 2010).

*Time/CNN.* "Truer Blue." Prime Archive/Partnership with CNN, 1986. http://www .time.com/.

*Wall Street Journal*

———. "House Panel Rejects Senate Bill to Reduce Cost of Auto Repairs." March 1, 1972, 32. Proquest Historical Newspapers. http://www.proquest.com/en-US/.

———. "Moss and Williams in Different Ways Act to Goad SEC Modernize Securities Industry." August 17, 1972. 28. Proquest Historical Newspapers. http://www.proquest.com/en-US/.

———. "FTC to Toughen Tactics Against Firms Practicing Deception Under New Statute." January 20 1975. 24.

———. September 3, 1968.14. Proquest Historical Newspapers. http://www.proquest.com/en-US/.

———. April 28, 1970. 1. Proquest Historical Newspapers. http://www.proquest.com/en-US/.

———. July 19, 1972, 10. Proquest Historical Newspapers. http://www.proquest.com/en-US/.

*Washington Post*

———. "Chemicals That Can Kill." August 29, 1976. 26. Proquest Historical Newspapers. http://www.proquest.com/en-US/

———. "Ex-Senator Warren Magnuson Dies at 84." May 21, 1989. D6.

———. Mintz, Morton. "No-Fault Bill Approved by Senate Unit." May 25, 1972. Proquest Historical Newspapers. http://www.proquest.com/en-US/.

———. Shifrin, Carole."Warranty-FTC Bill Voted by House Unit." May 23, 1974. A-5. Also see Proquest Historical Newspapers. http://www.proquest.com/en-US/.

———. Sinclair, Ward. "The Man Who Perfected Oversight." January 14, 1979.

———. January 8, 1975. D-8. Proquest Historical Newspapers. http://www.proquest.com/en-US/.

*Washington Post Times-Herald*

———. "House Committee Kills Proposal to Reduce Cost of Auto Repairs." March 1, 1972, A6. Proquest Historical Newspapers. http://www.proquest.com/en-US/.

———. Pearson, Drew. "House Group Listens to Auto Lobby." June 24, 1966. B15. ProQuest Historical Newspapers. http://www.proquest.com/en-US/.

———. October 29, 1972. A1. Proquest Historical Newspapers. http://www.proquest.com/en-US/.

White House. Bush, George W. (President). Statement. "President Bush Reaffirms Commitments in Iraq." May 10, 2004. See http://www.whitehouse.gov/news/releases/2004/05/20040510-3.html.

U.S. Bureau of Labor Standards. "Historical CPI Data." www.bls.gov/.

U.S. Department of Transportation, National Highway Traffic Safety Administration. "Relative Collision Insurance Cost Information Booklet, 2009." www.nhtsa.dot.gov.

———. "Table 2, Persons Killed or Injured and Fatality and Injury Rates Per Population, Licensed Drivers, Registered Vehicles, and Vehicle Miles Traveled, 19662008." *Traffic Safety Facts 2008: Early Edition*, National Highway Traffic Safety Administration.

# Index

# About the Author

**Michael Lemov** served as chief counsel to Congressman John Moss for eight years when Moss was chairman of the subcommittees on Commerce and Finance and Oversight and Investigations of the House Commerce Committee from 1970 to 1978. Before serving with Congressman Moss, he was counsel to Wright Patman, chairman of the House Banking Committee, and was general counsel of the National Commission on Product Safety.

Mr. Lemov is the author of several articles about the life of John Moss and his work on consumer protection and freedom of information, which have appeared in the *Sacramento Bee, The Hill, Politico,* and on *The Nieman Watchdog* website, among others. He is the author of "Consumer Product Safety Commission Regulatory Manual" published by Shepard's McGraw-Hill.

He was recently named by the governor of Maryland to the state's Consumer Advisory Council. He is a graduate of the Harvard Law School.

He writes and practices law in Bethesda, Maryland, where he lives with his wife, Penny.